37 SUMMERS

MY YEARS AS A CAMP DIRECTOR

by

ARTHUR SHARENOW

ZORBA PRESS
ITHACA, NEW YORK
WWW.ZORBAPRESS.COM

The stories in this book are based on true events. Though many of the names used are of the actual participants, other names, descriptions, personal characteristics, dates and places have been changed so that the persons portrayed are not recognizable. In other situations fictional factors have been combined with true events.

Published by Zorba Press
http://www.ZorbaPress.com

For more information about this work, and additional information including camp activities, visit the Zorba Press web site.

Release date (paperback): May 2012

ISBN+10: 0-927379-37-6
ISBN+13: 978-0-927379-37-3

Cover design by Susan Krevlin

Printed and bound in the United States of America.

For sales, permissions, and all other inquiries, please contact

Zorba Press by email: books@ZorbaPress.com

Printings: 2012–010203040506070809101112131415 16

Dedication

I dedicate my book to the three most important people in my camp life:

To my father, Alfred Sharenow, who encouraged and supported me in every important decision. He was my first and best baseball coach, a very important factor in my youth. He later endorsed my decision to become a lawyer. Finally, and most important, he provided both emotional and the initial financial support which made it possible for my dream of running a camp to become a reality.

My wife Judy, who was my support in the early years and my partner the decades that followed. Judy was very reluctant for us to get into the camp business at all, and agreed only because she knew I wanted it so much. But she came to love camp as much or more than I, and played an ever more important role in camp with each succeeding year.

Phyllis Dank was my confidante, my collaborator, and the person who seemed best to understand my idea of fun. She brought her spirit and enthusiasm to camp on a full time basis. Every camp should have a Phyllis, but very few are so lucky.

Special Thanks

To my wife, Judy, who plowed through the final proof reading, and helped to discover and correct several thousand errors, to my daughter, Susan Krevlin, for her really attractive cover design, and to Michael Pastore, who agreed to publish and edit my originally massive and unorganized manuscript.

Foreword

When I began this project, I had no idea where I was going. I knew my subject matter was camp. My first inclination was to write a novel, but I rejected the idea. I already had experience as a failed novelist, having written one many years earlier. It was a story set in fictionalized version of our 1969 camp season. For that novel I was able to find an agent, a former counselor, who graciously gave his time and best efforts to get it published, but after seventeen rejections, he and I both decided it was a lost cause.

Several years ago, just after we sold camp, I decided, rather than a novel, I should write a history. I forced myself to sit down to write day after day. The result was one hundred eighty-six pages of camp history, from our purchase of camp in 1959 up through 1963. Doing a quick calculation, I determined the total history would work out to just thirteen hundred seventy-four pages, which might well prove to be a negative.

I decided to give the history a few months rest period, after which I would edit and shrink my handiwork into more manageable dimensions. Several months later I did indeed come back to it with fresh eyes. To my dismay, my new eyes told me that what I wrote was not only too long it was also boring. If I found it boring, I couldn't expect others to be interested.

Then I did something revolutionary. I took my first ever writing course. It was a Memoir writing course offered at Brandeis University as part of a "Senior" Education" program called BOLLI (Brandeis Osher Living Learning Institute). My first teacher was Marlyn Katz Levenson, from whom I learned quite a lot in a short ten class exposure. She was both informative and encouraging. Over the next five years I had ten weekly writing sessions with Ruth Harriet Jacobs. Ruth has also been encouraging, but she is also more critical, and has been an enormously helpful tutor for me. I started writing memoirs, and tried to write each in story form, to hold the interest not only of my teacher, but also of my class-mates. One or two of my first stories were about incidents and people at camp. Some of the members of our little writing group had their own experience as campers when they were kids, but others had no camp experience of any kind. They all seemed to be interested in my first few camp stories, and that was all the encouragement I needed

I dropped all of the other memoirs, and started writing an Anecdotal history of camp, with the goal that each "Chapter" should be able to stand alone. The goal of each small chapter is to be both true and interesting. It has not been my goal for the stories to add up to a history. Nor are they necessarily presented in chronological order.

Along the way I have had to consider ethical issue of writing about people who were once either in my care or in my employ, without first getting their permission. Camp is first and foremost about people. And every story is filled with camp people. On my first draft of each, I used everybody's real names. I found it easier to recreate the situation in my mind by remembering the real people. When I realized I might actually complete a book, and attempt to get it published, the ethical issues came to the fore. I've resolved those to a degree. In any story which reflects badly on individuals, I've done my best to disguise the actual identity of those people, sometimes by just changing their names. Other times I have had to go further, even to combining the personalities and histories of two peoples' lives into one in an effort to better disguise the one featured in the anecdote. Then there are the heroes of stories. I can't resist using their real names.

Perhaps the most serious omission in this book is deliberate. Through the years I was never able to solve the issues related to questionable behavior by counselors when they were off duty away from camp. It was always puzzling and disappointing to me to discover that young men and women who were wonderfully responsible when working with their campers were quite capable of making bad decisions relating to their own health and safety.

I have done my best to recall with accuracy all the situations about which I have written, but these are memories, and memories are not entirely reliable. My memory is quite good, but several times I have started to write a story and found I had to fill in a missing piece with my best guess. Other times I've asked for help from my wife, Judy, or from Phyllis, our Head Counselor for so many years, or from our children, Susan and Robert. They've all had fun trying to supply some of the missing pieces. It is also possible that at times I have recalled things the way I prefer to recall them rather than as they actually happened.

I enjoyed writing these stories, but not nearly as much as I did living them.

Prologue
Thanks for the Memories

When I was a young kid Camp Kenwood, my third camp, was where I first felt totally accepted, where I came to feel competent and later even successful. It was my refuge through my Jr. High School years when my family fell apart.

I started at Kenwood during the war years, the big war, World War II. War was so much a part of everyone's lives, even to little kids like me, safe at camp in New Hampshire. One of our daily activities during the war was watching the trains go by on the clearly visible railroad tracks across the lake. It became a game for us to count the heavily laden freight cars. Then it became a habit, and finally our duty. Somehow, by counting, we became part of the war effort. Frequently the slow moving trains had more than a hundred cars, with flat bed cars shrouded in camouflage interspersed between tankers and regular freight cars. We didn't know what was in them or where they were going, but we knew it was for the war. Bobby Nason knew the engines by name. He counted the wheels on the engines, and spoke knowingly about them, as though they were old friends.

We had to bring our personal food ration books with us to camp, turning them in at the start of the summer so that camp could buy meat, sugar and other rationed items. They served a lot of "rabbit food" those summers. I discovered what turnips tasted like, and I was sorry I had. They usually came in stew, disguised as boiled potatoes, but we soon learned to avoid them, despite their disguise.

My counselor's name that first summer was Bruno Baer. He was a refugee from Italy or Germany or somewhere over there in Europe where they were fighting the war. He didn't speak good English. He tried to be nice, but he wasn't a very good counselor. He grunted a lot. He liked to sleep in the morning. We always woke up before reveille, and started talking. If we woke Bruno, he would throw his shoes at us. He didn't have very good aim, but we usually got quiet after the shoes started flying. According to Bruno, we weren't very good campers. Every day he told us how bad we were. Probably he wouldn't have been a counselor if it hadn't been for the war.

The counselor in Bunk Four was legally blind. His name was Guy Markesio. He had very white hair, a pink face and very thick glasses. I thought he must be around a hundred years old, but probably he was only about forty. He was a teacher at the Perkins School for the Blind. He tapped his way around camp with a white cane. He wasn't very good coaching sports. But he did play the accordion, and he was excellent at that. We called him Guy Squeezeboxio, but not when he was around. I don't suppose he would have been a camp counselor either if it hadn't been for the war.

Joey Goldberg (name for composite of underage counselors during the war) said he had been on the losing side in Maroon and Grey eleven years in a row. He was the bunk six counselor, and was about seventeen years old. He liked to give kids noogies. A noogie was a hard sock with a fist to the muscle in your arm, and you weren't supposed to show that it hurt when you got one. Nobody was allowed to tell. If they did, they'd get more noogies. Nobody told. He probably wouldn't have been a bunk counselor either if it wasn't for the war. But he was a good guy. He spoke our language and played our sports. He ran most of the activities we liked.

When we went out of camp, we traveled everywhere on foot. That was the only way. Gas was rationed, and couldn't be wasted taking campers places where they could walk. It was a very long walk through the woods to the bottom of Mt. Kearsarge and an even longer walk from there to the camping area most of the way up the mountain. We ate our sandwiches on the side of the trail just before starting up the mountain. They were peanut butter and jelly, or bologna or cheese, or sometimes mystery meat. The water in our metal canteens was warm by the time we started up the mountain. Sleeping at that campground was an adventure. There was only one outhouse, and it stunk. The park ranger always warned us to close the door because, if the door was left open, hedgehogs would come in. Hedgehogs like the taste of the urine soaked wood around the toilet. I never went to the outhouse alone at night. I was afraid of meeting a hungry hedgehog.

I was a camper in Bunk eleven when the newspaper came with the big headlines

ATOMIC BOMB DROPPED ON HIROSHIMA

We all read the front of the newspaper that day, instead of just the sports section. Nobody could figure out quite what it was all about, except that it was good, and the war would be over soon. What was an atom? How did they split it? How could that make it explode? How many Japs were killed? The counselors didn't understand it much better than we did, but that didn't prevent them from trying to explain it to us. A few days later the papers had another headline, another atomic bomb on another unpronounceable Japanese City. Then on August 15th, the best headline of all.

JAPAN SURRENDERS

It was over at last. The good counselors would be coming back to camp for next year. The Red Sox would get all of their good players back too. They were all in that war. We would soon have steak, roast beef and Hershey bars again.

The following summer, camp was amazing to us all. There were a lot more boys in camp, and we "Seniors" were going to live in a new part of camp called The Tent Colony. It was up next to the big ball field. We had never lived in tents before. I was pleased to discover they had real floors, and the cots were the same World War I surplus cots we had in Junior camp. We soon learned that the tents were cooler on hot days and warmer on cold nights than the bunks had been. You could roll the side flaps up all around to let in the breezes on hot days, and close everything tight and almost airless when it became frigid outside.

There were also negatives that went with tent living. We didn't have toilets in the bunks. That wasn't so good. It meant a long walk in the dark to the SBH (Senior Brown House) if you had to go at night. Some of the boys peed out of the back of the tents. It started getting pretty smelly back there behind our tent row. It was an area to avoid when we played Merry Chase at free play time. (Merry Chase was a rough and tumble combination of hide and go seek and hounds and hares.)

The other negative was not so bad. We didn't have any place to put our clothes. We lived out of our trunks. There were clothes at the bottoms of those trunks that never saw the light of day during the entire eight week camp season. But the trunks came in handy. They were our card tables at rest period. They were where you sat when you wanted a quiet talk with somebody. Usually during Rest Period we were lying on our beds reading. Most of us were engrossed in intellectually stimulating comic books, like Superman, Batman and Captain Marvel, but Arnie Rubin went to a tough school that made him read things like War & Peace. He took his assignment seriously. We felt a little sorry for him, but wondered why our schools didn't have us reading over the summer.

We had a whole lot of new counselors. Some of them had been in the Army and the Marines. Willy Shellnut, our new Senior Unit Leader, was a little older than most camp counselors. He was probably close to thirty. Willy smiled most of the time, spoke softly, and was really smart and nice. He wasn't a great athlete, but he played hard in Watermelon League. He always wanted to win, but he was amazingly fair. He sometimes even called himself out of bounds in volleyball. Arguments never got very far in games with Willy around. He always settled them, and everybody was satisfied because we knew he was always fair. After about a week, Willy lectured us about not peeing out the back of the tents, and after that there was a whole lot more of walking back and forth to the SBH.

Judge Goldblatt had leathery skin, bulging muscles, and a voice like a Sergeant in the movies. Though he was tough and sometimes stern, we all liked Judge. When Judge Goldblatt led us on a hike up Mt. Cardigan, he started at a trot. He didn't seem to mind that we were all carrying packs with bed rolls and food on our backs. I thought for sure I was going to die on my way up the mountain. But Judge found some great treats for us too. Half way up the mountain he heard a stream running.

"Let's go take a swim boys".

We left the path and followed the stream off to the side until it opened up into an amazing stone basin filled with clear water, the coldest water in the entire world.

I'll never forget that swim. It brought me back to life. We lay naked on the rocks to dry off before putting our clothes back on. Then we started climbing again. It was still a long way to go, but we felt better.

We got to the state park camp site and dropped our packs in a pile. Then we continued up the mountain. I'm not sure how Judge knew there were blueberries up there, but he did, and we spent an hour picking and eating blueberries. Then we reached the top and the whole world opened up before us. The path we climbed was on a steep slope from the campsite to the top. The top was an almost flat plateau of rock. But on the far side was a sheer drop of hundreds of feet. We crept close to the edge, and then sat, with our feet dangling out in space. We could see forever. Beyond the valleys and the hills in the foreground were the White Mountains, reaching to the sky and forming a backdrop for the horizon. Through the many years that have followed, I've never climbed or been at the top of a mountain without thinking of that day and Judge Goldblatt.

By my second year in Senior Camp, the name had changed from tent colony to Senior Camp. Willy Shellnut (army veteran) was back as Unit Leader. He came with his wife, and they lived in a cabin adjacent to Senior Camp, one he had built with his own hands, an amazing fact to us all. Judge Goldblatt (Marines) was still second in command. To round out the veteran group, Bill Riff (Navy) was added to the Senior staff. The rest of the counselors were normal Jewish college students and former campers who had been just a little too young to fight in the war.

We had a great baseball team. Baseball was king. All other sports were minor. We played soccer twice every summer, and I hated it. Only the tough kids liked soccer. Tennis was for sissies who were bad at baseball. Basketball was a New York sport, and the few kids from New York and New Jersey played it. Most of us from Boston had no basketball experience and played it badly. Baseball was a different story. At home we played on Saturday and every day after school, until we had to go home for supper. When we started in the Spring, there was still snow on the ground, and we played until the late Fall when it was so cold our hands were freezing.

At camp we had fielding drills or games almost every morning and batting practice in the afternoon if it wasn't too hot. I remember those blazing hot days on the senior ball field. The senior field is unforgiving on hot days. It is wide open with no shade at all except behind home plate. I would pitch batting practice every day for what seemed like an hour and then I finally got to hit. Hitting was the prize. We all took shots at lofting home runs over the cliff in short left field.

That first summer in senior camp, my cousin Joel joined me at Kenwood. Though he was a year older, we were in the same tent. It was good having my cousin there, but it meant I was not going to be in a tent with my two closest camp friends. So it was kind of a mixed blessing. But I did like Joel, and it all worked out well enough because we formed a reversible battery (pitcher-catcher, catcher-pitcher), following an old family tradition. My Father and his had been a reversible battery for the town team in Vineland, New Jersey back in ancient times. I tried to teach Joel how to throw the curve ball my Dad had taught me, but he never quite mastered it. He was the better catcher. When we played other camps one of us would pitch and the other catch. Most often I was the pitcher. Nobody from the other camps could ever hit my curve ball.

Joel only came that one summer. My second year in Senior camp I was reunited in a tent with my good friends, Donny Aronson and Arnie Rubin. We also had a new boy named Eddy Rosen. To make him feel at home, we called him New Boy all summer long. Though we liked him well enough, it was important that he not feel entirely comfortable. After all, he hadn't served an apprenticeship of years in Junior Camp. Eddy was a good kid, and we really liked him, but things got a little touchy when we had tryouts for the team, and he tried out against Donny Aronson for shortstop. Even worse, it was obvious to all of us that he was a better short stop and a much better hitter. When the team lists were posted before the first game, and Eddy was named the starting shortstop, Donny accepted his demotion to third base with good grace. The potential conflict was eased when it turned out that Eddy was also the best catcher in camp. Eddy was my catcher the rest of that summer and the following summer. Don reclaimed his shortstop position, and whatever tension there was between New Boy and the rest of the bunk disappeared.

What a team we had! We killed everyone. We beat our traditional arch rival, Camp Ragged Lake, 1-0 in the game at Kenwood and 2-1 when we played them at Ragged Lake. They had a pitcher named Joe North. He was big and strong and very blond. Actually their whole team was blond. We referred to them as the blond camp. We had trouble hitting Joe North, but we murdered the pitchers on all of the other teams. We didn't just stop at camp teams. We even played the Andover town team and beat them about 27-0. They were really bad. We had similar scores against Camp Crescent, Camp Wa-lu-la, and Camp Wingo.

We had a coach we hated that year. His name was Roger Walsh. Ken (The

Director) was going professional on us. Roger actually coached varsity baseball at Brookline High School. His great sin was thinking he could teach us something about baseball that we didn't know. He wanted us to do stupid things too, like running laps and doing stretching exercises. None of us every heard of such nonsense, and we were determined to put him in his place. We went to Ken (the director) to complain. We were shocked when he backed up the coach, and told us to do what Roger told us. Grudgingly, we went back to practice the next day, and did all of that stupid stuff. When we finished the camp season with a 10-0 record, we knew it was despite him, not because of him. Hmm!!! Is it possible he knew something? The next summer Roger was gone. We had practically our whole starting team back, and we still won most of our games, but we didn't do quite as well. But, without exception, we all had more fun at practices without the punishment runs and ridiculous exercises.

My third and final summer as a camper in Senior Camp, Donny Sherman joined our tent group. At home, Donny and I lived on different streets, but our yards backed up to one another. Donny came to the group very late in his camp career because he had to win a religious war before being allowed to join us at camp. Not only was his Father an observant Orthodox Jew, but his uncle was Rabbi at Conservative Temple Emanuel in Newton and the Owner/Director of a Jewish summer camp for boys. I can only imagine the endless conversations, pleadings and arguments that must have gone on in the Sherman household before Don was finally granted the right to join us at Kenwood, a nominally Jewish, but never religious camp. Unlike Eddy the previous summer, Don never had to overcome the "New Boy" label because we knew him from home.

We went from the four man tents we had occupied on the Senior Camp plateau to a six man tent that had been erected at the bottom of the hill and adjacent to the lake. It was eight or ten feet away from the swampy end of the lake. We spent a good bit of that summer fighting and losing the battle of the mosquito. Our proximity to the water also enabled us to fully appreciate the nightly serenade of hundreds of full throated bullfrogs, who were so close they sounded as though they were additional tent-mates.

Finally, I remember the five of us, Eddy, Don Aronson, Don Sherman, Arnie Rubin and me, sitting around calculating the fortune that Ken Huberman must be amassing as the owner of Camp Kenwood. We agreed that summer. When we grew up, we would buy the camp from him, and we would all be millionaires.

Part One
In The Beginning

1
Running A Camp

During all of my years as a Camp Director I always had Lou Gehrig's memorable lines in his retirement speech in Yankee Stadium as my personal mantra.

" ... I consider myself the luckiest man on the face of the earth ... "

After all how many young men, trained to be lawyers, are fortunate enough, as I was, to escape the endless arguments and intricacies of the law, and substitute for it the sheer exhilaration and excitement that comes with running a camp? How many people are lucky enough to understand that what they do and how well they do it can make a profound difference in the lives others. I always knew this. I always understood this. I was entrusted with the lives of other people's children, and it was my job to live up to that responsibility.

I can't even imagine any other occupation that provides the challenges, the excitement and the sheer fun experienced by a Camp Director at the opening of each camp season. The only experiences remotely similar would be the opening of a show for the Broadway Director or the beginning of the season for a Major League Baseball Manager. But even these two examples are pale shadows. After all, how many openings does a Broadway Director have in a lifetime? How many major league managers go into each season believing that they have the very best team in baseball?

I went into every camp season with the conviction and determination that it would be a winning season, a smash hit, a super banner summer. I looked at each camp season as a new adventure, a new challenge, and another opportunity to create our own perfect little world. I spent the entire year assembling the pieces needed to reach that goal. To me, nothing could match the absolute fun of meeting the daily challenges, getting to know the kids, watching their surprise and delight as a Special event unfolded, and building relationships with many of the counselors. Those of us who run camps have to have a lot of little kid in them.

As I approached the start of my first summer as a camp director, I was both excited and nervous. I had spent months hiring staff, experienced weeks of anxiety trying to get the physical plant ready in time for the camper's arrival, and a full week, working, playing and evaluating our counselor staff. I should have been exhausted, but no such thought crossed my mind as I stood on the side of the hill, revelling in my small kingdom. I was on an unparalleled emotional high. The curtain was about to go up on my first production. I could hardly wait to see how the plot would develop with me playing the lead role for the very first time.

That first summer and all of the years that followed, our campers exploded into camp on Opening Day. Almost all of them arrived at camp on chartered busses. Much of the staff plus a few scattered campers who had arrived earlier by car were in a state of suspended animation as we all waited on the steeply sloped side of the Hollow for the busses to arrive. The bridge on our camp road was the first to announce the approach of the busses. Its wooden planks screamed in protest at the weight of the vehicles. Word was soon passed up to the office. Then our Public Address system shouted out the glad tidings.

"The Busses are here!! The Busses are here!!"

As I watched the little boys come off the bus, I witnessed an incredible sight. Most of them had made friends on the bus. At the very least, the counselors on the bus were their new friends. They had been cooped up for hours, particularly the ones who came all the way from New Jersey and New York, just waiting for that magical moment when they would finally arrive at camp. Now they had come and they couldn't wait. They spilled out of their buses, in many cases forgetting hand luggage, stuffed animals, baseball gloves and the remains of travel snacks. They were ready for action. Within minutes we had them assigned to their counselors and cabin groups; they had gathered their hand luggage, and they were off to their cabins. The busses pulled out of the Hollow. It was empty now except for a few stray pieces of luggage and the unlucky Junior Counselors I had assigned the task of identifying, sorting and delivering the leftover treasures.

Within a half hour there were boys swarming everywhere in camp. In our little boys' area, called "The Compound", there were baseballs and Frisbees flying in every direction. The Intermediate boys, slightly older and with more easily channeled energy, were on their way to the gym for basketball. The Juniors headed out to the Junior Ball Field to play soccer. Some of our youngest cabin groups, populated largely by first year campers, were being given tours of camp by their counselors. One way or another, the boys were out of their cabins and totally immersed in their activities.

The scene when the girls came off their busses was only slightly less frantic; but the immediate result were similar. The girls' ball field, where they gathered after coming off the busses, emptied in minutes. By the time I walked over to the girls' side I wondered "where did they all go?" The whole girls' camp campus was empty. Just moments earlier it had been filled with girls hugging, laughing, screaming and crying. They had all disappeared into their lodges.

As I walked the length of the girls' campus, shrieks of delight came from Spruce Lodge, where our thirteen and fourteen year old girls lived in a constant state of emotional overdrive. I heard sobs coming from Bunk E in Pine Lodge, and I wondered which girl was so inconsolable about her bunk placement. Finally, as I approached Hemlock Lodge, I saw little girls and their counselors emerge, holding hands and doing a lot of giggling. Their counselors were taking them on their first tour of camp. The girls did a lot of running ahead and jumping about, but as I watched, I saw that they never strayed very far from their counselors. That first day of tours the little girls' counselors were like Mother ducks, proudly leading their small flocks into the great wide world of camp. Never again would the girls look so dependent or their counselors so omniscient.

Since that first opening day, I saw this scene repeat itself year after year, and always with the same excitement and enthusiasm. With this as the prospect every year, how could I not have " ... considered myself the luckiest man on the face of the earth"?

2

Harvard Law School
Or How I became a Camp Director

Harvard Law School was a big mistake! Probably the law was a big mistake. Why did I go to law school anyway? And why go to Harvard? Looking back on it now I'm sure I know the answers to both questions. The college years had proved to me, my family and a select group of well chosen professors that I was a good student. When you find something you do well, stick with it. I was a good student. Why not continue? Law School provided that opportunity. The only other thing I was really good at was baseball, and my Father had convinced me that the odds were very long against me making a living playing baseball. As for Harvard, how could I not go once they accepted me? After all, it was the best.

Judy and I got married the Sunday after I graduated from Brandeis in 1955. Judy had one more year before her Brandeis graduation. Both sets of parents agreed to provide the support for that first year. It was viewed by them as a fine investment in the future of the next Clarence Darrow. We lived in a three room apartment in an area called Charlesbank. It was right next to the Brandeis campus and Judy was able to walk to school. I commuted to Cambridge. After the first year of law school Judy had graduated and she started teaching school. We lived on her salary while I continued to study.

At Harvard Law there was a one day Orientation period. Dean Griswold spoke to us that morning. He didn't give us the traditional Harvard Law School

Speech. "Look to the right of you. Look to the left of you. One of you three will be gone before the end of the first year." He assured us "That was from the Bad old Days when Harvard Law School was a high pressure place." The clear implication of his talk was that Harvard Law was now a warm and fuzzy place. He then proceeded to tell us how brilliant we all were. In the course of his introduction to life at THE LAW SCHOOL, he did mention the importance of the Socratic Method. I conjured up a mental image of a Socratic professor in a long white robe surrounded by aspiring young legal scholars. They were sitting together under a shade tree. In the distance there were sheep grazing in green pastures. The kindly Professor encouraged his followers to give their opinions on a variety of knotty legal issues.

On the very first day of classes I was introduced to the Socratic Method, law school style. My first class was in Civil Procedure. Our professor's name was Abraham Chayes. He was young and reputedly brilliant. He had graduated from the law school just a few years earlier, clerked for Supreme Court Justice Felix Frankfurter, and was the law school's youngest professor. He looked quite ordinary as he walked into the room. He was long and lanky, needed a haircut, and wore a standard Harris Tweed sport jacket. But then he opened his mouth and started asking questions. He never gave answers. I hadn't a clue what the answers were. I didn't even understand the questions? In fact, I didn't understand one thing he said the entire hour. I have one whole page from that first class. It is full of long questions with question marks and no answers.

It got worse from there. Old man McCurdy was my Contracts professor. McCurdy was round with a red face and a shock of white hair. He smiled at us as he entered the room, and looked at his seating chart. He started by calling the boy at the end of the third row. He worked like a grim reaper. He started at the end of one row, and sure as death, proceeded around the semi-circle calling on victims, never varying from that row until all of the students were cut down to size. Unlike Chayes, he answered questions, but he did so only after humiliated students were unable to come up with the right answers.

Fortunately for me, the first two class sessions he picked on people far from my assigned seat, but on the third day of class he started at the end of my row. I was about twelfth in line. My notes are quite legible while the first two or three of my classmates were being "Socratized". My handwriting got worse and worse the closer he got to me. I hoped he wouldn't have time to reach me by the end of the class. It was a race of McCurdy against the clock. I watched the hand move toward the hour as he came closer and closer. Two minutes to go and I heard my name. By then I was so frazzled I couldn't have told him what day it was. I stammered out some sort of answer, enough to establish that I didn't know what I was talking about. He let me sit down in ignominious defeat just as the clock struck eleven.

Property law class was a show. Every seat was filled, and there was always a crowd standing in back to watch and enjoy. It was the James Casner theatre. He was director and lead actor. He always made his entrance from stage left after all of the seats were filled. He strutted in like a peacock. His voice was clear and cut through the room like a rapier. It was in Casner's class that I first realized why all of the rooms were shaped as amphitheaters. It provided a proper setting in which students could be thrown to the lions for the entertainment of the crowd. Casner knew everything there was to know about property law. We HAD to learn property law to defend ourselves. He had razor sharp wit and a barbed tongue. In his class you could be diced and skewered. He took no prisoners. On the other hand, he never failed to compliment brilliant responses when he heard them. I never was the recipient of one of those compliments.

The only respite in my schedule of carefully designed tortures was Constitutional Law. Our professor was Paul Freund. Not only did he write the book, but he was often quoted as an authority by Supreme Court Justices. He was a very kindly and gentle man. He spoke in a soft voice and never embarrassed anybody. As far as I was concerned it was a waste having such a nice person teaching the only course I really understood.

I was part of a group of eight or ten aspiring lawyers who gathered at a class break every morning to sit and have coffee. We all seemed to have that one open hour every day. Many times the discussion involved the relative merits of arcane points of law from cases we were studying. Some of it was interesting to me, but not nearly as interesting as the sports page, where I could catch up on how the Red Sox or Celtics had done the night before. "What is the matter with these people? Don't they get enough of this stuff during class and studying for classes? Can't we have a time out?"

Occasionally they humored me, and we talked about the previous night's game or Wilt Chamberlain or the fortunes of Washington baseball teams, but then the subject always went back to law. I probably should have gotten the clue then and there. But in some respects I am a slow learner.

I went through all three years of law school. The first year was truly terrifying. In that "warm fuzzy place" we had no papers to submit and no exams from September until the end of May. A single four hour exam in each course determined your grade absolutely. Until you received the results you never really knew where you stood. I worked long hours in law school. Some of my friends appeared to work many fewer hours and achieved at least as good or better understanding. That was more than a little deflating. The next two years were less confusing, but more demanding in terms of work load. But taken together, the three years were a fantastic education in self-discipline. Along the way I even learned a little about law.

I passed the Mass. Bar exam with ease, and got a job at a well known Boston law firm. Quickly I realized that I was bored to tears. I would not have believed it, but I missed the intellectual fervor of law school. In law school we had discussed and analyzed important and complicated cases. Most were Supreme Court cases. In our firm everything I had anything to do with was absolutely mundane. The most disillusioning thing was to be told time after time to go to the file cabinet. "We have a form for that". It didn't matter what it was. There was a form for everything.

Supreme Court rulings didn't play any discernible role in our firm's practice. Very little was intellectually challenging and even less was of importance to anyone in the world except the immediate parties.

During my first summer in the law office, I worked on a bankruptcy case involving a children's summer camp. Our firm represented two companies that had sold them meat, and got stuck with thousands of dollars of unpaid bills. I was very curious to see the camp. I had spent virtually every summer of my life in camp. Judy and I had both been counselors and became Head Counselors during the summers through college and law school. The camp we visited was in operation when we arrived. Balls were flying. Kids were running. The waterfronts were busy with splashing happy children. Sailboats were out on the lake. I loved the scene. It was my kind of world. What I didn't love was the physical facility. Judy and I watched the activities and the kids, remembering how much we missed camp. Right then and there I got the yen to get back into camping. Judy was intrigued by the idea, but she was much more wary of it than I.

From that point on, my body kept working at the law, but my mind wandered more and more frequently to the possibility of running a camp, our camp. Judy and I discussed and debated it for months. She finally agreed. Several months after our visit to that bankrupt camp we approached Ken Huberman, who was owner/director of Camps Kenwood and Evergreen, the camps in which we had spent all of those summers. He was getting old enough and had been at it long enough so that I thought he might be willing to sell. He said "yes!"

We bought our camp. We bought it with much optimism, little cash and a lot of debt. We experienced a great deal of financial stress in the early years, but we struggled through that. Camp came to play the central part in our lives and in the life of our family from 1960 through 2004. I have never looked back with regret to my abandoned career as a lawyer. I had found my calling.

3
The First Summer

1960 was my first summer as a camp director. It was also the first time in my camping years that I had ever worked with girls. I got a real education that summer, spending more time with Evergreen, our girls camp, than I had anticipated. Almost as soon as she arrived in camp I discovered that the young woman I had hired as Head Counselor, the most important job in camp, was not up to the job. An accomplished Head Counselor does all of the day to day programming, assigns and motivates counselors, deals with camper issues, organizes major all-camp activities, and makes them fun and exciting. It takes a talented and charismatic person to fulfill all of these roles. The young woman I hired for this multi-faceted job was just plain awful. She was not only unable to put together a coherent program, but she also managed to alienate most of her staff from the first day. For a while I tried to work with her, but after a couple of weeks I found myself working around her. Finally I decided it would be easier and less confusing to the staff if I just did it myself.

I was the only reasonable candidate for the job. My wife, Judy, who had been the Evergreen Head Counselor several years earlier, was busy being a new Mother to our first born child. Bernice Huberman, Evergreen's founding director, was recovering from the effects of an aneurism, which occurred the previous summer, making it impossible for her to resume stressful work. The remainder of that summer her husband, Ken, had worked with the girls' camp for the first time. He was not anxious to repeat the experience. So, despite being handicapped by being male, and thus unable to freely go in and out of the campers' cabins, and being further handicapped by my inexperience in working with girls, the job was mine.

Functioning as a brand new director of both camps and as Head Counselor for Evergreen was educational for me, but a disaster for the camp. I was not a brilliant success in either of my new capacities. I seemed to move from crisis to crisis on a daily basis. When I woke up every morning I held my breath waiting to see what would go wrong. Most days I didn't have to wait long. Many mornings I didn't even have to leave the house before the first problem literally came to my doorstep. Typically, one of our Evergreen counselors was sitting on my porch. She was almost always sobbing, frequently verging on hysteria. The cause of her distress could be a slight by another counselor or frustration in her own inability to solve problems within her cabin, or control her campers. No matter what the reason, she felt she couldn't wait to pour out her tale of woe until after breakfast. I learned to have my wakeup cup of coffee out of sight in the tiny kitchen of our cabin before opening my front door. Then I would open the door, and there she would be.

When I didn't have counselors crying on my porch I had Evergreen campers crying in my office. I got the feeling after a couple of weeks that I could get to know every girl in camp without ever leaving the office. It seemed that sooner or later every one of them found their way to me with an issue.

"I have to move to Bunk C. I can't stand another day in Bunk D. They're all mean." .....

"You've got to get _____ out of our bunk. She's ruining the whole summer for all of us." .....

"Marsha took my magazine and she won't give it back." .....

"I did a good job making my bed this morning then Roz came to inspect. She said I had sand in the bed, and she pulled the blankets and sheets off. It's not fair. It's just not fair. She hates me. That's why she did that."

I had some great fun with my new job too. Girls' campfires were a revelation to me. I loved the singing and enthusiasm, the hugging, the swaying circle of friends, the solemn candle lighting ceremony, the "traditional" tale of a camp that was only ten years old at the time. I loved playing softball and volleyball and hounds and hares with the girls. They were so much more emotional than the boys.

While I was getting an education in working with the girls in our relatively small girls' camp, I had little time available to spend with Kenwood, our considerably larger boys' camp. I counted on the veteran staff, largely filled with returnees from the past few summers. I counted on a Head Counselor, who had been in camp for years. I counted on a Waterfront Director, who had been in camp even longer. I also counted on Ken, my mentor, doing whatever directing was necessary in Kenwood. I was wrong all around. Ken viewed his role as being strictly advisory. He had no desire to participate in active management any longer. My inherited Kenwood Head Counselor, a very talented man who I had known for years, was resentful and disappointed at the change in management. He had been under the impression that, under Ken's continued ownership, he would be given a share of ownership. It was clear to him when we bought the camp, this was simply not going to happen. His lack of enthusiasm that summer was contagious. Our veteran staff in Kenwood did an uninspired job and I was barely aware as it was happening. From my limited view everything looked normal at Kenwood.

Evergreen suffered with a younger, less experienced group of counselors, working with an inexperienced Head Counselor/Director. The result was a general sense of dissatisfaction throughout camp, a concern that the camp was leaderless and a lack of certainty about the future. The next summer we opened with an unprecedented number of new counselors and thirty percent fewer campers. The drop in enrollment was almost as great in Kenwood with its experienced staff as it was in Evergreen, which had more obvious problems. It took us many years to inch back to our 1960 enrollment.

At the end of that first summer I did not feel that I was the luckiest man on the face of the earth. I felt I was perhaps a man who made a huge mistake in leaving the law. That was the only time I ever entertained such a negative thought.

Part Two
The Early 1960s

4
Homesick Sandy

Sandy was eight years old, away from home for the first time, and homesick. For the first three or four days of camp Jeff, his counselor, struggled to get him out of bed, out of the bunk, out to activities, and

"For God Sake, Sandy, please stop crying."

"I miss my Mommy. I want to go home."

"Sandy, give it a chance. You'll love the activities if you will just try."

"I don't wanna try. I wanna go home."

"Come on, Sandy, you know you like kickball. Let's go now. You can be on my team."

"I have a stomach ache. I can't play."

"Come on, Sandy, you don't have a stomach ache. You're just trying to get out of playing."

"I want to go home." This time it was not a plea, but a vehement statement of determination.

Variations on this conversation occurred several times each day.

In my experience as a counselor, I had worked with older campers, where homesickness was rarely an issue. Sandy was the first homesick little boy where I became personally involved in trying to affect a cure. Experience is the best teacher, and in working with Sandy I achieved a solution of sorts to his problem, but, in the process, created a big headache for myself.

I told Sandy's counselor to bring Sandy to me. I would talk with him. Jeff brought Sandy to my office, and asked if he should stay.

"No, Jeff, you go back to your group. After Sandy and I get acquainted, I'll bring him back to you." Jeff left, and I had a scared little boy sniffling in the corner of my office.

"Sandy, Jeff tells me that you want to go home."

"Yes, can I call my Mommy now? I know she'll come and get me." His voice was shaking and the tears streamed down his face. I handed him a box of tissues.

"First thing, Sandy, you've got to stop crying and blow your nose. I can't let you talk to you mother now. The way you sound, she will think something awful happened to you. She'll be very worried. You don't want to worry her like that, do you?"

"If I promise not to cry, can I talk to her?"

"Maybe you'll be able to talk to her in a few days, but not now. We have a camp rule. No parents can call for the first ten days of camp and campers can't call them either."

"But I have to talk to my mother. I feel terrible. I have to go home."

"Why do you have to go home?"

"Because everybody in my bunk hates me, and the activities stink, and the food is awful. If my Mother knew how terrible it is here she'd want me to come home. She would come right up and get me."

"Well, you can't call home. Those are the rules, but I'll tell you what you can do. You can sit at my desk. I'll give you paper and pencil and an envelope. You write to you Mother, and tell her everything that's wrong here at camp and all of the reasons you want to go home. You fold it, put it in the envelope and seal it. You can address it, I'll put a stamp on it, and then the two of us will go to the post office and mail it. When she gets the letter, she'll know exactly how you feel."

He sat at the desk, sobbing and staring down at the blank paper. Finally he started to write. When he was through, we drove to the Potter Place post office. Of course, it was closed mid-day, but he watched me put his letter through the slot in the front door. He was satisfied that it was on its way. I took him for a ride to our local highlights. We stopped first at the covered bridge in Cilleville. We got out of the car, and climbed down onto the rocky ledge under the bridge.

"Some of our campers are going to canoe here right from our camp lake this summer. The stream that brings the water here comes right from our lake. Here, under the bridge, the water is deep, and it's a great swimming hole. I swam here when I was a camper."

He didn't believe me at first when I told him I had been a camper just a year older than he was when I started at Kenwood. But he was interested. Next we walked through the covered bridge, down a dirt road, and came to that wonderful rickety old general store where they sold corn cob pipes, comic books and candy. It was closed. The sign on the door said "Open Noon-5 PM."

"When I was a camper, I bought a corn cob pipe here. In fact every kid in my bunk bought one. Of course, we didn't really smoke them, but we liked the way they looked sticking out of our mouths. We all wanted to look like General MacArthur. He was a famous general in World War II, and he smoked a corn cob pipe. Maybe you'll buy one here someday."

We walked from the store the short distance to Johnson's Lumber. He liked walking between the high stacks of lumber, some already cut into finished lumber, others with boards still rough hewn.

We got back into my car, and I drove the long way through Wilmot Center, back to our dirt road, and finally to my favorite place, the Old Mill Stream. I showed him where he and his friends would start their climb a little later in the summer. From the starting point where we stood, I was able to point out my favorite little waterfall.

"When it's time for your group to come here, I'll come with you, and I'll be right there next to you in that pool below the waterfall. I'll help you get through the waterfall, so that you can stick your hands out the front of the waterfall, and wave to your friends. You'll like that. Everybody does, including me."

His eyes lit up. He was excited at the prospect.

"Can we climb a little on the rocks now?"

I looked at my watch, and shook my head no.

"I'm sorry, Sandy, I have to get back to camp. Besides, I promised Jeff I would get you back to the group. First activity is already over. Your group is at swim now. You'll have to miss that too, but I want to make sure I get you back in time for third period. I think you have arts & crafts third period. Do you like arts & Crafts?"

The animated look had disappeared from his face. "Ya, it's okay."

We drove back slowly over the bumpy dirt road. As I walked him down to the crafts shop I asked how he liked the morning.

"I liked it. Camp may be alright if I can just stay with you."

"That won't be camp if you just stay with me, but I'll tell you what. Any time you feel really upset, you can come and find me, and we will spend some time together. We'll do something nice. You'll be my special friend."

"Jeff won't let me come to you any time I want."

"Maybe not any time, but I'll talk to Jeff, and make sure he understands we have a special arrangement."

Sandy's Mother eventually got his tear stained letter, and responded as mothers do when they receive letters like his. She called camp in a panic. I had forgotten to call her to warn her about the letter headed her way. During our conversation she was skeptical when I assured her he was doing much better, and asked her to call again if and when she received similarly bleak mail.

In his own fashion, Sandy did adjust to camp that summer, and I had a special friend, who I came to think of as my shadow. I don't believe I got through a day the rest of the summer without Sandy by my side some part of the day. No matter where I went, he came too, like a faithful puppy. I tried to wean him, and was partially successful. But it was an arrangement I was never foolish enough to repeat in all of the years that followed. It was clearly a mistake, but was it worth it? Sandy was a camper and Junior Counselor with us for eight summers. He and I always did have a special relationship, but after his initial camp season he became a fully integrated camper. On the other hand, I learned subsequently, there are better ways to work with homesick campers.

It was early 1970s, a few years after Sandy's last summer at camp. One of our Evergreen counselors came to the office to tell me she had picked up a hitch hiker at the Danbury General Store.

"He saw my camp shirt, and came right over to me. He asked for a ride to camp, said he was a camper here for years. I found it hard to believe he was ever a camper here. You'll see what I mean when you see him. He said his name is Sandy and that you and he were good friends. "

I knew at once who she meant. I was pleased and intrigued at the prospect of seeing him again. I hadn't heard from him since his last summer at camp, and I wondered what ever happened to him.

I went out the office door to greet him. If I didn't know who it was, I would never have recognized him. He was dressed in shabby jeans and a work shirt, neither of which looked clean. These were augmented by muddy boots and a canvas back-pack. His shaggy hair and scraggly unkempt beard were matted and looked dirty. He smelled bad too. But he broke into a smile when he saw me, and so did I. He was my boy Sandy after all.

After a shower and a change of clothes he was quite presentable, but his world was far removed from camp and from the Brooklyn neighborhood where he grew up. He seemed a little foggy, perhaps even dazed as we reminisced. Then he regaled me with tales of his current life, most of which involved "his old lady" and various "pads" they had briefly occupied around the country. As he said goodbye to me the next morning, he pulled a familiar looking corn cob pipe out of his pocket.

"Remember this? I always keep it with me, wherever I go. It reminds me of camp."

Homesickness is the number one early season problem for camps. It is a painful malady, frequently accompanied by a very real physical issue like a stomach or headache. It can manifest itself as soon as a new camper gets on the bus to camp, at his first camp meal, or at bed-time that first night. Happily, most of those so afflicted are "cured" in a matter of days, as they begin to feel a part of their cabin group, get so busy with camp activities that they forget to feel alone, and come to accept their counselor as a substitute parent or reliable older friend.

We have to be both flexible and creative in our approach with homesick campers. We have used "Big Brothers" and "Big Sisters" effectively many times. We have used special programming. On rare occasions, when nothing else worked, I even resorted to "hypnotism". I cannot actually hypnotize anyone. Nonetheless some "homesick campers" are wonderful candidates for "positive suggestion." But without any tricks or gimmicks, the most effective cure of all is the passage of time. We just have to be able to get that poor sad child as active as possible until he or she gets themselves over the hump. One day they wake up, and realize that camp is okay and so are they.

5
Appointments With The Campers' Parents

Enrolling children for camp is the very life blood of the camp business. This was my primary and most important job in Fall and Winter. To me, the winter was necessary work and the summer was my reward. I was not comfortable as a salesman. I doubt if I could have sold anything that I didn't believe in as much as I did camp. But even loving camp and believing in it, I found selling difficult. In the early years I had to quiet my nerves to make phone calls to prospects. Having succeeded in making an appointment, my heart would flutter and my blood pressure would rise as I came to the front door. A kind of anticipatory terror seized me as I rang the bell. Fortunately, that extreme degree of disquiet lessened with experience and the passage of time.

The visits themselves were usually pleasant, parents receptive and hospitable, and children enthusiastic and welcoming. I always felt considerably better leaving the home of a new camper prospect than I had on entering. On the other hand, I rarely walked away with signed applications and deposits. Though I did eventually enroll a good percentage of the prospective campers I visited, there was always suspense. The campers' applications reached me by mail weeks after my visit to their home.

Typically, the parents' goodbye line would be one of the following.

"Thank you so much. It was so good meeting you."

"It looks like you have a lovely camp. We have to think it over."

"We have just one more director to interview before we make a decision, but we're leaning your way."

" We'll have to sit down, and talk and see if we can really afford it."

"I don't know what to say. We love your camp, but she really wants to go with a close friend from home. We'll try to change her mind"

"We're not sure whether your camp has enough athletic competition for him."

"We're just concerned that your camp may be a little too competitive."

"I'm not sure about sending her to a coed camp."

"You seem very set on segregating the boys and the girls"...

I enjoyed revisiting the families of returning campers far more than "selling" or being interviewed by brand new families. Most often I was I invited back because they were planning to enroll their second or third child. I had very little selling to do. Their older sibling had already done that for me, and the parents already knew and trusted both me and our camp. Returning campers welcomed me as though I was a visiting celebrity.

I understood and appreciated that camp parents had entrusted their children to us, and I tried to live up to that trust. I also knew that parents only wanted what was best for their children. If some of them made difficult demands or occasionally seemed unreasonable, it was because they were so concerned about their children.

Through the years, I had positive relationships with the parents of most of our campers and developed close relationships with a few. Many became friends. They were a part of our camp family and we were viewed as a part of theirs. But those visits to enroll new campers were always a challenge for me, and none more so than my very first appointment.

My First Camp Appointment

That first camp appointment in the New York area produced a nightmare scenario. The prospective camper was an eight year old boy who lived in Douglaston, New York. My wife's parents' apartment was my New York office. It was way uptown on the west side. I had never heard of Douglaston and had no idea where it was in relation to upper Riverside Drive. I did know it was somewhere on Long Island. I got directions from a family friend who had on occasion ventured into the outer precincts surrounding "The City." He advised me to allow plenty of time because the roads might be crowded at rush hour. My appointment was for seven o'clock. He suggested that it would take at least forty-five minutes. So I allowed some extra time, and left at six.

The Triborough Bridge at rush hour can be a pretty scary roadway. It was even more so to me that night in a heavy downpour. I went through the tolls and found myself was in the wrong set of lanes to ease onto Grand Central Parkway, a fact that was brought home to me by the blare of horns and squealing brakes as I attempted to shift across three lanes. The other drivers were not in a charitable mood toward a trouble maker from Massachusetts, who was slowing their way home. On the other hand, Grand Central Parkway gave me plenty of time to think about my next exit. It was a virtual parking lot. My heart was beating faster and I felt myself sweating as the minutes were rapidly ticking away while I peered through my fogged up windshield for the exit marked Northern Boulevard. It was ten minutes before seven when I got to the top of the ramp onto Northern Boulevard, and entered another line of creep and stop traffic. It took me a few minutes before I realized I was headed back toward Manhattan. I could hardly U-turn. Northern Boulevard was four lanes wide, with no divider and heavy traffic in both directions. The rain slicked road was a reflective nightmare with glare from neon signs and headlights creating a crazy quilt pattern on the road surface. Finally I was able to turn onto a side street with a traffic light and get back on facing East. I was already ten minutes late, and I wasn't sure how far I had to go to reach the illusive Douglaston. Cell phones were a few decades in the future at that time and the heavy rain made outdoor public phones an uninviting place to stop to make a call. I looked for a store likely to have a pay phone, but didn't see any. I plodded ahead, seemingly inch by inch.

When I reached Douglaston I had trouble finding the street, but finally located it and rolled to a stop in front of the prospect's house at eight-fifteen. I was an hour and fifteen minutes late. I had never been so late getting anywhere in my life. I felt frazzled, and even worse when I realized the house was dark. There were no outside lights on and the interior was dark on the ground floor. The only light I saw was in a second story bedroom.

I rang the bell, and heard nothing. I rang again and heard footsteps coming my way. The light went on in the front hall. The outside light came on. Mr. Cohen greeted me.

"Are you the man from Camp Kenwood? We gave up on you half an hour ago. We thought you forgot the appointment. What happened? Why are you so late? Why didn't you call?" I explained as best I could, and he took pity on me. He invited me in.

"My wife just left for a meeting at the school. She won't be home until at least ten o'clock. She's the one who'll make the camp decisions. There's no point in you making a presentation to me, and it's too late for Johnny. He's already in bed. Why don't you give my wife a call tomorrow and plan to come back some other time."

I learned an important lesson that night. Never again would I drive to Long Island, New Jersey suburbs or even nearby Westchester County in the evening for an evening appointment. I would drive to the designated town early in the afternoon, locate the actual address of my evening appointment, and then spend time at a local library or movie, have dinner, and arrive right on time. Over the course of the next thirty-five years, I can remember being late for an appointment only once.

6
Accordion Boy

In 1960 I was a brand new Camp Director, but could recognize trouble when it came my way. I saw trouble headed right toward me in Grand Central Station. I was standing with my camp sign, surrounded by a group of young counselors. The boy coming toward me appeared to be about twelve years old. He looked soft and flabby, very pale, and was dressed completely wrong. He wore a pair of neatly pressed slacks, brown and white saddle shoes and a white long sleeve shirt. To compound these problems, he was carrying an accordion. I groaned involuntarily.

I had never seen him before so I was able to maintain a momentary hope that his Mother was leading him toward the wrong camp, perhaps the Camp Kenwood in Connecticut. No such luck. His Mother was striding determinedly straight toward me like an arrow. She offered her hand.

"Mr. Sharnoff, I'm Sophie Spiegler and this is my son Stephen." Then she turned to her son "Stephen, shake hands like I showed you." I was soon shaking Stephen's sweaty limp hand. After a few seconds, I released his hand, and it fell to his side. I realized then that he must have been enrolled months earlier by Ken Huberman. "You should hear Stephen play. He's really excellent on the accordion. He could play for you right now."

It was all I could do to restrain an audible groan. I was saved from hearing his recital by the simultaneous arrival of several other sets of parents and children. As I happily greeted the newcomers, one of our counselors stepped forward and led Stephen and his mother toward a group of boys Stephen's age. I had no time to think about him again until we were actually on the train.

As campers and their parents started to pile into the Grand Central waiting area, our once generous looking plot of floor began to shrink. Camp groups were tightly packed against one another. In those days Grand Central Station was a madhouse on camp opening days. Each camp was assigned a cordoned off position and given a sign. Parents were sent a map of Grand Central, showing where their group was to meet. It was their job to plow through the crowd to the right location. There must have been eighty camps meeting their campers in roped off area. From there we would pick up the surrounding rope, and use it as a mobile corral to make our way to the tracks.

I prayed silently that we wouldn't lose anyone along the way. The children were now inside the ropes with the parents holding on from outside, hugging, kissing and saying tearful goodbyes as we made our way toward our train. I breathed a sigh of relief when we were safely in our private car. A quick roll call established that we had all of our campers and happily none of their parents on board.

I busily rearranged the kids so that they were all sitting with others their own age, some of whom would be their bunk-mates. I also had to make sure each age group had a counselor nearby. It was their job to make the new campers feel welcome. A few of the new campers were crying, homesick before we even rolled out of the station. They really needed comforting. The New Haven railroad was doing its best to make the trip unpleasant even before we were underway. It was instantly clear that the air conditioning wasn't working. That was to be expected. But the drinking water faucet wasn't working and toilets would not be unlocked until we got out of the station. I knew The New Haven used equipment for camp openings that they had no need for the rest of the year, but that knowledge didn't make the discomfort any more palatable..

The music came from the far end of our car. I looked down the isle. There was Stephen, standing with his accordion spread across his chest, playing "Funiculi-Funicula." He actually played well, but his voice was another matter. It was high and squeaky, and decidedly off key.

I knew his performance would not endear him to his future bunk-mates. Twelve year old boys don't often sing solos in public, unless urged on by adults. The other campers were remarkably restrained in their reactions. Nobody jeered him or told him to "Shut Up." But they were all talking about him and laughing at him, quietly and politely, but laughing nonetheless. Stephen was now officially notorious. I scurried down the aisle.

"Stephen, you have to sit down now. The train is about to start. I'll help you put the accordion away."

Reluctantly, he stopped singing and playing. Together we secured the accordion in the luggage rack. I sat down next to him.

"You should just hold off on the accordion while we're on the train. Let me introduce you to some of the other boys. The boys sitting over there are your age."

"Oh, Okay."

I took him over and just as I began introductions, the train started with a lurch. Stephen lost his balance, and wound up toppling onto Harry Schwartz' lap.

"Get off me. I can't breathe. Get this fat tub off of me!"

Stephen got off as fast as he could, slipping into the one vacant seat in the two facing benches. That was not an auspicious introduction to the group. I didn't know then, but I suspected that things would only get worse.

By the time we arrived at camp, his reputation was established.

That very night I received my first delegation of the season. It was Stephen's bunk-mates.

"He's awful. He's going to ruin our summer. "

"Give him a chance. You don't even know him yet. All the rest of you are friends. One boy can't ruin the summer for a whole bunk of friends, but you can and will ruin his if you don't give him a chance. Right now he probably knows you're here, and knows you're talking about him. How do you think that will make him feel?" I could see my logic was unlikely to change any minds.

"Can't you move him to another bunk?"

"Why should we be the ones to suffer?"

"Please!"

I knew Stephen would not be a desirable bunk-mate, but I was upset that the boys weren't even willing to give him a chance.

"He's not moving! Get that straight!" I'm sure that if you give him a chance, in just a few days he's going to become a member of the group. It's simply not fair to shut him out after just a few hours in camp."

They trooped out of my office grumbling. The next night after supper, during free play time, I heard screams coming from one of the bunks in the Junior Unit. I ran to see what the problem was. By the time I got there, two counselors were holding Stephen and Josh Levine apart. Josh had a big bump on his head and Stephen had a bloody nose. Josh was red in the face and Stephen was crying. I never did find out what actually started the fight. But the physical facts were agreed upon. Stephen had thrown a rock and hit Josh in the forehead. Josh retaliated by punching Stephen in the nose. Josh had a big bump emerging on his forehead and Stephen's nose was bleeding profusely. Throwing a rock at another kid was an inexcusable offense, but both boys were clearly in the wrong so both lost the privilege of going to the evening activity that night.

Later that night, after the campers were in bed their counselor came to my office. He had no question who the guilty party was. "He's pretty awful. He doesn't even try to get along. He wants everything to be on his terms. I can't blame the kids for getting angry. I don't think he can really last the summer in our bunk."

"What does he do that's so awful? I have to call his Mother. Give me a couple of examples."

"At rest period he walked over to Eddy's bed and deliberately farted in his face. It was lucky I was right there or they would have piled on him. After things calmed down, he went to change into his bathing suit. He came back into the room and threw his dirty underwear on Josh's pillow. He's just looking for trouble. He doesn't want them to like him. Then, at super time, he poured the whole bowl of French fries onto his plate before anybody else had any. The kids were really upset. Do you need more?"

"No. I get the picture and so will his Mother."

I called his Mother to alert her to the fact that Stephen was having serious problems in camp. I was as gentle as possible, but wanted her to know there had been some bad episodes.

"So nu, I'm not surprised. There's always a problem with Stephen. That's why I picked your camp. Ken Huberman told me that you were very good at working with kids with problems. Right now he's your problem. Anything you have to do is fine by me. This is my vacation. You don't need to call me every time there is a little problem."

A few days later Stephen pushed Sammy Cohen down the front steps of the bunk. It was only five steps, and it wasn't a serious injury, but we had to take Sammy to the hospital for an X-ray of his wrist. Sammy's mother was very upset when I told her how it happened. I agreed to move Stephen to a different bunk the next day.

There were only eighteen boys in Stephen's age group. That meant only three bunks of six boys each. The new bunk was right next to the old one. The boys were well aware of Stephen and his problems, and not happy to have him moving in. But they were good sports, and he moved in. It took only two days before I got a delegation from bunk ten asking to have Stephen removed. The counselors were all in agreement. Stephen should not be in camp. Stephen was a menace.

I had another wonderful phone conversation with his Mother.

"You have to keep him until Visiting Day. I'll take him home then."

"That's two more weeks. The situation is getting very tough here now."

"I can't get there before then. You'll have to work it out somehow."

"Alright, we'll work it out, but I want to make sure you understand that Stephen will be going home with you at the end of Visiting Day?"

"Yes, yes. Yes." She hung up.

That night I called Stephen aside, and told him we needed to have a conference. He was uncommunicative as I led him down to the waterfront path. We sat on the bench, looking out at the lake. "Stephen, you know things haven't been going well with the other boys. Can you think of something you can do to improve the situation?"

There was no response. "Stephen, answer me. I'm hoping we can come up with something that will make the rest of the summer go better for you." Stephen turned his head away, and mumbled something. "A little louder, Stephen, I just couldn't hear you."

"I hate it here. I want to go home." There was a catch in his voice, and I saw tears streaming down his cheeks." We sat for a while and his gentle tears turned to heaving sobs. "I want to go home." Over and over he repeated it. Eventually he quieted down. I told him about the move the next morning, and that he would be going home on Visiting Day. We both agreed he could make it until

Visiting Day.

Stephen was moved to Bunk twelve the next day. I knew it was only temporary, but hoped that it could be workable for the next two weeks. I appealed to the other boys' sense of fair play. They tolerated Stephen, but they made it clear that they hated him. We assigned one counselor just to Stephen so that he wouldn't have to go to the activities where he had problems. Removing him from many of the athletic activities and letting him spend time at Arts & Crafts at least provided several hours a day of much needed separation from the other boys.

Visiting Day came. So did Mrs. Spiegler. "Hi, Mrs. Spiegler, I'm so sorry things didn't work out better for Stephen this summer. I hope the two of you will be able to spend the whole day with us before you head back home. All of his things are packed and ready to go. You can either take them with you or we will ship them home Railway Express."

"That's very considerate of you Mr. Sharnoff, but Stephen won't be coming with me today. I'm afraid I have to go to Boston to visit my Brother. He's just had a heart attack, and he's in intensive care at Mass General. As soon as he's out of immediate danger I'll come back and pick Stephen up. It will be either Monday night or Tuesday morning." This was an unexpected development. I knew that Stephen and the kids in his bunk would be very upset, but I couldn't do anything about it.

"We'll look for you Monday night. I hope you enjoy Visiting Day with your son. And I do hope your brother-in-law is going to have a quick recovery."

Monday night came and went. Tuesday came and went. Tuesday night I placed a call to Mrs. Spiegler at her home in Brooklyn. She answered. "Mrs. Spiegler, what happened? You said you would come back to pick Stephen up and take him home with you."

"I'm sorry. After visiting my brother I got sick, and I thought it best to go right home." This was a ploy. I was certain of it. The whole business with her brother had been a lie. I was really furious with her.

"Mrs. Spiegler, Stephen cannot stay in camp. If you can't get come here to get him, we'll just send him home. Here's what I'll do. Tomorrow I'll send one of our most reliable counselors down on a train with him to Boston. He'll get Stephen to South Station, and put him on to the train headed to Grand Central. I'll call you in the morning to tell you what time to meet the train. You just have to get to the station."

"I'm sorry; I won't be able to meet him at the station. I'm just not well."

"You must have some friend or relative who can meet him at the station."

"No, there's nobody. I'm all alone. I'm afraid he's yours for the rest of the summer. You contracted to take care of him for eight weeks. You're just going to have to do that."

She hung up. I couldn't believe it. I dialed her number again and again.

She refused to pick up the phone. I had to find a solution. We have a camp doctor for July and a second camp doctor comes for August. A few days before Visitors' Day, I learned that our August doctor was hospitalized with Hepatitis, and would not be coming to camp. It was clear that we could no longer inflict Stephen on any of our campers. Stephen spent the rest of the summer, living in our vacant Camp Doctor's cabin with a counselor who represented a different kind of failure. They both lasted the summer, and actually did quite well together. Tom Lightfoot was a success working with Stephen Spiegler. Stephen, relieved of the pressure of having to get along with his peers, appeared to be content if not happy the next four weeks.

That happened in my very first summer as a camp director. In the subsequent thirty-six summers, I enjoyed working with many hundreds of campers and their parents. In all of those years we had perhaps five or six other campers who presented serious behavioral difficulties comparable to Stephens'. None of those was with us for more than a few days. But, in all of those years, I never again had to deal with a parent as selfish and intractable as Mrs. Spiegler. I will never forget her or her son!

7

Pauline the Mean

In 1962 I hired Pauline Grande as our Girls camp Head Counselor. She was a gym teacher at a grammar school on Long Island. Her school gave her rave references. She also had camp references. Most of her camp references were good, but her most recent one was considerably less enthusiastic than the others. Since I knew, and had little respect for, the camp she had been with, I took little stock in a negative reference coming from them. We talked about it at length during the interview.

Pauline had been Girls' Head Counselor the previous summer at Camp Chippewa. Chippewa was one of our closest neighboring camps. We competed against them in sports. I had personally visited there the previous summer as coach of our girls' softball team. I was appalled by what I saw going on there. It seemed their girls and boys were drifting all over the place and didn't have any particular schedule to follow. I was even more put off by the fact that their unsupervised teen age boys were allowed to hang around the ball field to watch their girl friends play our girls. If all they did was watch it would be one thing. But they teased their own girls and made fun of ours. Our girls took softball seriously and played reasonably well. We almost always won; and, against badly coached teams like theirs, scores like 20-0 were not uncommon. Their boys' catcalls were insulting and laced with sexual innuendos.

I didn't remember Pauline from that experiences, but she remembered the occasion well. She had been the home plate umpire. She remembered being embarrassed by everything about her camp that day. She assured me that it was not unusual. She had spent the whole summer debating whether or not to quit. She had found herself powerless to function as a proper head counselor in a camp where the directors failed to set a pattern of acceptable behavior. We talked for a while about the kind of camp she would run, and it was just exactly opposite to everything I had observed at Camp Chippewa. She and I were clearly on the same wave length. I offered her the job on the spot, and she accepted. All winter I was thrilled by the prospect of having a truly Professional Head Counselor for Camp Evergreen.

In our early years running camp we continued our predecessor's practice of holding pre-camp parties late in the Spring for the children who would be joining us at camp that summer. We invited Pauline to come to the New York girls' party, which we ran at the Roger Smith Hotel in White Plains. We thought this would be a good way to introduce her to the camp and the camp to her. She would meet some of the girls and counselors and help us run what was always a challenging party.

Pauline arrived looking uncomfortable in a tailored suit. After introductions and initial greetings, she said little, plunking herself down on a chair in the back of the room, seemingly as far from the action as she could decently get. The party went on all around her, but she might as well not have been there. It was now very late in the Spring, with the start of the camp season just around the corner. Judy and I were now worried that Pauline was going to be a catastrophe as Head Counselor. Clearly the party had not been her arena but we still had hopes that camp would be.

As soon as we got to camp, and Pauline started to work with her counselor staff, it was clear that camp was her place. She was great. She was a no nonsense woman in her late twenties, who had years of camp experience. She knew right from wrong. Schedules were not a puzzle to her. And she had the knack of getting her counselors to do what she wanted most of the time.

If Pauline saw an activity not going well, she joined the activity, added a new twist to make it fun. Her very presence in the game seemed to energize girls who had been listlessly going through the motions prior to her arrival. If our oldest girls didn't emerge quickly enough to suit her when the activity call sounded, she went bounding into Spruce lodge. They came right out and moved quickly to their activity.

Pauline had a commanding presence, naturally broad and muscular, she tended to dress in a way that reinforced the impression of strength. She was quickly dubbed "Pauline the Mean" by the boys and their counselors. I think the boys really were afraid of her. But there was a soft and gentle person hidden beneath a formidable outward appearance. Pauline had a wonderful knack with homesick little girls. I would see her walking with them from the ball field, waterfront or tennis court. They would be weeping or wailing. She would be holding the little girl's hand as they walked toward her cabin. Her "homesick conferences" always took place in her cabin where the sad little girl could munch on a candy from Pauline's candy bowl. She could spill out her tales of woe while sitting on the floor cuddling and petting Pauline's dog Gypsy. A short time later the tears would be over and Pauline would walk the little girl back to join her group.

Pauline the Mean she might be, but the girls respected her, and many even loved her. She was the person most responsible for turning Camp Evergreen around. Prior to her arrival on the scene we had survived a couple of rocky camp seasons under my inexperienced leadership. I knew a lot about working with boys and male counselors, but it was Pauline who showed me how a girls' camp could and should be run. Equally important, she set an example of how to be a Head Counselor for her ultimate successor, a dynamite young counselor named Phyllis Margil.

Saturday Night Socials

When we bought the camp, we inherited a lot of good things, and some things that drove me crazy. Saturday night socials were always my least favorite camp activity. But the socials we inherited involved not only our teen-agers, but reached down to the nine and ten year old boys and girls as well. After our first summer running camp we abolished socials for all of the camp units below Seniors. There were howls of protest, but we stuck to our convictions. The Senior socials, which we did retain, took place as far from the rest of camp as we could place them, at the furthest end of camp, in Kenwood's Senior Lodge, which was a small Recreation Hall designed to be used for night time activities for our oldest campers..

Our camp is in the woods, in a part of New Hampshire largely by-passed by civilization. It is located on a dirt road about a half mile in from the blacktop. Eagle Pond Road, actually connected to a spider web network of dirt roads, but in those days had virtually no traffic except vehicles headed to or from camp. When you drive in from the blacktop the first signs of life are our camp buildings on the right. On the left is an impenetrable forest. The camp is strung out in a line along the lake. It is between the lake and the dirt road which roughly parallels the lake. You first reach Evergreen, followed by Kenwood's Junior Camp and finally the Senior Boys area. The Kenwood Senior Lodge stood at the most distant corner of Kenwood's Senior camp and was isolated from everything in camp except that dirt road which ran close behind it.

I was not at the Senior Social that night. I was running a program with our younger boys in the camp's main Rec Hall. I was in the midst of leading a song when one of the Evergreen senior counselors burst into the room, coming up to me in the front of the hall. She was breathless. It took a few seconds before she could do anything but gasp.

"Arthur, Billy sent me down to get you. He said come right away. We have a big problem at the Senior Lodge. Some tough looking guys came into the dance and they wanted to dance with some of the girls. They reeked from beer. Billy told them to leave, but they refused. They were still in there swearing and arguing with Billy when he sent me to get you."

I ran with her up to Senior Lodge, leaving the Junior Camp counselors to continue the Rec Hall program. We were both breathless when we arrived. The kids were excited and agitated and so were the counselors. But the mysterious tough guys were nowhere in sight. The strangers had just scooted out a minute or two before we arrived. The counselors were sure the intruders were drunk. Billy, our Boys' Senior Unit Leader, was really upset.

"I didn't want to get in a fight with them, but it almost came to that before they finally left. I know they're around here somewhere. They haven't left camp." That sounded ominous. In fact, it sounded like those kids were going to present us with a great big pain in the neck the rest of the night.

"Just keep everyone in the building and block the door. I'll track them down." I searched all around the lodge. There were no signs of life. Then I realized that if there was any real danger it would be for our younger girls. The Seniors were all in the Senior Lodge with their counselors, and the Junior Camp boys were all in the Rec Hall with plenty of counselors. On the other hand, our younger girls were back in their individual lodges where their counselors were not even aware that there was a problem. Who knew what kind of mischief these drunken teen-age boys might cause. As I ran down the road toward Evergreen, I came first to the Girls' softball field. From a distance I saw a flashlight beam playing on the field. As I got closer I saw three young men caught in the beam. I heard Pauline's voice.

"Don't you move! Don't you dare take a step until I tell you that you can.!"

I directed my flashlight at them from the road. We both had huge flashlights with sealed beams like auto headlights. Our beams intersected, and we both moved slowly toward them. They stood like statues. It reminded me of a WWII movie with the Nazi searchlights pinning escaping refugees. They didn't know who or how many of us were behind those lights, and I could see they were scared. They stood stock still waiting for us.

As we got close enough to talk I could smell the beer on their breath and emitting from their clothes. There was no doubt. They were drunk. But the bravado and fight they had displayed at Senior Lodge had deserted them, at least for the moment. We walked them to the corner of the ball field where there was a softball backstop, and beyond that to the Evergreen gate, which signaled an entrance to the road. I wanted them out, and as fast as possible. They all looked big and menacing in the dark. The tallest of the boys was clearly their leader. I shined my light in his face. The light was intense, and he shaded his eyes defensively with the back of his hand. He didn't look so threatening at that moment.

"Where is your car?" He grunted an answer I couldn't make out. "I asked you a question. I want to hear the answer."

"It's in the bushes up by that other building where they're dancing."

"Okay, you come with me. We'll get your car." I then turned to Pauline. "You watch these two, and don't let them out of your sight. If they give you any trouble at all call the police." This was at a time before anybody ever heard of cell phones. Pauline would have had to run to the office to make that phone call.

I walked up the road with one sullen but chastened young man in search of his car. It's a very lonely dark road. As we approached Senior camp, we were surrounded by woods on both sides of the road. I was a little nervous thinking that this kid could jump me, and I had absolutely no way to protect myself. Recognizing my own danger, it suddenly dawned on me that Pauline was at greater risk. I had left her with two of them. They might get their courage back at any minute.

We recovered his car without incident, and drove back to the Evergreen gate, where Pauline waited with the other two charmers. When we reached them the two boys were sitting on large boulders by the side of the road. Pauline stood over them holding her big flashlight on them, as one might hold a gun on captured bandits. Clearly they were her prisoners and were not about to move until she said they could. I got out of the car and the other two climbed in. Pauline had some final words of advice.

"Now get out of here, and don't come back. If any of you ever show your faces around here again, we will call the police. You'll find they're not as kind as we are." The driver stepped hard on the gas pedal, and they left us in a cloud of dust. I turned to Pauline to ask how she was. She was shaking like a leaf, and she started to cry. I had never seen Pauline cry.

"I was never so scared in all of my life. How could you leave me with two of them? Do you realize that the big guy had a broken beer bottle in his hand? I told him to drop it, and he did, but he could have killed me."

I apologized and was shaken myself to realize I had fallen into the habit of thinking of her as "Pauline the Mean" just like the kids. I thought there was no situation she couldn't handle. I also realized that I had never before seen her show any emotion other than excitement during ball games.

Pauline was wonderful, and I thought she would be with us forever. She seemed to love camp just as much as we loved having her. She was with us four summers. After her fourth camp season, she seemed to disappear for a few months. Finally in January I got a letter from her.

"....I enjoyed my years at Evergreen, but I just can't come back this year. You'll be fine without me. Phyllis is grown up enough now to do the job." I regretted her decision, but she was certainly right about Phyllis.

I still wonder occasionally, whatever happened to Pauline. I never did get to tell her how very important she had been to me and to Camp Evergreen.

8
Evergreen Softball

When we bought Kenwood and Evergreen they were very separate camps with quite different philosophies and policies. Kenwood had been a traditional boys' summer camp, with a heavy sports program which emphasized athletic competition. That was the camping environment which served me well as a camper and which I enjoyed as a counselor. Kenwood had been a camp since 1930. Evergreen was only ten years old when we came into the picture as Directors. Evergreen was directed by Bernice Huberman, whose philosophy of camping was almost diametrically opposed to her husband's. Evergreen emphasized individual activities rather than team sports and individual accomplishment rather than competition. In fact, actual competition was officially not welcome at Evergreen. During Bernice's years as Director, Evergreen was altogether a much quieter place than Kenwood.

Over a period of time I came to see great value to both approaches, but when we first took over the camps I thought the Evergreen approach didn't make much sense. How could you hope to instruct sports without competition as a stimulus? "Nonsense" I said to myself "the only way girls will have the desire to learn and get good at sports and really to care about them is to provide the incentive of competition."

Softball was the obvious place to start for two reasons. First, I was a baseball player, and had been coaching boys in baseball and softball for years; so I had no hesitancy in coaching girls. I wanted to do it myself rather than finding a competent softball coach among our counselors. I knew I could teach and would coach well. Perhaps more important, if I coached the girls, I would get closer to these strange new creatures called teen age girls. It was a great policy decision. I loved working with the girls. We certainly got to know one another in those early years and in all of the years that followed. It took me awhile, but I came to almost understand them, and to appreciate their emotional highs, their fantastic cheering and their never ending singing. I came to learn that the morale boost of singing better and cheering louder than the other team was at least as important to many of the girls as the outcome of the games.

The second reason to choose softball was recent camp history. The year before Judy and I bought camp, Bernice had suffered a life threatening illness early in the camp season. Because of her illness that summer Ken had taken over and ran Evergreen his first and only time. Under Ken's auspices Evergreen fielded its first inter-camp team, playing softball against Camp Wilmot, our closest neighbor just a few miles down our dirt road.

I made a few phone calls, and scheduled two games for our oldest girls. Then I announced try-outs for the team. Twelve or thirteen girls came for try-outs. Of course, they would all make the team, but try-outs were important. It announced to the kids that it mattered and that making the team was not automatic. In those early years we had just a few girls who had actual ability and experience, and I learned that the first rule of try-outs is to make sure you don't wind up getting too many people hurt.

My first pop fly ball to the outfielders resulted in a quick run to the infirmary. The ball easily eluded a nervously outstretched gloved hand and landed squarely on the top of a girl's head. That caused me to quickly re-evaluate my approach. All of the girls were brought in close, and I tossed a few very easy lobs to each of them. Some had virtually no experience and were hopelessly inept. They were clear candidates for the next infirmary run if I was not very careful. With the infield candidates I tapped the balls very softly. Several of the girls were clearly afraid of the bouncing ball. Only one ball hopped far enough over a waiting glove to locate a defenseless nose. By the time the girl with the bleeding nose reached the infirmary with her accompanying counselor, I saw the first girl coming back with her counselor. They were taking turns holding a bag of ice cubes on the top of her head. This try-out was certainly a smash success. By the following summer I was equipped with spongy rubber soft balls for those first tryouts.

Very early it was clear that we had three actual ball players. Phyllis Margil was our star. She later became a star counselor and finally matured into a wonderful Head Counselor who ran Evergreen program for decades. She is now Evergreen's Director. The other two, Marilyn Grossman and Gail Koff, disappeared from the Evergreen scene after their graduation as campers. We had several other girls who lacked experience and ability but whose enthusiasm was contagious and endearing. We had many practices. Together we proved that anybody who is willing to work at softball will get better at it, and they all did.

After a few weeks of practice our team was ready to go. The whole camp was excited at the prospect of a real team playing another camp. We went down the road to play Camp Wilmot, our closest possible rival. I was shocked when I got there to see that their softball field was laid out on such a slant that if a ball was put down on the ground at first base it would soon start rolling, pass the pitcher's area, roll next to third base and continue down into their pond. With the intuitive instinct of a true coach, I concluded that we were not going to play a softball powerhouse that day. We went through our by then snappy pre-game warm up. I hit softies to the more tentative fielders and challenging ones to our pitcher, short stop and first baseman. Then I watched as the Wilmot girls warmed up. Their pre-game warm up resembled our very first try-out. They looked pathetic. Comparatively speaking, our girls looked like pros. The game was mercifully stopped after two innings with Evergreen having an astonishing lead of thirty runs or so. I took our champions out for ice cream. I called camp from the restaurant to relay the result and final score. We were met on the Evergreen ball field as conquering heroes by the whole camp. EVERGREEN SOFTBALL WAS BORN!

A week later we traveled several miles to Camp Chippewa. Though several of the Chippewa girls clearly knew how to play softball, the disparity between the two teams was just as great as it had been at Camp Wilmot. Our kids, whatever their skill level, actually knew what they were doing. The Chippewa girls clearly did not. But the game was not nearly as much fun. Camp Wilmot was a nice small girls' camp, like Evergreen. Their girls were really nice kids. They cheered, clapped and sang. They just didn't practice or care much about softball. Camp Chippewa, by contrast was a larger coed camp. Their boys were allowed to hang out around the field without any male counselors in sight. They teased their own girls for their softball inadequacies and made fun of ours for being capable. Worse still, they commented on our girls physical characteristics in stage whispers that grew louder with each new batter.

"Their shortstop looks like she needs a shave"...."Here comes the one with zits all over. I hope they're not catchy."..."look at the boobs on that one."

I complained to the umpire in the first inning. She walked over and scolded the boys. The game resumed, but nothing changed. The boys didn't leave and they didn't stop. After I concluded that the umpire was unwilling or unable to control the boys, I took our girls off the field and we headed back to camp.

I made two policy decisions that day. First, our Kenwood boys would never be present at Evergreen games and our girls would not be spectators at our boys' inter-camp games. Neither boys nor girls needed the additional pressure of worrying about what their boy friends or girls friends might think of their play. Nor should the girls have to consider how they looked while playing. The second decision was that our girls should only play other girls camps and not coed camps.

I was able to maintain the policy of no coed spectators at games or practices for the next thirty-six years. Though it was an unintended consequence, I believe it was a contributing factor in turning Evergreen into an athletic powerhouse. I was unable to maintain the second policy decision, though I tried. Through the years more and more camps dropped by the wayside and were out of business. As the years went on we traveled at ever increasing distances for inter-camp competition. At first it seemed that the all girls' camps that were geographically closest to us were among the earliest to fail. So we wound up playing coed camps that were not too distant. Then they started going out of business, and we traveled farther away from home and found a new group of all girls' camps.

When Judy and I bought Kenwood and Evergreen in 1960 there were 22 camps within about a twenty miles radius. When we sold the camp thirty-six years later Kenwood & Evergreen and only one other camp had survived. It was sad watching so many camps close. In the 1970s there just were not enough children to fill them all. Only the strong could survive. In the 1980s retiring camp directors discovered that their camps were worth more as vacation properties than they were as camps, so those camps too disappeared. Both Camp Wilmot and Camp Chippewa were among the casualties. In the early 1960s Camp Wilmot became "Light of the World Camp", a church owned property with varied groups occupying the camp each week. They would no longer be interested in inter-camp sports. I was disappointed. I was less distressed when I learned, in the mid-1960s that Camp Chippewa was out of business. There were signs on the property advertising their campers' cabins for sale.

After the first few years of searching for other camps to play, and hoping to find some, we developed some regular pleasant rivalries. In the process we indulged in something girls camps called "Play Days" where several sports would be played on the same day. It was a wonderful concept because with enough sports involved we could get virtually all of our girls, even the least athletic, into at least one of the games.

One of the camps we played on an annual basis from the mid-1960s to the present is Camp Robindel, then a much larger girls' camp located in distant Center Harbor, New Hampshire (an hour bus ride). They had wonderful tennis players and swimmers, and we usually lost in those areas. In the early years we always lost to them in volleyball because we wouldn't let any girls who were on the softball team also play intercamp volleyball. In softball they always presented a real team and usually they had several superior players but minimal team coaching. Frequently we had good games with them, but we usually won. We also played off and on against Camp Wi-co-su-ta, which was located on Newfound Lake and was only a thirty-five minute ride from

Evergreen. They were also a much larger camp than Evergreen in the 1960s and 1970s, with perhaps twice as many girls. They consistently had strong tennis, gymnastics and volleyball teams. Their softball teams would vary from decent to awful, depending upon the year. I don't believe we ever lost to their girls in about thirty years of inter-camp softball play, but it is possible that we lost one somewhere along the way.

Our nearest and dearest rival camp was Camp Kearsarge. Camp Kearsarge was located in nearby Elkins, New Hampshire, a fifteen minute ride from Evergreen. I loved it when we played Camp Kearsarge and so did our girls. First, they were close. Second, they were the same size camp as Evergreen, give or take a few girls. Third, I really liked their Director, Rhoda Booth. She loved camp, as I loved camp, and was sincerely devoted to her girls. She was also a very interesting and colorful character. We had play days with Kearsarge, and both camps won their fair share of competitive tennis matches, swim meets, and volleyball games. We almost always won softball, usually by lop-sided scores. But, regardless of the outcome, the girls always enjoyed the day.

Rhoda ran a camp with a more relaxed schedule than ours, and she had a more elastic sense of time than I. If we arranged a day at Evergreen with the first activities to start at 10:00 our fields were ready, our greeters were at the Evergreen gate, and our girls were ready to play. By 10:30 our girls were getting hoarse from singing and cheering. I phoned Kearsarge. They were on their way. At 11:05 they would arrive. All of the scheduled activities would have to be shortened to get them all in. But somehow it worked out. The softball game, which was usually first activity in the afternoon, generally ran less time than allocated because the score would become so lopsided in our favor that there was little point in continuing.

One day we went to Kearsarge for a full day of activity. We arrived at the agreed upon time of 9:30. There was not a soul in sight. We went to the tennis courts since that was the first scheduled activity. Nobody was there. I went back to check at the dining room, which also housed the camp office. Rhoda met me on the dining room porch. She was in her robe, which was clearly covering pajamas. Her hair was in curlers under a net. She hardly presented a glamorous image of a female camp director. With the dining room door open, I heard the chatter of a dining room full of Kearsarge girls. It appeared they were still at breakfast and not quite ready for the opening volley. Rhoda apologized.

"I'm so sorry, Arthur. Dear me, I don't know how I forgot you were coming today. I must have neglected to write it down. Tell me now what we were playing? I'll have the girls come right out." She was always so pleasant it was hard ever to be angry with Rhoda.

Our counselors and girls all were astonished that the Kearsarge girls were still having breakfast at 9:40. At Evergreen our girls were usually through with breakfast, had cabins cleaned, and were into activities by 9:00. The Kearsarge schedule sounded very relaxed and luxurious. Our girls were amused. Our counselors, on the other hand, were envious. A few minutes passed and six Kearsarge tennis players came running to the courts. I don't remember who won those matches. They were interrupted by two kinds of hysteria. Their clay courts were home to a large number of hornets' nests. Just as the matches were about to start, the hornets emerged from their holes in the clay. The girls who were warming up on the courts at the time became hysterical as the swarm of potential stingers buzzed around them. They raced off the courts, and hid under as many layers of clothing as they could find at court side.

A Kearsarge counselor was dispatched to find Rhoda. She came, breathless, still nattily attired in her robe and curlers. She was holding a can of insect spray, and ran on to the court ineffectually chasing individual hornets around and around. I don't think she downed any of the invaders. It was a very funny sight. Our girls were rolling on the ground laughing. Their girls were suppressing laughter behind their hands. Finally the maintenance man came to the rescue with a large commercial spraying machine. We left the tennis courts, and went to play volley ball first while he disposed of the hornets.

By the late 1960s, our girls were getting better and better. I could now field softball teams where our starting lineup no longer had any girls who were in danger of getting injured by balls hit to them. Our camp was a little larger now than in the early 1960s which created a larger talent pool. Even more important, we were gaining a reputation as a girls' camp that actually instructed in sports, so we started to interest parents of more athletic girls. By the early 1970s almost all of the girls in camp had an interest in softball. At least they all professed an interest.

In 1974 we had seventy-seven girls in camp, and sixty-three of them were on age appropriate softball teams. The problem was finding games for all of these girls to provide an incentive and a reward for all of the practicing. Finally I arranged a play date with Camp Kearsarge involving several sports in three age groups: girls age 13-15, 11-12 and 9-10. Our girls were eager and enthusiastic at all ages. All sixty-three girls were going to be able to play softball that day. By this time Rhoda was no longer running Camp Kearsarge. She had retired and turned the camp over to her son Gil. Unlike his Mother, Gil did not love running a camp, but he was doing his best, or so I thought until that day.

We waited by the tennis courts, and six Kearsarge Senior girls came out with their coach. "Ok" I thought, "our Senior girls will start with tennis." I asked their tennis coach what else was scheduled for that period. She didn't know of anything else. I asked for Gil. He finally came out, and I questioned him as to which activities our 10 year olds and 12 year olds would be doing first.

"Sorry, I meant to call you. We really haven't had time to practice with the younger girls. Only our 15 year old teams will be playing, but we will compete in all three sports."

"But Gil, I have over sixty girls here. They've been practicing and they came to play. They'll be terribly disappointed, particularly if they don't get to play softball."

"Sorry, we're just not going to be able to accommodate you."

"It's not a question of accommodating me. This is what we agreed to weeks ago on the phone. If you weren't going to be able to do what we arranged you could at least have called a little in advance and let me know so I would not have brought all of these girls along and told them they were playing."

"I know, but times have changed. This is the way it has to be. You know we don't have to play any games. If you don't like the way I've set things up you can take your girls back to camp. There are other camps for both of us to play.

"Gil, of course we don't want to leave. Our two camps have been working together for years. Can't you get your girls out just to play some games, even if they haven't practiced? You've got more girls than we have." By this time the tennis was ending, and the girls from both camps were moving to the volleyball courts. They had nine big girls ready to play. I heard swim call over the PA, and watched as all of the younger Keararge campers trooped down to the waterfront for swim. "What am I going to tell my girls? They came over here to play, and you won't let them do anything?"

"You can play whatever girls you want against my softball team."

"OK, Gil, thank you."

I didn't want to say anything else because I was so furious with him I wasn't sure what I would say. But he did give me an idea. After volleyball there was the usual pause for lunch and rest. During that "Rest Period" I took all of our girls and counselors down to the softball field. I started running very short practice sessions with each of our teams. Then I sat them down to talk.

"Here is what we are going to do. They only have their Senior team ready to play. All of you will play against them. You are all good ball players. Our Seniors will play the first two innings. Our Juniors will play the next two and the Sophomores will play as many more as we have time for.

The game started with the usual cheering. We had a good Senior team. Though defense was always my first criteria in setting up a team, many of our girls could hit too. We scored five runs in the first inning. My daughter Amy pitched the first inning for us, and shut them down 1-2-3 with two strike outs and a weak ground ball. I replaced seven of our starters with pinch hitters in the 2nd inning. Our substitutes came through with three more runs. Amy's friend Sara Bloom pitched the second inning for us and again shut Kearsarge down 1-2-3.

At the start of the third inning, I replaced all of the Seniors with our eleven and twelve year old Juniors. This lineup was filled with smaller girls. They were less powerful, but happened to be even better athletes. Our twelve year olds scored twice, raising the score to 10-0. Our very best pitcher in camp that summer was twelve year old Betsy Friedman. A skinny little twig of a girl, Betsy could whip the ball in faster than any girl, boy or counselor in camp. The three Kearsarge batters she faced were terrified as all three struck out without touching the ball. Now the substitutes on our Junior Team came to bat, and they failed to score. Betsy paralyzed three More Kearsarge hitters. We had completed four innings and it was time for our sophomore team.

Our Sophomore team came to bat. They were all tiny. They were presumably a team of ten year olds, but at least half of them were eight or nine. They looked mighty small against the Kearsarge fifteen year olds. We were shut down without touching the ball. Our good little pitcher was a wonderful kid. She was able to get the ball over the plate. Against other ten year olds that would have been enough. But against fifteen year old girls it was not nearly enough. The Kearsarge girls stood up at bat with complete confidence. They hit the ball often and hard. They finally won the game in the last of the sixth inning. Both teams delivered cheers for the other team, and we trooped back to our bus. We could see that the Kearsarge Senior girls were embarrassed to have won a game like that. But Gil was pleased.

"Play as many girls as you like." He said. "We always enjoy winning."

I wasn't sure I had done our little girls any favor having them play and get beaten so badly. But my doubts were dispelled on the short bus ride back to camp. It was clear that they were very pleased that they had gotten to play. Many of them wrote home to their parents bragging that they were now on the Senior team and had played against the Seniors of Camp Kearsarge.

Our Evergreen softball teams got better and better as time went on, and the caliber of opponents also improved. More girls' camps were now coaching, not only tennis, swimming and individual sports, but softball, soccer and basketball too. In 1978 I decided to start a girls' softball tournament, modeled after the long standing Boys Tri-State Softball tournament, which had begun in 1958. It was time for the girls. The concept was foreign to girls' camps, and I had to sell hard. The first year we only had four camps, and it was not a surprise when we won. The second year we had six teams, and again we won.

In 1980 we now had a camp of one hundred girls. It was the third year of the tournament. It was my tournament. I invented it, and I expected us to win every year. After all, how could we lose? I was the coach. By then it was well established that my teams were supposed to win. Well, somehow it didn't always work out according to plan.

We were playing Camp Robindel in the Finals. Neither team had a dominant pitcher. Not surprisingly there was plenty of hitting on both sides. Unfortunately the score was nine to five in their favor going into the last of the fifth (the final inning). We loaded the bases with two outs. We had one girl who had not yet played that day, and I sent her up as a pinch hitter. Karen Kramer was a wonderful girl. She was sweet, bright, creative and altogether as charming as a fourteen year old girl can be. She was tall and her coordination had not yet caught up with her growth. She was questionable in the field, but at bat, when she connected, she was capable of hitting the ball a long way. I hoped this would be such an occasion.

On the first pitch, her bat connected, and the ball went flying beyond the center fielder. Our girls were jumping up and down and screaming with excitement. The three runners on base scooted around to score, and awaited Karen at home. Karen flew around the bases, arms and legs akimbo. She was so excited that she neglected to make contact with any of the three bases as she circled triumphantly. She was mobbed by her adoring team-mates at home plate. Unfortunately, the other coach saw what I saw, and had the ball thrown in to the first baseman, who stepped on the bag, and the umpire called Karen out. We lost the game and the tournament by one run. The girls were very disappointed, particularly Karen, but nobody was upset with her. They spent the ride back to camp consoling her. By the time we arrived at camp she was the heroine again. She had hit the longest ball of the day, and that was a triumph all by itself. We celebrated our second place finish that night just as though we had won. Our traditional pizza and ice cream treat was as joyous as ever.

In 1983, 1984, 1985 we had such powerful teams in all sports that there was virtually nobody around who could play us. We had about twenty-five real athletes in our Senior unit, and two of them, Abby Karlyn and Kari Rosencranz, were about the strongest female athletes who had ever attended Evergreen. They came together as friends from home, and they were totally dominant in all team sports. Abby pitched for us and Kari played short stop. Our two best players always played pitcher and short stop. Several of the girls in that group of Seniors went on to play high school sports. Kari and Abby became varsity athletes in college. Abby was still pitching years after camp. Another of the athletic girls in that group was Lynn Meterparel. She had never played softball before joining us at camp. Soccer was her sport, but she made herself into a softball player too. Some years later, Lynn went on to become the first female general manager of a men's major league soccer team. Many years later Lynn is back at camp filling the role of Evergreen Head Counselor.

In 1990 we lost a game. That was shocking in itself. We were not used to losing. We had a really good team that year. Deena Maletz was our pitcher. She had pinpoint control and good speed and never seemed to get flustered. We had Jennifer Russo who could hit for distance and we had two really accomplished bunters, Hillary Dockser and Emily Luskin. Bunting and running was always an important part of our offense. Every position was held by a girl who could field and knew what to do with the ball. This was not a team likely to lose.

It was the final game of the Tri-State tournament. We played a camp new to the tournament, Camp Bernadette. Bernadette was a Catholic girls' camp located in the strangely named town of Gilmanton Iron Works, about an hour away from Evergreen. Early in the day, on breaks between our games, I watched Bernadette destroy their early opponents. I knew we would be meeting them in the finals and they would be trouble. They were big and strong and knew how to play. But most of all they had a pitcher. She was the first windmill pitcher I had ever seen in a camp game. She could throw hard enough to strike fear into the heart of any batter at the girls' forty-foot tournament pitching distance. Early in the day, while her team was playing against another camp, one of her fast pitches broke her catcher's hand. We took that girl to the emergency room at the New London Hospital. During the game just before they were to play us, she was pitching to a new catcher, who was clearly afraid of the ball. Several pitches passed her by without a touch. They went right to the backstop. One of the missed pitches broke and went through a two inch board in our backstop. Unfortunately, our whole team was watching when this happened, and they were not too enthusiastic at the prospect of batting against her.

Bernadette was good, but so were our girls. We just didn't have any answer for their pitcher. In the first two innings our girls were actually shaking when they went to the plate. I didn't blame them. Bernadette scored a run in the first inning on a long home run by their third batter. The second, third and fourth innings neither team could score. In the top of the fifth and last inning, Bernadette scored again. As we came to bat I called our girls into a huddle.

"She's been pitching all day. She's must be getting tired. I want you to wait her out. No swinging unless you have two strikes called. Make yourselves small at bat. Crouch. Pretend you're going to bunt. Do anything to make it hard for her to throw strikes." Our first batter went down on three strikes. Then, unbelievably, we got our first real hit of the game, a double. Our next batter hit a weak ground ball toward first base. Our runner who was on second base ran right through Jacki McCarthy's stop sign at third base and continued on home. She should never have scored, but their first baseman was so surprised to see her going that she threw late and high to home plate. That was our entire rally. Our next batter struck out, and we lost 2-1.

But something new had been added to the game, the Windmill pitch. It was no longer going to be good enough just to have the best team. We were going to have to learn how to hit a really fast pitch, and we were going to have to develop girls who could throw like that. Eventually we were lucky enough to have a few of our girls develop into windmill pitchers.

Our best ever was a girl named E.B. May. E.B. was our star in 2004. When she threw her windmill her hand slapped her leg as she released the ball. It sounded like a gunshot. The batters were afraid before the ball ever left her hand.

We continued to have wonderful girls and stronger and stronger athletic teams. We also found stronger opponents to play, but still we won almost all of the time.

I had so many joyful years coaching our girls' softball team. I loved to see them jumping up and down cheering. It was a treat for me to see them willing to work to make the team. It was personally rewarding to see the girls try so hard to improve, and to learn what it means to be part of a team. But most of all, I just came to love and feel close to all of those girls through the years. The bonus for camp was that so many of the members of the softball teams later returned to camp as counselors. Year after year they tried to recreate for their girls the same sense of fun and enthusiasm and team work they had experienced as campers.

9

The Hat Man

It was 1963 and we were getting better at running camp. Our percentage of returning campers was reassuring evidence, but it was clear that I needed help enrolling new campers. Apparently I wasn't very good at it. The best way to get such help, I decided, was to hire a person who had a record as a camp recruiter. That person would also play a key role in camp. Stuart Goldberg became a vital player in our comeback years. He answered my New York Times ad for a "Camp Representative".

When I first met Stu, he seemed almost perfect for the role. He had been a Head Counselor at a camp in upstate New York, and had successfully enrolled campers for them. Before that he had been a waterfront director for years at a very large camp in Pennsylvania's Pocono Mountains. He was a Junior High School teacher in an upper middle class town on Long Island. He had a young family, which seemed to promise the likelihood of longevity in camp. He appeared very old and experienced to me at the time, though he and his wife Sarah were only a few years older than we were and very likely not yet forty.

In our first interview Stu made it clear what kind of camp role he wanted to play. He no longer wanted to be a Waterfront Director or a Head Counselor. He wanted to be something we had never had before, something called an Assistant Director. At the time we were desperate for campers, so I was willing to buy into his concept of an Assistant Director. Stu was good at enrolling new campers, and we needed campers. I also needed some experienced help in camp. He would provide it. His primary responsibility would be working with the Kenwood Head Counselor, Charlie Epstein. I would devote much of my time to improving the operation of Evergreen, our girls' camp.

Stu had an overtly expansive personality, with lots of highly visible good cheer. He looked like a happy guy, bursting with enthusiasm. In public, he always wore a smile. It lit up his ruddy complexion. He worked at creating a persona for himself. He was a self-made colorful character. He came to camp with a hat collection, which became his visible signature. Each day of the summer he wore a different hat, from standard baseball caps, to a fireman's hat to a bee keepers screened shroud. He even had a deep sea diver's helmet.

In addition to experience, Stu also brought some great camp programs with him. He had his own activity that became identified with him. He was the chief Polar Bear, the guy who would go around early in the morning waking up kids who wanted to be members of the Polar Bear club, going on a pre-reveille swim. After their swim, he took them to the dining hall porch where they had hot chocolate, and were then sent back to their bunks to rejoin their bunk-mates for the start of the day. It was a wonderful experience for kids.

Of course, early morning swims were a camp tradition long before Stuart Goldberg made his appearance, but we had never made the most of it. He built it up and institutionalized it. The kids who went on the early morning swims earned "Polar Bear" patches. They had their names read off at morning lineups. It became a big deal. He had a sense of drama and dress-up that brought a new dimension to camp. Everything he did became a big deal. That was his way.

Stu revitalized our camp carnival. Camp carnivals have been standard in many camps for a very long time. In a typical camp carnival, each bunk or unit creates a booth with some sort of game. Once the Carnival is built, campers take turns being in charge of their bunk's booth, and going around to other booths. We've had some pretty elaborate ones through the years: water slides, miniature golf courses, dunk the counselor games and horror houses. Some complicated booths require campers and their counselors to work for several days building, testing and trying them out before the actual carnival. Decorating and building the booths becomes a morale building activity.

Since almost everybody works on its' construction, there is no way the basic contents of the carnival can be a surprise to any but the very youngest campers. Stu Goldberg brought us a way to make that day a surprise.... He may not have invented it, but it was brand new to us. He introduced "The Big Top". It was erected at dawn, before reveille. When the campers came up for morning assembly they saw it for the very first time. What was the Big Top? It doesn't sound like much, but it was enough for imaginative kids to feel it was something special. We positioned a big pole in the ground in the middle of the carnival.

That was the hub of a wheel. The spokes were multi-colored streamers of plastic pennants, like the ones they use at used car lots.....strung out from the hub to shorter poles sixty feet from the center. It created the illusion of a colorful Big Top. In the center was the centerpiece, a huge papier-mâché figure of the theme character for the carnival that year. The one I associate most clearly with Stu was our very first big top. The theme of the carnival that year was cowboys. He arrived at assembly that morning dressed in clothes and hat identical to our paper–mâché giant cowboy. Since his day we have had some more imaginative costuming, but he actually gave us a start in that direction.

Stuart also introduced "Rope Burning", a spectacular evening event that we have used ever since as the culminating event of our all-camp Apache Relay race. I doubt if the Apaches ever had a relay even remotely resembling the race that has borne its name for generations of campers. Though it may currently sound politically incorrect, the name is likely to stick forever, in the same way that boys will "Indian Wrestle" forever. There are some descriptions that are too choice to abandon. In a Rope Burning contest there are two or more teams of four senior campers whose object is to build a fire whose flame will burn and break a rope suspended between two poles ten feet above the ground. As a camp activity, Rope Burning has many rules and traditions about when the wood may be gathered; how large pieces of wood may be; how many matches are allowed; whether a team may protect a fire by holding blankets on the windward side; whether or not tennis rackets can be used as bellows to fan the flames of the fires in their infancy, etc., etc. etc.

But imagine two, three or four fires brightening the night; the whole camp gathered behind a safety rope cheering their fire builders. "Burn fire, Burn".... "Burn fire, Burn" .... "Higher fire higher". The teams chant with the fire builders. The chanting gets more intense as the flames get higher. The fire builders, drenched with sweat from exertion, dragging more wood on to the fire; fanning the flames; throwing dry pine needles on to help the flames leap higher, ever higher. The cheering comes to a fever pitch as the flames lick against the rope, and finally the rope catches, sizzles, and breaks. A great cheer erupts from the successful team. Tradition keeps the other team or teams still working so that their rope too will burn. Lesser success merits fewer points, but still they work and sweat, and their team screams encouragement.

For the first few years only boys were allowed to build the fires. It was my impression that girls in the early nineteen sixties were not interested in getting that sweaty, working that hard or getting that dirty, but that all changed a few years later. Girls became more assertive, and argued that they should have the same rights and activities that the boys had. They were sufficiently convincing that we changed our policy, and girls too became fire builders. We had to make sure that all participants, boys or girls, had their hair tied back. The hose man, always a responsible counselor, whose job it was to keep fires from spreading, spent most of his time dousing the hot heads of the fire builders until the last rope was burned.

Stu was with us for five summers. He could have made a place for himself for many more seasons if he had wanted to dig in and take over an area of camp responsibility. In his first few years it all worked. He helped inject some new life and spark into camp, and he helped to pick up some of the slack for Charlie, who got tired and tended to run down toward the end of the summer. But after his first two or three years, we were already a lot better organized. As camp was getting better and better, he appeared to remove himself from active participation. It seemed there was not very much that he wanted to do.

He wanted to be an Executive. Our camp was still a small camp, and we were barely breaking even. The concept of a non-working executive was not only inappropriate, but it was also personally galling to me. Between his commissions for camper recruiting and enrolling campers and his salary as Assistant Director, I paid him more money than I was able to take as a salary for myself. I worked year round for camp, and during the camp season I worked unbelievable hours. I loved what I was doing, and never felt over-worked. But, it was irritating to see him doing less with each passing summer.

And so the Stuart Goldberg era ended after five years.

10
The McCarthys

"Hello, Mr. Sharenow, my name is Dot McCarthy, and I have two boys who want to go to your camp."

We chatted for a while, but I wanted to make sure she knew before we hung up.

"Mrs. McCarthy, are you aware that almost all of our campers are Jewish. I assume you're not Jewish."

"Of course, I know that. I live in Great Neck Estates. All of my neighbors are Jewish. My boys' two best friends are already your campers and the four boys want to go to camp together."

This was 1961. In those days you didn't find names like Smith, Jones or McCarthy on temple membership lists. I had bought a camp that had a 100% Jewish clientele. That's the way it was in camp in the nineteen forties, fifties and sixties. Jewish kids were not at Christian camps, and Christian kids were not at Jewish camps. These patterns changed dramatically in the late sixties and seventies, but Mrs. McCarthy's call was an extraordinary one in 1961.

When I visited the McCarthy home to show slides of camp and tell the boys about it, I discovered a boisterous household with not two but nine McCarthy children. All who were old enough gathered around to watch the slides and ask questions. I had come to tell Bryan and Gregg about camp, but Linda, who was ten, and older than both Bryan and Gregg, wanted to know why she couldn't come too. Mrs. McCarthy said "Maybe next year. This is just for the boys this year." I left the house with applications for Bryan and Gregg. Mrs. McCarthy's only concern was that the boys attend church every Sunday. Since there was a Catholic church in Potter Place it would be an easy request to satisfy. I left the house feeling wonderfully triumphant in every way. It wasn't often that I signed up campers on the spot in those days.

Bryan and Gregg were both terrific campers. Gregg was more rambunctious, but well within the limits of normal camp behavior. He was a fun loving and high spirited kid. Bryan was a fantastic athlete and such a good boy. He and his friend Ricky Cohen were such positive leaders that every bunk they were in all the way through their camp turned out to be "the best bunk ever." I remember a letter Bryan's counselor, Dave Holsinger, sent to The McCarthys. The exact words are gone, but it went something like this.

"Your son Bryan is the nicest boy I've ever met. I hope someday when I get married I have a son just like him." That was quite a tribute from a twenty year old camp counselor. I suspect they were pleased to receive this letter. Of course, Dave wrote the exact same letter to Ricky Cohen's folks, but he didn't realize he had written the same letter. He really meant it...both times. He loved those boys.

Linda and little sister Cindy joined us the next year, bring our McCarthy family to four. They were doing wonders for our non-Jewish percentages. Cindy was a lovely little girl. She was in our youngest bunk. I didn't really get to know Cindy as well as I did the boys and her sister Linda. Cindy just fit in well everywhere, never making waves.

Linda and her bunk-mates were lucky. Their counselor was Phyllis Margil, who was Evergreen's best and most enthusiastic counselor. Linda was a big strong girl for her age, at least as big as Phyllis. In her bunk were three wonderful but tiny girls her age, Nina Bauman, Debby Lieberman and Joan Mamelok. When the bunk-mates walked anywhere together it was almost comical, Linda was so much bigger than the others. It would have been easy to mistake Linda for the counselor. Phyllis agreed. "She not only looks like a counselor, right now she's as good a leader as any counselor in camp."

On Friday nights we had a liberal Jewish, service at our camp. Bryan and Gregg had gone to the service each Friday night the summer before, sitting with their bunk-mates. I assumed the same would be true with the girls. I knew it was all right as long as we got them to church on Sundays. Our services featured a volunteer choir of campers. I looked up on stage that first Friday night, and there was Linda McCarthy singing in the choir. "Oh, my God, what will Mrs. McCarthy think of that?" I called her that night to apologize and assure her it would never happen again. She laughed.

"I don't think it will hurt my kids to sit in on your services. Whether they participate or not is up to them. But at least it will give them a few minutes to sit still. Linda can keep singing if that's what she wants. Last year when the boys came home I wasn't sure whether Ein Keilohenu was from services or a Color War cheer. It didn't sound so different from Akalaka Ching Alkalaka Chow. Everybody in the family knows the words to both."

In 1966, Randy McCarthy joined us at Kenwood, and little Jacki McCarthy came to Evergreen. I think Mrs. McCarthy lost track of Jacki's age. Her application form said she was seven. Jacki said she was five. Jacki was right. There were now six members of the McCarthy family at camp. Danny McCarthy was next in line, starting camp in 1973. The McCarthys were a presence.

On Visitors' Day in a year when there were six McCarthy children in camp, Mrs. McCarthy had a race with her son Bryan from one end of the camp to the other. She was winning (or so she said) as she ran into my office through one door, plopped several thousand dollars down on my desk, and ran out the other door. I knew she was going to be paying that weekend but hadn't expected the payment to be quite so casual.

The McCarthy clan kept coming and kept growing. By the 1990s we always had at least ten or twelve members of the second generation of McCarthys and their relatives at camp. Even oldest brother Glenn, who never went to camp himself, sent his children. None of this younger generation attended church in Potter Place on Sundays, nor did they attend Jewish services on Friday nights. Our non-Jewish contingent was now so large that we ran alternate activities during the Jewish service.

Every one of the children of the first McCarthy generation was an outstanding camper. All of the girls became counselors at Evergreen, but the family ethic required the boys to leave camp and get "Real world jobs" as soon as they were too old to return as campers. The McCarhy girls were among our very best counselors.

Little Jacki, who started camp at age five in 1966, will be returning for the 2012 season for her 40th year at Evergreen. She was Unit Leader for our oldest girls for many years and has been the athletic director at Evergreen more years than I care to count. Of all of the McCarthy clan, I know Jacki best. After she got over her homesickness as a very underage camper, she became a Camp Director's dream. She was wildly enthusiastic about all sports, a very strong and vocal leader, and quite a good athlete. During her years as a young counselor she was both an enthusiastic bunk counselor and a very strong athletic coach. On the other hand, Jacki was never reticent; she had a strong opinion about everything. I loved her on the ball field, but she was not my favorite person at counselor meetings. Sometimes she questioned camp policy out loud, and that was annoying enough, but other times, she would voice her objections under her breath for those around her to hear, creating a disruption in my well-orchestrated staff meetings.

Jacki coaches all land sports. She knows the sports and tries to infuse the campers with her own enthusiasm. When she coaches soccer or basketball, she never sits down and never stops yelling, instructing, directing and exhorting her girls to be better, and she usually succeeds. Neither her yelling nor her teams' successes have endeared her to the athletic directors of the camps we play. The other Camp Directors hate her, but that has not stopped several of them from trying to get her to change to their camps. For years, Jacki was my assistant coach for our softball team. In that sport, she had the chance to not only drive other camp's coaches crazy, but she drove me crazy as well, because I could never get her to stop shouting. I am quite a vocal coach as well, and it is confusing for the kids to have two people yelling instructions at the same time. As annoying as that could be, I loved working with her. How could I not? The kids loved her, and always responded positively to her exhortations. Now I am retired and its her team. Nobody will ever try to keep her quiet again.

She and her husband, Bob, (now Kenwood's athletic director) and their children are definitely a camp family. We were invited to Jacki and Bob's wedding. I felt so badly that we were not going to be able to attend. I called to explain to Mrs. McCarthy that a niece of ours was having her Bat Mitzvah in Newton, Massachusetts the same day as Jacki's evening wedding in Tarrytown, New York. "You have to come. Jacki will be very upset if you and Judy can't come. When is your niece's party? If its afternoon, you can fly to New York when it's over."

"I would love to do that, but we still won't make the wedding on time."

"Don't worry, we'll wait for you. I'll have a limousine meet you and get you to the wedding on time."

We did, and she did, and we got there, just on time. Among the guests was a large contingent of past and present camp people. That was hardly a surprise. Jacki included all of her campers from the camp season just concluded. Fifteen of our senior girls came to this rather formal wedding which took place at a very elegant country club. Despite the trappings, it was a wonderful, boisterous, funny wedding.

The Club where the wedding and reception were held was both resort and a hotel. Most out of town guests stayed over and had breakfast together the next day. After the ceremony and party, and after most of u s had gone to sleep, Jacki and Bob stayed up with her campers almost until dawn, playing ping-pong and pool and reliving tales from camp. This was so typical of Jacki!

Last year Judy and I received a Christmas card from Dot McCarthy, as we always do. But this card had a long note inside.

Dear Judy, Arthur & Family,

It's that time of year when families get together more frequently. At each and every one of our affairs the Kenwood-Evergreen group takes over. Old stories become new and the joy and laughter is as hearty as it was the first time the story was told.

I sit and watch and listen with tears in my eyes. I thank the Lord (I'm a firm believer, just not in what form "it" exists) that Arthur came to our house and won our childrens' hearts. The joy and memories you both have instilled goes on. Their times spent around Eagle Pond were the best times of their lives. It just...well it sounds corny, but it makes my heart want to burst with joy. ....

Just this past week, amidst the hustle and bustle of planning for the holiday, plans were made for Winter weekend at camp and memories were shared and I thanked the Lord again.

So, dear people, if you ever had any doubts about the path your life took, let me be one of the many to tell you there are thousands of young minds and hearts that are thankful to have met both of you and the fabulous experiences at Kenwood & Evergreen. My one regret is that we were not able to send all of my grandchildren. The difference is noticeable.

Stay well and happy.

Love, Dot

11
Ansel & Sons

Ansel, our head maintenance man, was one of my favorite people in the world. I knew I could trust him and count upon him one hundred percent of the time. He had grown up and started working during the great Depression, when men considered themselves lucky to find work. He knew only one way to work, very hard and until the job was finished. As a young man, during the Depression,he had not been able to find a paying job, and had apprenticed himself to a carpenter, where he learned skills he needed for a lifetime of employment. Ken Huberman, had hired Ansel as a carpenter and part time maintenance man in 1946. By 1960, when Judy and I became camp owners, Ansel was THE maintenance man, who knew everything there was to know about our physical plant.

Ken Huberman assured me, "You can rely on him positively. He's knows everything and he's honest. He's so honest he even tells you when he doesn't know something, and you'll find out that's a rare trait." I learned a great deal from Ansel.

Camp had been built in the early 1930s, the very depths of the great Depression. Consequently, the plant was put together as inexpensively as possible. The camp population grew slowly in the 1930s and early 1940s, but then experienced explosive post-war growth in the late forties and fifties. The original plant, which was a hodge podge of makeshift systems, had not anticipated and did not properly serve such significant growth. The result was a series of crazy quilt temporary solutions that nobody understood, except Ansel.

He was the only one who knew that when the lights went out in the arts & crafts building, the critical fuse box was in the infirmary. He was the only one who knew that the dry well (cessspool) for bunks four and seven was located under the clay basketball court which had been built behind those bunks. He was the one person who knew how to start the auxiliary gas powered water pump when we had an electric power outage. I learned all of these things and much more from Ansel through the years.

Ansel had gained his expertise during a period when everything had to be done in the least expensive way. The first couple of years we owned the camp, I took my lead entirely from him, and perpetuated the pattern. Some of his problem solving turned out to be short sighted and costly, but, through the years, his ability to keep things running as inexpensively as possible saved me a great deal more than it ever cost. Even more important, he gave me peace of mind. I knew that no matter what went wrong, he would fix it or find the help he needed to make it work.

Water

I had always thought of drinking water as something that came out of faucets. I knew as a fact that we had two monster water tanks under the dining room. I also knew we had pumps in our pump house that somehow were responsible for getting the water out of the ground and into those tanks. But I didn't truly appreciate them until the first time we ran out of water.

The year was 1963. It was two o'clock on Friday afternoon when Ansel found me. We were busy sprucing up the camp for Visiting Weekend. By nine-thirty the next morning we would have a few hundred parents and relatives visiting their children and judging our camp. If ever there was a time when things had to look good and run smoothly, it was Visiting Weekend.

Ansel found me on the Junior ball field. "Arthur, we've got an emergency. We don't have any water. The pump is still running, but no water is coming. I think the well points must be clogged. You've got to announce for everyone to stop flushing the toilets until further notice, and no showers either. If they don't stop right away every toilet in camp will be plugged. After the announcement, meet me at the pump house." I was stunned, but I didn't ask any questions. I followed instructions.

When I got to the pump house, Ansel was there and so was his helper Jimmy, a local kid from Danbury. The pump house was a ramshakle structure, containing two powerful looking but ancient pumps. The shack was lit by one sixty watt bulb hanging from a white porcelain fixture attached to the roof by one screw and some peeling duct tape. Jimmy stood at Ansel's side as he unscrewed the pipe that connected to the electric pump, and attached it to the gas model. He worked with a huge pipe wrench. It looked like it took all of his strength as he pushed and pulled the wrench to secure the pipe to the gas pump.

"Well, we'll know in a minute." He started tugging the chord. The motor turned over, but didn't start. He pulled again and again. Finally it caught. The gas motor released a cloud of fumes, and finally starting chugging. "Jimmy, when I tell you, I want you to open that valve over there. I want you to open it all the way. Arthur. Could you go around back? There's a pipe that comes out and goes up the hill toward the dining room. There's a faucet off that line. When I tell ya, you open that faucet, and let's all hope water comes pouring out."

Jimmy did his job. I did mine. And nothing happened. "No, Ansel, no water. Nothing's coming."

"Give it a minute." I gave it more than a minute.

"Sorry, still no water."

"I know. I'd hear it if it was coming. I was hoping it was the pump. I could have called Clayton Miller (The camp plumber). He would have had some sort of motor I could use, but it's not the pump. It's those blasted well points." He used the word "blasted" only in extreme situations. "Blasted" was the closest he ever came to swearing. With "blasted" I knew we were in trouble.

"We're going to have to send someone down to Capitol Plumping in Concord before they close." He started writing a description and numbers on the corner of a cardboard box. He tore the corner off the box. "Tell them this is what we need, and they'll have it ready for whoever you send. Meanwhile Jimmy and I will start work pulling up the old well point. "He thought for a minute. "These points are pretty dear, but you might want to buy two of them just in case."

Two hours later I backed the station wagon down the back path to the pump house. The new well points were sticking out the tailgate. Ansel and Jimmy had pulled up three muddy eight foot sections of pipe. The old well point would be next. As they turned the wrenches, they grunted with the effort. Finally the old well point, caked in mud, emerged above the cement cap. Ansel laid it on the ground. With a wire brush and rags he and Jimmy wiped it clean.

"No wonder we're not getting any water. See this." He showed me the pointed pipe. It was ringed almost its whole length with eye shaped screened openings. The screens over the eye sockets were completely clogged with mud. "We'll have to go a few feet deeper, and see if we can get to a spot where the water flows clean." The new well point came out of the box. I could see the eye holes were clean and clear, and I understood it was through these holes that water entered our system.

It was about ten o'clock that night when the new well point started producing clean clear water. I felt like dancing. "Great work, Ansel. You too, Jimmy. Thank God you got it going." We were all gathered in the pump house with our flashlights trained on the water flow from the test faucet. I turned to our Head Counselor. "OK, Charlie, pass the word. We have water. In a few minutes, when the pressure builds up in the tanks under the dining room, you can tell the counselors they can start flushing toilets again."

I don't remember how many times Ansel had to replace those well points over the years, but I remember very clearly when he came to me during Work Week in 1978 and announced "We need a new well. Our well has run dry." This was shockingly bad news, but I was grateful it was still Work Week and not during the actual camp season when we would have had hundreds of people to worry about. "OK, Ansel, where do we go from here?"

"You may have to go artesian. Let's see what we can find. We must have water under the grounds somewhere, not just in this one spot. Old Clarence Ford is pretty good with the witch sticks. I'll go get him. I think I saw his rig over in Wilmot Flat this morning. He'll come right away. He doesn't charge much, and, if we've got water here, he'll find it."

I couldn't believe that in the late 1970s with modern technology available, our future water supply was going to be dependent on an old man with a quivering tree limb. It sounded like Ansel was proposing witchcraft.

An hour later I was following Clarence and his forked branch around camp. Several fascinated counselors, attracted by the spectacle, had joined our entourage. Clarence and Ansel kept up a steady stream of chatter, relating stories of water found on other people's property, gushers in some cases, trickles in others. We were about fifty yards from our now defunct well when his branch started to quiver. the branch started dancing up and down. It was positively gyrating. I kept my eyes on Clarence's hands to see if they were moving. They weren't. He just held the branch loosely and it did its thing. We all stood still, watching a miracle. After a minute or so, Clarence looked up.

"We'll mark the spot. You got water here, all right, but it's a long way down. Let's see if we can find something closer to the surface. With this here spot, you'll need an artesian well. It will cost you a bundle to get at it." We continued our tour around camp. The branch, held out in front of Clarence, didn't shake a bit. Finally he gave up. We could keep looking, but I think you'll have to bite the bullet, and go artesian in that spot we found right at the start.."

Ansel had worked with Digger Phelps some time in the past. Ansel made the phone call. Digger and his rig were in camp the next morning. The drilling went on all that day and into the early afternoon the next day. Then a shout went up.

Water!!! We've got it!! Looks like a gusher!" This was Digger shouting at the top of his lungs. Since he had stopped the drills we heard the news all over camp. Orientation Period was about to start that afternoon. We were lucky. They hit water one hundred sixty feet below the surface. I was told we had an unlimited supply, and could pump a hundred fifty gallons a minute if we wanted. I breathed an enormous sigh of relief. That well has been providing water for camp for over thirty years now, thanks to Clarence Ford and his witch stick.

In the off season, when winter sets in and the weather got too cold to continue outdoor work, Ansel would set up a wood burning stove in the Red House, where he would build cubbies for the boys' bunks, scrape and paint windows from the girls' bunks, varnish canoe paddles. He would repair and build anything he could physically move into the Red House. He was so conscientious, that I knew he would work full days right through the winter. I didn't need to check on him. But he needed me to come up periodically so he could show me what he was doing, and get my approval.

In January 1972 snow banks on the side of the dirt road were ten feet high.

The path to the front door of the Red House was more tunnel than path. The smoke curled in the air from the pipe out the living room window. Ansel greeted me at the door. After a few minutes of normal chatting, I sensed that he was more subdued than usual. Something was on his mind. Maybe he was getting depressed working in such isolation. Several times he almost started to say something, and stopped, and went back to describing a project. I knew that sooner or later he would tell me what was on his mind. I knew he just couldn't be rushed, and I was willing to give him all the time he needed. We went to lunch at the Black Water Diner. After we ordered, he cleared his throat and began. It all came out in a rush.

"I'd like to get my plumbing license. You're paying Clayton Miller and his boys a fortune, and they do everything wrong. If I had a plumbing license, I could drain the pipes for you, better than he does, and we wouldn't have all those leaks to repair every Spring. When you build new bunks, I could do the plumbing." He went on describing the various ways his plumbing would save me money. I had no doubt he was right. Then he got to the part that had caused his hesitation.

"I have to take a course to get my plumber's license. It's pretty expensive. The course is $150.00 and the license will be another $50.00. I can take the course at night or on weekends so it won't interfere with work. But I'm hoping you'll pay for the course and the license. And, after I get it, I'd like you to raise my pay by twenty-five cents an hour. I'll be worth it to you. I promise I will." He ran out of steam, and just stopped talking, waiting for my reaction.

There was no doubt in my mind that my answer would be "Yes", but for him I needed to think it over before giving an answer. I had finished my hamburger and was on my second cup of coffee when I smiled and nodded my agreement. Ansel smiled, picked up his hamburger club sandwich and started to eat. It was then I realized he had not taken a bite while he awaited my decision.

"Thank you. You won't be sorry." I knew I wouldn't. Ansel did all of our plumbing from that time on for the next fifteen years or so until he couldn't work anymore, and had to retire.

I thought it was my camp, but I knew it was also Ansel's camp. He let me use his camp every summer. He cherished it. He worked so hard to get it ready every year, and then I would move in with my counselors and we would mess up his hard work. It was even worse when the campers came. They didn't respect the property the way he felt it should be respected. Litter on the ball field was viewed as a personal affront. The screen door of a cabin broken during a stick ball game was vandalism. A dirty paint brush returned to his shop was a high crime. The worst indignity of all occurred when some counselor borrowed one of his tools from the shop and failed to return it on time and to its' exact right place.

He never shouted and never screamed. He just got so upset that he could not stand bad behavior another minute. On at least three or four Staff Orientation Periods, he got so upset he just left without saying a word. He would pack up his personal tools, get in his pick up truck, and head for home. I would find him there that night, and listen to his recitation of the many counselor sins he had suffered that day. I always pleaded with him to return, promised that the scoundrels would be reprimanded, and guaranteed there would be no recurrence of those crimes for the rest of Orientation. He always agreed, and came back the next morning. I knew he had to. After all, he wouldn't trust anyone else to take proper care of his camp.

12
Scythe Swingers in the Spring

The sun was just peeking over the horizon as I drove down the rutted dirt road. It was not yet choked with dust, as I knew it would be in a few short hours. Last night's heavy fog left a blessed, but short lived layer of dew on the road. The fields of hay on either side were coated with a glistening blanket, giving the illusion of brilliance and prosperity, a land of plenty.

I uncapped my thermos, and took a gulp of energizing morning coffee. I needed that coffee to face the long day ahead. My days were all long in the spring, as we began our annual battle against time and elements to get camp ready to open for another year.

My ancient workers were there, as I knew they would be. They were waiting for me or for whoever would come along to offer them work that day. They always got in the first car that reached them in the morning. There didn't appear to be a commitment that would extend beyond each day's sunset. They were my labor force. Some days I reached them first. Other days we were short handed.

There was Gussie, sitting on the stoop in front of his nondescript shack. He had dressed in his usual scarecrow apparel, tattered overalls, plaid shirt and straw hat. He always needed a shave, but somehow his unkempt facial hair never quite became a real beard. It was hard to guess his age. I knew he had years of hard drinking behind him, and they had taken their toll. Ansel, our head maintenance man, had told me stories about Gussie's wild youth. I'd loop back and pick Gussie up last. That way his body odor would assail his fellow passengers for a shorter period of time, and it would be less likely to permeate the seats of my old Town and Country Ford wagon.

John Currier's house was around the next turn. His farm house had deep blue shutters, emphasizing the whiteness of its clapboard siding. All was in order. The barn looked freshly painted. His small herd of Holstein cows congregated in a corner of the fenced field, munching contentedly. Yet, there was John, sitting on the top step of his porch, waiting to be hired, waiting to do a day's work. Did he need the money or did he just need to be busy? I thought probably a little of both.

John was always neatly dressed, enhancing his natural good looks. His snow white hair set off a ruddy complexion and fresh scrubbed look. I always thought of him as an elderly gentleman rather than a day laborer. He was articulate and a good conversationalist, but he had a particular brand of New Hampshire twang in his voice. The first time I spoke with him I was sure he was putting me on with his exaggerated accent.

"Good morning John."

"Morning Artha"

"Are you up to a little mowing this morning?"

"Ehya, I'll get mya scythe."

I once tried to use a scythe. I swung that giant blade around me so hard that I almost fell over. My efforts were mocked by the field. The tall grass bent, but never broke. I gave up after three or four more back wrenching swings. The grass refused to yield to my amateur efforts. Yet it would surrender to these old men. They would swing those scythes hour after hour, clear one field, stop for lunch, and go back out to clear another before the day was done. I secured the scythe to the roof rack, and went on.

Fred Laffey was next. His family farm had a neglected look, but was still functioning. The rusted tractor and two defunct television sets, sitting in his front yard gave an unmistakable clue to the Laffey family fortunes. Yet the fields adjacent to the house were plowed and planted. I could see freshly laundered clothes hanging on the line. The house itself looked as though it was losing a long battle of attrition against harsh New Hampshire winters.

Fred's age was hard to determine, but I felt sure he was on the far side of seventy. His clothes, like his house and barn, had seen better days. They were well worn but clean. He always wore a faded red kerchief around his neck. Later in the day, when the sun was high, he would untie the kerchief and use it to mop sweat from his brow. Fred was a nice guy. He didn't speak much. But when he did, he was soft spoken and unfailingly polite.

"Looks like anotha nice day. Tell ya, we should get that senya field of yours all mowed off before lunch." That was it. I never heard another word from him all day.

I drove a few hundred yards to my next worker's house, but the front steps were empty. There was no point knocking on the door. Someone else beat me to it. I wouldn't have Jimmy with me today. It was getting late. The others would all be gone by now. Reluctantly, I headed back toward Gussie's shack, confident that he would still be available. He was not anybody's first choice. Predictably, he was there waiting.

As I drove through the Hollow and pushed my tired station wagon up toward the dining room, I could see a few of our young counselors trooping toward breakfast. I'd join them in a few minutes. Ansel was waiting for his crew as I pulled in next to his shop. He greeted John Currier warmly. John was his friend. You had to be able to read Ansel's face to know he had given John a warm greeting. His face had the slightest hint of a smile as he said "Hello, John". By contrast, Fred Laffey got a "Mornin, Fred" without the smile. All he could spare for Gussie was a nod.

They all brought their lunch boxes into Ansel's shop. His shop was like a cave under the dining room, and it always felt like winter in there to me. One wall was the side of a granite ledge. The other three walls were banked dirt held at bay by rough pine boarding. The shop had been excavated under the dining room by hand shovels many years after the dining room was built. The men's lunches were safe from the blistering heat that had been promised by the weather man.

As I went up the path and around the corner toward breakfast in the dining room, a breakfast I would share with my eager young counselors, our aged work force piled their tools into the back of Ansel's pickup. John sat in the front with Ansel. Fred and Gussie climbed onto the bed of the truck. The truck started down the hill, heading toward the overgrown Senior Camp ball field.

Another day of work had begun.

13
My Favorite Cook

Jack and his wife Anna came with the camp. Jack was Chef. Anna was Dining Room Manager. For the next eight years I lived in relative bliss. I didn't realize how lucky I was. I didn't have to think about the dining room or kitchen. I arrived at meals and sat down at my table. Food came out of the kitchen and we ate our meals. Jack did all of the food ordering, and the kitchen costs always stayed within the budget. I heard rumors from other directors that kitchens could present problems. As I heard their stories I smiled smugly, feeling very superior to these poor directors, who clearly did not know how to run a kitchen.

Jack ruled the kitchen with an iron hand. He brought all of his help with him; his assistant cooks, his teen-aged schleppers and dish washers. They all owed their jobs to him, and if he said "jump" they jumped. His cooks worked with him at Connecticut College where Jack was one of the senior chefs. The boys who mopped floors, lugged groceries and washed dishes were all sons of his friends and acquaintances from New London, Connecticut.

The fact that Jack's food was rather bland and uninteresting was unimportant. He knew how to produce it. He knew how to get it out to the tables on time. And he never ran out. The campers were happy enough with his food even if the mashed potatoes were lumpy, the roast beef was tough and the chicken was dry.

Of course I did hear some shouting from the kitchen occasionally. Every once in a while I would see one of the kitchen boys running out the back door of the kitchen. They always looked as though they were running for their lives. One day there was more shouting than usual in the kitchen and I decided I needed to go in and see what was happening.

Jack was waving a meat cleaver over his head while he chased one of the dishwashers. The boy dodged around the chef's bench, past our massive Hobart Mixmaster, past the dishwashing runway, and escaped through the screen door to the outside. Jack threw the cleaver just as the screen door slammed behind the running boy. The cleaver lodged in the door jamb, quivered and stuck. Jack was so angry he looked ready to explode.

"Damn that kid. I'm calling his parents tonight. He's out of here tomorrow. I won't put up with his nonsense any more. What's the matter with the rest of you? Why are you standing around? The show's over. Get back to work. The sooner you get this place cleaned up the sooner you'll get your time off."

I found this side of Jack somewhat disconcerting. I couldn't ignore what I had witnessed. I had a talk with him later that day, telling him he shouldn't be throwing things at the kids, particularly not knives or meat cleavers. He assured me it was a rare occurrence and he wouldn't let it happen again. My conversation with the Second cook also made me feel a whole lot better.

"Don't worry." He said. "He's not like that all the time. He rarely gets that angry more than once a week. You don't need to worry about the boys. They've learned how to move fast when Jack's in a rage. He'll never catch them. I'm not sure he even wants to, but they don't know that."

I came to believe that perhaps our kitchen was not the paradise I had supposed. It was clear that Jack did have his little peccadilloes. Years later I was to look back longingly on Jack's years in the kitchen as part of our kitchen's golden age.

14
Bagels 1960–1996

"What do you mean you don't have bagels at camp? You have to have bagels on Sunday morning. It's Jewish law. Most of your campers are Jewish. They have to have bagels. I bet Benny Friedman has bagels at his camp on Sunday mornings." (Benny Friedman was owner of Camp Kohut in Maine, and he was frequently cited by my father as the ultimate authority on how to run a camp.)

"I know, Dad. I would like to have bagels, but there are no bagels in the state of New Hampshire. Our supplier in Franklin never heard of bagels. Cricenti's Market in New London didn't even know what I was talking about. When I called Associated Grocers in Manchester, the salesman said he had heard of frozen bagels. He could order some for me. I said no. They'd come in with our delivery on Tuesdays and I would have to figure out where to store them until Sunday. So, no bagels."

My Dad was not to be thwarted in his bagel promotion.

"I'll buy bagels for you in Brookline on Saturday, and drive them up to camp that day. I'm sure you can get cream cheese from one of your suppliers. What do you say?"

"It sounds like a solution, but what about lox (smoked salmon)? What good are bagels without lox?"

"I'll check it out."

The year was 1961, my second year running camp. We had lots of problems trying to run a successful camp, and bagels on Sunday morning was not on my list of top ten camp priorities.

It was five o'clock in the afternoon the following Saturday when I saw my Father's powder blue Cadillac pull up our gravel and dirt driveway in a cloud of dust and park next to the dining room. I could see bags of bagels filling both the front passenger seat and the entire back seat. What a sacrifice he made for me. Not only was he giving up a beautiful Saturday, when he could have been playing golf, but he was subjecting his immaculate car to the dust and ruts of our camp's dirt roads. I knew his first stop after he left camp would be at a car wash. He would never allow himself to be seen in such a disreputable looking vehicle either at his club or in his neighborhood.

I ran out to greet and thank him, astonished that the bagels took up so much space. Not only were the seats filled, but the trunk of the car as well. Jack, our chef, sent a couple of the kitchen boys out to help us haul the bagels up to the kitchen. Jack had already made it clear that he and his crew would have nothing further to do with Bagels. He had plenty of experience dealing with bagels and lox as a chef at Connecticut College. If I wanted such a labor intensive product in camp, I would have to figure out how to deal with it without his help. I had already bought blocks of cream cheese from Crockett's Dairy, and even frozen lox from Manchester.

Now all I needed was a delivery system. We had two different Sunday morning breakfast procedures. For Evergreen, I had inherited a tradition of "Breakfast in Bed" for our girls, while the boys had breakfast at their regular dining room tables. Of course, breakfast In bed was not really breakfast in bed. It just meant that the food had to be packaged and delivered to the Evergreen office porch where the girls would pick up their food, and picnic either in their lodge living rooms or outside on their campus.

There were serious mechanical problems in both venues: the danger of the cutting of the bagels and the time delays associated with smearing of the cream cheese. We clearly could not let loose a bunch of sharp knives either to the boys' tables or to the Evergreen campus. Further, the cream cheese, sold to us in big five pound blocks, would take forever for individual campers to smear if it was set out on a buffet table.

A solution came to me. "If there are any Senior boys who do not want to go to the Social tonight, send them to me. I have a job for them." I knew there were bound to be boys who found Socials painful, and would be very enthusiastic about avoiding one. Socials were problematic in my mind at best, and I was happy to offer the reluctant boys a way out.

My recruits couldn't wait to find out what I had in store for them. They all had to wash their hands first before they could even learn their destination. This was a clue they had no trouble interpreting. Then we headed into the kitchen. The long prep table was ready. We had bags and bags of bagels at one end, blocks of cream cheese with multiple butter knives along both sides. Toward the far end were trays of thawing Nova Scotia salmon. There were lined cardboard boxes at the very end of the table, waiting to receive the finished products. Charlie Epstein (our Head Counselor) and I were at one end, with sharp knives in our hands. Four Kenwood Seniors were on each side, and the ninth boy was at the end ready to pack the boxes. It was easy to pick the boys who would be entrusted with the responsibility of inserting the lox into the open faced bagels that came their way. Larry Rabinowitz and David Levine became positively giddy when they saw the lox coming out of the walk-in refrigerator, and were enthusiastic about the prospect of being the ones to handle it. The empty boxes at the end were already pre-labeled: "Evergreen with Lox", "Evergreen no lox", "Kenwood with Lox" and "Kenwood no lox". My best guess was that at least half of the kids and counselors would not want lox. It turned out to be more like two thirds, and we adjusted for that by the second Sunday.

My boys and I had a good time. They smeared the bagels. They smeared their hands. They smeared the table. They chatted and laughed, and were clearly having a much better time than they would have had at the social. But while they enjoyed their tasks, they also worked with surprising efficiency. It didn't take much more than an hour to complete the job. Their bonus at the end was a bagel sandwich any way they wanted it, together with a can of soda (a very rare treat at camp in that era). The payoff for me was great. Not only did we get the bagels ready for the morning, but I got to know these eight or nine boys, who were mostly kids I would never really have known had it not been for the bagel and lox brigade. I had my Saturday night bagel brigade for several years, as long as Jack was our chef. When Jack retired, and Bob replaced him as major-domo in our kitchen, Bob was very happy to take care of bagel prep work, and my bagel team days were over. I rather missed them when they were gone.

Bagels and lox were a big success at camp, perhaps not quite as important as my Father thought, but still, a big success.

As the years passed, my Father was replaced as our bagel delivery agent by Phyllis' husband, Mickey Dank. Phyllis and Mickey lived in Natick, Massachusetts, the home of Eagerman's Bagels. Mickey, a lawyer by trade, would come to visit camp and Phyllis every weekend. He was a willing volunteer for the bagel run. He would do anything and everything he could to help at camp. For years, he was our bagel man, faithfully delivering bagels from Boston to the bagel desert of New Hampshire. He would drive up to camp in his sporty little convertible entirely engulfed in a sea of bagels. He never lost a bagel along the way.

Years passed, and the times changed. Bagels went from being an ethnic

Jewish food to a popular American alternative to English Muffins and donuts. The most convincing sign of the changing times was the 1990's opening of a bagel shop in New London, New Hampshire, our neighboring town, where they had never heard of bagels two decades earlier.

15
My First Neighbor
Avery Sanderson 1960

It was clear we would never be able to expand our camp unless we could purchase additional land. Of course, in those early years the practical issue was not expansion. It was trying to fill the cabins and ball fields we already had with campers. But I had hopes that it would not be too many years before the need to expand would become a real issue. Our sixty-five acres were sandwiched between Eagle Pond on our right and Eagle Pond Road on the left. Those were going to be immutable boundaries. Oh yes, we had a hundred or more acres on the other side of the road. Those wonderful woods would be great for hiking trails, for a campfire area, for an out of camp overnight sleepover spot for younger campers. But I hated to contemplate the nightmare scene of groups of kids running across the road for regular activities held on the other side. Sure, if we set up an activity there, the counselors would be cautious the first year, and the campers would be intimidated into waiting for road crossings. But by the third or fourth year, when the novelty had worn off, kids would bound across that dirt road without a thought. So I concluded our camp was not going to be expandable, unless....

Unless .... We could somehow buy the eighty acres adjacent to our property at the far end, just beyond our Senior Camp area. If we could acquire that property, we would not only control that end of the lake, but we would also be able to move the boys' camp further along, have more play area and expand our girls' camp. That would be the answer. That was my long range plan.

That land had lain vacant and unused for at least the past ten or fifteen years. Sheep once grazed there. I remember how exciting it was for me as a camper when we would sometimes wake up in the morning to see dozens of sheep grazing on the Senior Ball Field. By the time we bought the camp I was sure that the old man who owned that land must be very old. He didn't graze sheep there any more. I told myself he should certainly want to sell that useless land before he dies.

The old man's name was Avery Sanderson. He lived in a great old rambling farm house just across the lake from camp. Ansel, our head maintenance man, who seemed to be related to everybody in the area, numbered Avery among his cousins. He warned me that Old Man Sanderson was pretty crotchety. That was a unusually extreme statement from Ansel, who was a man of many skills, but verbosity was not high among them. I decided to telephone rather than just drive over to visit.

"Hello, Mr. Sanderson, my name is Arthur Sharenow. I'm your new neighbor. I just bought the camp from Ken Huberman."

"Hmm, yes? " There was a pause. I waited, and then plunged ahead.

"Mr. Sanderson, I would love to come over and say hello. Now that we're going to be neighbors, I thought we ought to at least meet."

"Hmm!" A long pause followed. "I never had much to do with Huberman. We don't have to be friends you know. We're just neighbors and we're lucky we've got a whole lake between us. Just keep your kids off my property, and that will be good enough."

Undaunted, I plowed ahead. "I wanted to talk to you about that land you own at the end of the lake."

"There's nothing to talk about. It's not for sale. I'm tired of talking now. Maybe I'll talk to you again in a year or two after I see how you and your kids behave." I heard the phone click off.

"So much for that" I thought.

A year passed, and I tried again. "Hello, Mr. Sanderson, this is Arthur Sharenow calling again. Remember I called you last year..." He cut in.

"You don't have to remind me. I know who you are."

"I'm calling to see if we can get together...." I didn't get to finish my sentence.

"Tomorrow morning, ten o'clock. My house." He hung up.

Sanderson greeted me at the door. He looked his part, the hard bitten Yankee farmer. He was tall and lean, almost gaunt. His ruddy complexion advertised outdoor living and good health. His scalp shone through his thinning white hair. He wore faded dungarees, a flannel shirt, and leather moccasins. I held out my hand, which he ignored, as he led me in through his kitchen.

It was a great old house. The floors creaked, and the wind whistled through the walls, insulated a century earlier with old corn cobs. He escorted me in through the breezeway that connected to the barn in the rear. No words were wasted in the process. The braided oval rug in the living room was muted earth tones. There were caned rockers on either side of the stone fireplace. Two rebuilt carriage seats faced the fire.

I exclaimed what a wonderful room it was as he ushered me into the living room. He grimaced, or perhaps that was his smile. He motioned me to sit.

"Okay, what is it you want?" He knew what I wanted. I had told him a year earlier, but he wanted me to say it again. So I did.

"Well, actually two things. First we've been neighbors for a year now, and I just wanted to say hello and give us a chance to get to know one another." I paused giving him an opportunity to say something. He didn't. I moved ahead. "I understand that you own the eighty acre parcel down the end of the pond. It doesn't look like you are using it any more, and we certainly would love to have it for the camp. Would you consider selling it?"

"I might consider selling that parcel for the right price."

"Do you have a price in mind?"

"I do, but you tell me what you want to pay. I'll tell you if it's enough."

This was an unusual opening gambit to a real estate negotiation, but I was excited. I had come over with no expectations at all. Now it sounded as though he might actually consider selling it to me. I knew the going rate for unimproved land on back roads in the area. I knew it was going for about thirty dollars an acre. For his eighty acres that would amount to twenty-four hundred dollars.

I figured if I offered him a thousand dollars more than the going rate he couldn't turn it down. I offered it.

"Sorry, young man, that's not enough. That land's been in our family for a long time and it doesn't cost me much in taxes to hold on to it. "

"How about four thousand?" I knew I was stretching to go that high.

"Nope, that's still not enough to make me want to sell."

"Are you sure you can't consider my offer. I just can't afford more than I offered. I just took on a huge mortgage to buy the camp." He shook his head "no", and that was the end.

"Thanks for your time, Mr. Sanderson. We'll do our best to be good neighbors, and I know you will too." He directed me out the back door and sounded almost friendly as he said goodbye.

"Well, that's the end of it," I thought. "I'll have to wait until he dies to get another crack at that land. He says he wants to sell, but I don't think so."

Six months later I learned I was wrong. I received a business letter from a William B. Grant.

"... I understand you have an interest in my land at the end of Eagle Pond. We've got eighty acres of prime forest land with 300 feet of frontage on the Pond. It could be developed into very desirable waterfront property. I've been thinking about developing it myself as a resort, but I decided that you might be interested in that parcel....." I read on with increasing interest.

"Who is this guy? And how did he get that land? What does he want?" The last paragraph of his letter gave me a clear answer.

"....and twenty-five thousand dollars would seem to me a fair price for the land..."

The rest of the letter was not important. I couldn't consider his highly inflated price. Our mortgage payments were so high that I had determined that anything else I might buy would have to come out of our operating income, no more loans for me.

I already knew Ansel well and trusted him completely, but I was sure he must have some idea what was going on. I peppered questions at him. "If your cousin wanted to sell the land after all, why didn't he get back to me? How did this guy Grant get the land? Who is he? How much did he pay? What's his game?"

He was reluctant. He was embarrassed. He was ashamed. But finally he blurted it out.

"Avery Sanderson would never sell to you unless he was desperate for money. He wouldn't do any business with a Jew if he could help it. Edna and I both tried to talk to him, but he wouldn't listen. I'm sorry to say that there are still plenty of people around here who think like him."

I trusted Ansel, but what he said didn't really seem to make sense to me. Though Sanderson hadn't indicated any friendship for Ken Huberman, who had been his neighbor for many years, nonetheless I knew that this same man had sold part of the camp property to Ken years earlier. Do people's prejudices really develop that fast? But I also remembered his response to my initial overture toward a relationship.

"We don't have to be friends you know. We're just neighbors and we've got a whole lake between us."

However, I reluctantly became convinced that Ansel's appraisal might be correct. I checked with the Registry of Deeds and discovered that Sanderson had sold the land to Grant for twenty-five hundred dollars after turning down my offer of four thousand. Thinking about it years later I still have my doubts that Sanderson would act against his own interest on account of prejudice. Perhaps there was some pre-existing relationship between Sanderson and Grant that he wanted to keep to himself. Since neither of the men is still alive I will never get the clarification that has puzzled me through the years.

16
Drama At Camp

A convincing case can be made for the concept that every camp season was a Dramatic Show with a cast of hundreds on stage. Each season we had triumphs and tragedies, tears and laughter, tension, fierce competition, humor, personal disappointments, and, almost always, a happy ending. At the end of each summer, my mind gravitated toward the triumphs and the humor. Frequently our formal Dramatics program provided some of the best laughs.

Drama was a very important program to me. Like ceramics, arts & crafts, debating, "logic games", quiz games, spelling bees, and even riflery, drama gave us an opportunity to find areas of success, and perhaps even stardom, for children whose lack of coordination would never allow them to become stars in sports. I enjoyed being in plays when I was a camper.

I was fourteen. The play was "The Monkey's Paw". I entered from stage left. A terrible storm was heard off stage. The lightning and thunder recording was pretty effective. The line in the script was

"Come in quick. Give me your stick."

In response, I was to hand my walking stick to my host, who was played by my friend Arnie Rubin. He greeted me at the door. We rehearsed this entrance over and over. Every rehearsal Arnie's line came out

"Piss quick. Your pants are on fire!"

As fourteen years olds, we were convulsed with laughter every time. Our long suffering dramatics counselor, Elliott Silverstein, didn't think it was so funny.

"If you keep rehearsing it that way, you'll never get it right the night of the play." He was right. Arnie brought down the house with his "Piss quick, your pants are on fire." When the laughter subsided there I was holding a useless walking stick. Ken Huberman, our camp director, looked sternly disapproving. I think Elliott Silverstein must have been seriously called on the carpet for our adolescent laugh line. Our next play was "The Devil and Daniel Webster", and he didn't let us clown around at all. Nor did Elliot return to camp the following summer.

That's how the drama program worked when I was a camper. The kids, like me, who enjoyed being on stage, would act in several short one act dramas during the course of the summer. Since there were relatively few boys who were eager to be on stage, those of us who were, became frequent performers. That was before there was a Camp Evergreen; before girls made their appearance on our camp scene.

The scene changed "dramatically" in 1950 with the introduction of girls in camp. There were now plays for both boys and girls. Some were coed, but most were designed specifically for one or the other. It seemed that almost all of the girls wanted to be onstage, and though, in Evergreen's early years, there were many more boys, girls dominated the footlights.

Don Emerson came with the camp. We inherited him as drama counselor in 1960 when Judy and I became directors of Kenwood & Evergreen. He had already set a longevity record for drama counselors by that time. I knew Don during my summers as a counselor, and I knew he was a great guy, but I didn't fully appreciate his ability until I saw him in action with a camp director's perspective.

What a wonderful man he was! He was the perfect drama counselor. He was serious about putting on good shows; and yet he had a sense of humor and a sense of proportion that made him the ideal person to work with kids. During his tenure at camp, he wrote and directed two original musicals for children. His "Tom Sawyer" went "big time". It was too big for our cramped Recreation Hall Stage so it was shown on stage at the Andover, New Hampshire Town Hall. All the camp's neighbors were invited. Those who accepted the invitation were pleasantly surprised by the production, which had a huge cast of boys and girls ranging in age from twelve to fifteen.

Don taught music and drama at a well known prep school during the ten months of the year when he couldn't be at camp. He was my ideal of a camp Dramatics counselor. If only he could have stayed on for the next thirty or forty years, our drama program would have been a true delight for our camp and campers. Unfortunately, most good things must come to an end. Don retired from camp after our first summer as directors. He assured me it wasn't the change in administration. It was the work load. His job at camp was physically much more challenging than his work at school. At camp he had to do everything himself. He was producer, director, scenic designer, costumer and makeup expert. At school he was a member of a talented arts faculty, several of whom had assisting roles in his productions.

Through the next thirty-six years I tried, but I could never find anybody who was quite as perfect for the job as Don had been. But we certainly had some memorable drama counselors through the years.

Our Dramatics Counselors faced a very difficult assignment. As a matter of camp policy, I wanted every group of boys and girls in camp to put on a play of some sort. Every child was strongly encouraged to be in his group's play. Most were delighted, but for some children being on stage can be more traumatic than beneficial. It was important that they be given a way to participate without actually going on stage. They could be in charge of props, or lighting or even just pulling the curtain, as long as they were included somehow in this group effort. For the seniors, aged twelve to fifteen, there was to be a Broadway musical in which every senior boy and girl would be encouraged to participate. Since our camp was small in the early nineteen sixties, the cast of the senior show was only thirty or forty campers. All-cast rehearsals were difficult then. They became far more challenging in later years when chorus numbers could bring seventy or eighty teen age campers on stage at the same time. Through the years, Dramatics counselors came for a year or two, and left. Some were more or less successful, and a few were notable.

Next Came Dilger

H.S. Dilger was one of the most extraordinary people ever to work for me or probably any-one else as a camp counselor. I was twenty-nine years old and a Camp Director. Hiring counselors was still a new experience to me. I was enormously impressed by Mr. Dilger when he answered my ad for a dramatics counselor. But I offered him a job with some serious reservations. On his contract he had crossed out the words "drama counselor" and inserted the words "Instructor of Histrionics.

H.S. Dilger is an Indian, a Sikh, who was already a published author, a radio personality, and an impresario in his native land. He was also married and had several children. They remained in India while he was in Boston working toward a Ph.D. Technically he was a student like most of our other counselors. But he was very unlike most of our student counselors. He always called me Mr. Sharenow and to me he was always Mr. Dilger.

He represented a lot of firsts for our camp. He was the first counselor who spoke precise and flawless English. He was the first in our history to wear a turban. He was certainly the first and only counselor who ever brought his personal student with him to camp. Judy, my wife, answered the phone when Dilger called with that request. I had told her all about what an incredible personality Dilger had and how impressive he was.

"Mrs. Sharenow, do you think it would be acceptable to Mr. Sharenow if I brought a student of mine with me to camp?"

"I don't know. If he can do some camp job, I'm sure Arthur would be happy to interview him."

"You misunderstand. My student is a woman, Mrs. Wallace Krakowitz. She studies histrionics with me. We share a house together, and she has expressed an interest in continuing to live under my tutelage this summer as well. Mrs. Krakowitz is the Dance Instructor at Beaver Country Day School. I'm sure that she would be a fine dance instructor for your camp. "

"I'm sure Arthur will be interested in meeting your friend and discussing the possibilities with her."

"Good, then it is settled. You can meet her when you come to my house for dinner. I would very much like to cook dinner for you and Mr. Sharenow. I would hope to show your husband and you that fine Indian cooking is not all curry and hot spices. Perhaps Mrs. Krakowitz and I shall prepare an entertainment for you as well". Judy consulted her calendar, and a date was set.

The address was in Brookline. I thought I knew all of the streets in Brookline, but I had never heard of this one. My street directory led me to one of the shabbier areas of Brookline. Shabby in Brookline is faded but respectable older homes, built originally for working class men and their families. These houses, once the pride of their original occupants, were now down at the heels, many showing paint several years past renewal time and gardens both scraggly and untended. An occasional freshly painted house stood out among its neighbors. Some of the houses were still occupied by one family, but many had been broken up into oddly shaped and oddly sized apartments. These were inhabited by a cosmopolitan mix of students, laborers and immigrants.

Dilger's house sparkled. The shrubs that surrounded the front porch were full and healthy looking. Colorful blossoming tulips trimmed and framed the shrub beds. The window shades were drawn. The ones facing the street had an exotic quality, painted to portray a night sky, with moon and planets and shooting stars. The doorbell chimed musically, and Mr. Dilger ushered us solemnly through a beaded archway into the living room. He indicated we should sit together on a love seat which faced another beaded arch. As we sat down we could hear muted oriental music from the back of the house.

Mrs. Krakowitz made her entrance in dramatic fashion through the beaded arch. She was a pale woman whose whiteness was accentuated by every aspect of her apparel, from a multi-hued scarf wrapped flowing around her head to a brilliantly colored flared skirt. She entered the room dancing. The music was louder now. Her dancing, like the music, had an Oriental quality to it, and was very professional. She was really good. But it was a very odd feeling sitting there, an audience of two in someone's home being entertained with a formal performance. When she completed her dance the three of us applauded and she made a stage bow. Then Dilger introduced her.

"It is my very great pleasure to introduce Mrs. Wallace Krakowitz, dancer extraordinaire. Mrs. Krakowitz, it is my pleasure to introduce to you Mr. Sharenow and Mrs. Sharenow, who have been so kind as to join us for a simple repast. And now, if you will excuse me, I shall return momentarily."

When Dilger returned he had on a silky black robe and a Merlin style magician's hat. He entered, bowed, and started pulling brightly colored kerchiefs from his sleeves. They were knotted together, separated and then together again. He cut them into pieces; tied them together again; pulled the ties tight and they were whole again. This act was followed by several other slight of hand tricks, and he bowed again. It was absolutely incredible; not the tricks themselves, but the fact that we were sitting in his living room and he was performing for us as he might before an auditorium filled with people. After the entertainment he announced it was time to dine.

The meal was delicious. During dinner and the visit that accompanied it, Dilger kept up a steady stream of interesting conversation. There was never a gap. He did almost all of the talking for the four of us. By the time we left the house, it was settled. Mrs. Krakowitz would be on our staff for the summer as a dance instructor. They had simply charmed us into a patently ridiculous decision. Dilger had neglected to mention that Mrs. Kramer spoke virtually no English. She was from Austria.

Dilger and Mrs. Krakowitz came to camp. It was clear from our discussions that Mr. Dilger, who loved children, would like to live with campers. I had him assigned to live with some of our oldest boys. What was unclear was that he and Mrs. Krakowitz both came under the impression that she would be living with him. This was totally impossible. Mr. Dilger was to live in a four man tent with three fourteen year old boys. Mrs. Krakowitz had been assigned to live in a cabin in our girls' camp with three other female specialty counselors.

To their credit, they survived the shock of separation, and each started on a camp career. Mrs. Krakowitz was a wonderful dancer but a complete failure as a dance counselor. We had to assign a counselor just to interpret for her and to keep even the youngest girls in good order. She was hopeless in every other aspect of camp life. She and Dilger met at dawn for early morning walks and lessons in histrionics throughout the summer. Both of them came to the dining room with the campers during meals, but they did not eat. They then went to our Infirmary which had a small kitchen, and prepared their own meals.

Mr. Dilger was getting mixed reviews. It was clear that our boys were very impressed by him. On the other hand, they didn't really know what to make of him. He was not the kind of counselor with whom they felt they could let loose. Nor was he a counselor in whom they could confide. He wasn't really fun in any traditional camp way. During free play time he never went out to play with the boys, but during rest period, when they were all in the tent together, he taught them card tricks and close up magic. They had all mastered the tricks by the end of the summer. I sometimes saw him watching his boys in athletics. He really did get into the games, and constantly yelled out encouragement.

"That was a fine effort, Mr. Kunen."

"You exhibit wonderful skills, Mr. Schwartz."

As a drama counselor he was surprisingly successful. Once our kids, boys and girls, got over his strangeness, they liked him. He had plays for them that were mostly original stories he wrote himself. They were beautifully written sensitive plays. His classes and rehearsals went well. Opening night of the drama season was a smash success. The first plays of the summer were presented by our youngest campers and the rest of the camp loved them. They also enjoyed Dilger's performances before and after the show as well as between the two plays. He did a dance, a song, and a magic act, and did them all very well. He was a first rate entertainer. The seven other plays that summer were equally successful.

The three boys who lived in his tent were three of our best and brightest, but were too young to fully appreciate his charm. They were perhaps looking for something that he could not give. But he apparently gave them things they never expected to get in a summer at camp. They all returned to camp the next summer. A few years later I got a letter from one of them telling me that his summer with Dilger was the best of his eight years at camp. Dilger was only with us that one summer.

Several years later I received a play bill from a Theatre in India. The playbill had a velvet cover. The cover was embossed in delicate gold leaf

"H.S. Dilger Presents".

Stan Berman

Stan Berman joined us as Drama Counselor in 1966. Stan was a professional, a veteran school teacher. He had previously indulged his love for the stage by directing two different Community Theatre groups for several years. He was a nice man who brought his wife and two children with him to camp. They lived upstairs in the Red House, just a short distance down our dirt road from the main campus. He was serious about dramatics, and ran an excellent program. There was never a danger that his cast wouldn't know their lines. They rehearsed and rehearsed and rehearsed. Stan produced "Oklahoma" as the Senior Show during his summer with us. The Senior girls and boys respected him, but complained about having to rehearse the same songs over and over again.

One night the camp top brass was gathered in our living room for a late night snack and chat. We did this at least a couple of nights a week. Our camp administration was very small in those years. In addition to Judy and me, there was Phyllis, Evergreen's Head Counselor, Charlie Epstein, Kenwood's Head Counselor, Norm Laakso, Waterfront Director, and Bob Kramer, Camp Doctor. That night their respective husbands and wives were with us eating, chatting and laughing. Things were going well in camp, and we were collectively in a silly mood. We got around to Stan Berman and "Oklahoma". I don't know who suggested it. It was either my idea or Phyllis'. We debated the wisdom for a while, but finally, throwing caution to the wind, we decided to do it.

Phyllis went to the Senior Girls' Lodges to get them up. Charlie (Kenwood head counselor) woke the Senior Boys. They got dressed, and we met just a little way from the Red House, where Stan and his family lived. The kids were giggling and whispering. They loved it. They couldn't believe that Head Counselors and Directors would lead them on a "Raid". We whispered instructions and then silently tip-toed right next to the Red House and directly under Stan's window. Then, voices raised on high, we started to sing.

"Oh, what a beautiful morning....Oh, what a beautiful Day.... I've got a beautiful feeling, that everything's going my way." Stan's lights were out and the house was quiet when we started. By the start of the 2nd time through, the bedroom lights came on; Stan opened his window, stuck his head out, and started conducting as though he was running a regular rehearsal. The kids cheered him when it was obvious that he had gotten into the spirit of it. We sang two or three more songs from the show, with Stan leading the singing from his open bedroom window. Then we escorted the kids back to their bunks and lodges. It took them a long time to settle down, and get back to sleep, but it was one of the things those boys and girls remembered most fondly from that summer at camp. Moreover, it humanized Stan Berman for them, and they worked with him to produce a wonderful "Oklahoma."

That little adventure probably served to enhance my reputation with the kids as well. But, by the time I got into bed that night, the realization struck me that I had taken a terrible gamble. Had Stan awakened in a bad mood, which was entirely possible, and come out screaming at the kids, it would have undermined him and probably would have destroyed the drama program the rest of the summer. But his reaction was great, we were heroes, and all was well. I can only shudder as I recall my youthful follies.

Part Three
The Late 1960s

17
Integration at Camp

The year was 1968. It was not a good year in America. The country was bogged down in Southeast Asia, in a war that seemed never-ending. Our college campuses were held hostage by student protesters. At the same time in the slum areas of many of our cities, poor blacks rioted and in some cases burned and looted the very neighborhoods in which they lived. The Black Panthers were a disquieting presence in the cities, and Hells Angels were terrorizing innocent people on the Highways. The nightly news was filled with frightening and horrible images. What was happening to my country? Was there any hope? What could we do to change things?

I couldn't do anything about the war. I had limited sympathy for and even less influence on the student protesters. But perhaps I could do something that would make a small constructive difference in black areas of the city. Camp would be the vehicle. It was my ambition and my conceit that we could help to foster some of the sorely needed black leaders of the future. Too many black kids grew up without the kind of experiences or education that prepared them for constructive leadership roles. Most of them had no personal contact with the white middle class world and values.

We would take a few children out of the city slums every summer and bring them to camp. Camp was far from their burning cities and danger. I wanted them to feel safe, to learn to know and trust their counselors, young adults who would care about them and care for them. I wanted them to experience all that was wonderful about camp: the sports, the mountain hikes, early morning swims , being on stage, learning songs, and most a of all, making friends they would trust.

I wanted them to catch the spirit of camp and make it a part of them. We could make an impact in their lives. Was this too much to hope for? How could I make it happen?

I decided we would start with six black boys from the slums of Boston. We would integrate them into camp with no cost to their parents, and those same six boys could keep coming, just like our traditional campers, as many summers as they wanted to come. Some of them would eventually return to camp as counselors, as many of our campers did. They would go to college. They would have real career choices. Some of them might even fill the leadership void that I saw in the black community. The idea was to make this a program that would run forever at camp.

These were worthy goals, and even ground breaking at the time. For the next twenty-eight years we always had six, seven or eight black children on full scholarships at camp. When we eventually sold our camp, we sold it to a wonderful young man who was one of our former campers, who was already sold on our goals. To his credit, Scott Brody has continued the scholarship program through his years as Director.

I didn't know, when I started down this path, just how challenging it would be. Happily we never faced the kinds of problems faced by communities integrating schools. After all, Parents didn't have to send their children to our camp. I'll never know how many new white campers we failed to enroll those first few years because of our new policy, but we did lose a few returning campers. Their parents might sympathize with our goals in the abstract, but not when it actually involved their children. Interestingly, though the first few black campers were eight, nine and ten year old boys, it was primarily parents of girl campers who expressed their concerns about the future of their children in our camp. The few who defected for that reason disappointed me, but I was not shocked that some reacted as they did. In other ways as well, our integration program fell short of fulfilling all of our intended goals. But that first summer was one I'll never forget.

Six little dark skinned boys, aged eight, nine and ten entered our all white world that summer. They were so excited. They were also scared. For them it must have seemed like an alien environment. Our job was to transform their understandable fears into a sense of belonging over the course of the next eight weeks.

The second day of camp I checked with the counselors of all of our new boys.

I wasn't worried about Chuck S. at all. He was the only one of the six boys who had a "middle class" background. His Mother worked in the office of one of the big grocery chains. She was a very intelligent woman, who had gotten Chuck into the METCO program in Boston, a program which brought inner city kids to suburban schools. She also had "found" our program for her son, whereas we had "found" the other boys by working through a social service agency. As expected, Chuck was doing fine.

Mark Sebell, a very enthusiastic veteran counselor, was the first to report on his new campers. His boys were eight years old. "Glenn was afraid to go to sleep because we didn't lock the cabin door. He was afraid if we didn't lock up 'some drunk might fall in'. I assured him that it wouldn't happen. Eventually he fell asleep. But only after I promised him I would not leave the bunk that night. Billy (the other new black boy in Glenn's group) didn't seem as scared. Maybe he lives in a safer neighborhood."

I spoke with Jeff Cokin next. He gave me a rundown on his campers, especially Melvin.

"Mel tried to run away last night while I was changing my clothes. I had to chase him in my underwear. I caught up with him just outside the door of the cabin. He was scared and started scratching and clawing trying to get away from me. I wound up practically sitting on him to calm him down. After a while he did. We talked quietly for a few minutes, and he finally told me what made him run."

"It was when you took your belt off. I knew somebody was gonna get a whuppen. I know I'm always the one who gets it in our house."

"He told me all about uncles who used their belts for whippings. I told him I would never use a belt to whip him or any of the other boys. I told him I was sure I would never hit him, period. I don't think he fully believed me, but he did calm down, and came back into the bunk."

Steve Baron reported that Jose was doing well, and seemed to make friends right away. Big Al Silverman (six foot nine) told me that Ronnie cried himself to sleep the first night, but seemed fine. Ronnie had a twin brother at home, from whom he was separated for the first time. The four counselors involved were all optimistic about their own campers.

The adjustment year had both humor and pathos. In the good humor department I offer two short anecdotes.

First. I heard clapping and cheering as I came around the corner of Bunk four. There was a crowd gathered around the ping pong table. Music came from inside the bunk, but it was largely drowned out by cheering and clapping. In the middle of it all, there was Mel, up on the table, dancing with wild abandon and real talent. The other kids loved his show and the counselors couldn't get enough of it. I wasn't sure how healthy it was for him to be "The entertainer". It seemed like such a stereotype. But he clearly loved the attention, and I wasn't going to take that away from him. Later that summer, Mel was a sensation at our annual camp talent contest with a similar dance routine.

Second. Steve Baron was Jose's counselor. Steve was a very good and caring counselor. He was also a good looking young man, who took pride in his tan. Steve had a sun reflector, and, when he had a free period, he would lie on the dock with his reflector, working on his tan. One day I saw Jose lying out on the dock with Steve's reflector. He was also working on his tan, which required very little help.

Some of our saddest moments that summer involved little Melvin. Just a little more background will help me to frame the picture for you. He was one of twelve or thirteen children in his family. His Mother was a loving Mother, but constantly overwhelmed. There had been a succession of men in Mel's life, but usually for short periods of time.

In the middle of the summer we have a Visiting Day. All of the Parents come to visit their children, reassure themselves that their children are healthy and happy. and to see the progress they have made in the first four weeks of camp.

The campers are eager to see their parents and the parents can't wait to see and hug their children. Visiting Day officially starts at 9:30 on Sunday morning. The first Visitors try to get into camp about an hour earlier. Half of them are there by nine. All but a handful have arrived by 9:30. Always a few are delayed a little by traffic, by miscalculations of distance or just plain getting lost. If Parents are not there by 10:00, we place calls home to make sure all is well.

Nobody was home at Mel's house when we called at 10:00 o'clock. I assured him his Mother was on her way and would be there soon. Mel was looking very sad by lunch time. Another camper's parents welcomed Mel to join them for a picnic lunch with their family. By mid afternoon Mel had given up hope. There was still no answer on the home phone. At 4:30 the campers' Parents started to leave camp, and make their way home. By five o'clock the camp belonged to the campers and counselors again, and the kids were back at more usual play.

At five o'clock a banged up Ford sedan came in through the gate. I can't tell you how many people were in that car, but it was quite a number. We paged Mel over the PA system. He was angry with them. He was embarrassed that his family was the only one to come so late. At that moment he seemed more upset with them than he was glad to see Mother and brothers and sisters. We got them all the picnic box lunches that everybody else had hours earlier. Mel sat with them. When It was six o'clock the bugle call for Assembly brought the camp to the dining room for dinner. Mel rejoined his bunk-mates, and his family got into their car and headed for home. All day I felt sorry for Mel. That night I felt worse for his family.

Two days before the end of the camp season, the empty camper trunks and duffle bags that had been put in storage for the season, are brought back to the cabins. The counselors of the younger children started to organizing and packing with their campers. Jeff, Mel's counselor, came to tell me that Mel refused to pack. He had insisted to Jeff that he was not going to go home.

I decided that I would have a talk with him. "I want to stay here all year. "

"Mel, you really can't stay. There won't be any other kids here. Everybody is going home. It will be lonely."

I'll stay here with just you and the counselors."

"I'm sorry, Mel, but the counselors go home just a day or two after the campers leave. Jeff won't be here. Mark won't be here. They have to go back to college."

"I'll stay with you."

"Judy and I don't live here year round either. We go home after a couple of weeks. There is no heat in the bunks. It's going to get very cold here soon." He pleaded for the next two days, but then came departure day.

On the bus back to Boston, Mel sat on Jeff's lap almost the whole way. Our Boston kids went with counselors by chartered bus to Riverside MBTA station in Newton. Parents came and picked them up there. All of the Parents were there except Mel's. Our counselors waited and waited. They tried to reach his Mother by phone. There was no answer. The parking lot was now virtually empty. But Chuck's Mother had stayed behind with Chuck to see what would happen. She knew where Mel's family lived and took him home. She promised she would make sure he would get safely back to his Mother. That was quite a welcome home for Mel!

Mel was with us for thirteen summers as a camper and later a counselor. He got himself into the METCO program when he was in Jr. High School. He worked very hard to get himself an education. Mel is a pharmacist now and has worked himself up to be a store manager. He has kept in touch, calling every year or two just to say "Hello". Just a few years ago Mel called me, and told me to look for some mail from him. He had a present for me. In the mail were two tickets to "Fiddler on the Roof" and a gift certificate for dinner for two at Legal Seafoods. I opened that envelope with tears in my eyes. It was a wonderful moment in my life and his as well.

There have been many scholarship campers since those first six, but I will always remember them. None of our boys or girls has run for President or even Governor yet. But one of them will some day. Perhaps more important, many are successful human beings.

18
Jay Lambert

Jay Lambert was an extraordinary little boy. Both of his Parents were deaf and, though well educated, including speech lessons, they both spoke in a way that required great concentration on the part of the listener. They were barely intelligible to people who didn't know them well and didn't care enough to make a real effort. Even for those who tried to understand it was difficult. They were terrific people, but they needed help in dealing with the hearing world.

When I first met Jay, he was ten years old, and the family spokesman in dealings with the outside world. Stu Goldberg, our Assistant Director, was the one who actually had the first connection with the Lambert family. With wonder in his voice, Stu related his first contact to me. The initial call had been made by Jay.

"Hello, Mr. Goldberg, my name is Jay Lambert, and I want to go to your camp. How can I make my application?" Stu heard a young child's voice on the other end.

"Jay, do you mind telling me how old you are?"

"I'll be ten before summer."

"I'm sure we would be happy to have you as a camper, but usually I speak with the parents first. If things are agreeable, we set up an appointment, and I come to your house and show slides and tell you all about camp. Do your parents know you're making this call?"

"My Mother asked me to call. Both of my parents are deaf, and can't talk on the telephone. They asked me to call you. My Mother is standing right next to me now, and she has marked the available dates for an appointment."

Stu made the appointment; came to their house; showed his slides; and talked about camp, with Jay serving as interpreter for his mother and father. At the end of his presentation and questions, the Lamberts asked for and filled out an application for Jay. Jay's little sister, Serina, joined him at camp a few years later. Sarina, like Jay, had normal hearing and speech. During the course of the conversation, Stu learned that Jay had heard about the camp from some other neighborhood boys who had been at camp the previous summer and were planning to return.

Jay had not been at any kind of camp before, but he did attend the local elementary school in Little Neck, New York, and seemed to have normal contacts with other kids. So I had a high degree of confidence that he would do well in camp. My only concern was communicating with his Parents if there was any kind of a problem.

Jay came to camp and fit in with other kids very well. Unfortunately for him, he had terrible large motor coordination, and hence was really limited athletically. He found team sports particularly painful and did his best to avoid them. Tennis and archery were not quite as much of a struggle and he was very enthusiastic about arts & Crafts, drama, and nature. He frequently came up with mysterious stomach aches, nosebleeds, twisted ankles and anything else he could think of when it was time for softball, soccer or basketball.

Early in his first season at camp, Jay and I came to an understanding. He agreed he would try his best at one athletic activity a day. In return, he could go to arts & crafts in place of any other sports that came up for his group that day. In addition, he agreed to go to swim instruction and general swim. Swimming was another area where he had his problems, but it didn't present the competitive failures that team sports did. I wanted to ease Jay out of failure situations as much as possible, but wanted him to stay with his group enough of the time so that he would be accepted as a member of the group.

Somehow it worked out for Jay. He never got better at sports, and he even occasionally ducked out on General Swim, but he made a small circle of friends, and became happy in camp. His particular interests were in music and drama. He was very willing to spend endless hours in the Rec Hall rehearsing, and additional hours helping the drama counselor with sets. He was also a star reporter for the Kenwood Scroll, our camp newspaper that came out twice a summer. Jay was with us for six summers as a camper.

As a matter of policy, we made our campers go somewhere else and do something else the summer after the tenth grade in school. They were then allowed to return to camp as Junior Counselors after the eleventh grade. Some took cross country trips. Others went to Israel for the summer. Some got jobs at Day Camps or spent the summer baby sitting. After their summer away our returnees were always eager and enthusiastic to return as newly minted Junior Counselors. It is a good and wise policy from which we rarely deviated.

However, in the year that Jay completed 10th grade we made four exceptions. Jay and three of his bunk-mates were allowed to return. It worked out much better for Jay than it did for his three friends. Jay became assistant in the camp Canteen while they became three very unhappy waiters in our dining room. Jay didn't assist in the Canteen for long. He received a battle field promotion to Canteen Manager after we fired the young man who had been hired to do the job. It was a great slot for Jay. It was my impression that he would never be a bunk counselor in our camp because our bunk counselors live in cabins with their campers, and go with them to all activities. That includes general athletics, leading some and helping in others. Jay was not capable of leading or even helping with sports. On the other hand, he was bright and personable and we wanted to have him continue in camp. So the Canteen and Jay seemed like a perfect match.

Our "Canteen" was like a satellite office, which had lots of potential functions, but only five that actually were exercised by the Canteen boy on a regular basis. Answering the telephone was number one; playing bugle calls and making announcements was number two; third was dispensing athletic equipment; fourth, giving out candy on "Candy sale" nights before the campers went in to see a movie or a play at the Rec Hall; last but not least the Canteen boy picked up, sorted and distributed the mail. Jay loved the job, and made the most of it.

Over a period of years Jay went from Canteen boy to Canteen Manager to Office Manager to Administrative Assistant. In fact, he didn't just change titles. I came to rely upon him as a hard working, highly responsible young man who could and did help in many ways. He color coded my schedules, edited and published the Kenwood Scroll, turning it from an annual 6-8 page paper into a seventy page summary of everything important and unimportant that happened in camp each summer. He also took care of important errands in and out of camp. Among other things, Jay completely re-wired our Public Address system throughout camp, upgraded our antique intercom network, produced a counselor show version of South Pacific, Starring Jay Lambert, and served as producer and master of ceremonies at our annual Talent Show.

During his summers at camp Jay met Linda, his future wife, who was one of our Evergreen counselors. It was Christmas break during Jay's Junior year at the University of Rochester when Jay and Linda came to visit Judy and me at our house in Lexington. After a few minutes of chatting, Jay got down to the reason for the visit.

"Arthur, I'd like to come back to camp again next summer, but I really won't be able to. I have to get a year round job."

This was a surprise. I had certainly expected Jay would be with us through his college years. But that was not the last of his surprise announcements that day.

"I'm leaving school. I'm not going back next semester. So I'm looking for a full time job now."

That was a shocker. I just couldn't understand why he would do such a thing.

"... why with only one academic year to go? Why would you drop out now? Are your parents having financial problems? Jay, this doesn't sound like you. There must be something that you're not telling me."

"My parents finances have nothing to do with my decision. In fact, they were very upset with me with I told them. I've just had enough of school. A few months more of school isn't going to make me any smarter or better prepared to do a job in the world."

"Jay, you're smarter than that. It doesn't matter what you might learn in these next few months. You're so close to graduating and getting your degree. That

Bachelor's Degree will be very important for the rest of your working life."

At this point Linda, who'd sat very quiet since they arrived, chimed in.

"That's what I've told him, but he won't listen to me. I hope he'll listen to you."

"I know this, but my mind is made up."

I knew Jay. He could be stubborn, and nothing I could say would change his mind, so I switched to a more welcome topic.

"Jay, what do you think about working for us with our Winter Camp program?"

Just the previous year we had winterized some of our facilities, and embarked upon two programs designed to make year round use of our camp facility. Weekdays we ran a program of environmental education, working with public schools. On the weekends we had an incredibly diverse clientele, ranging from a retreat for Episcopalian Monks on one end of the spectrum to a ski club from Cape Cod on the other. We hosted an encounter group from The University of New Hampshire, and several Jewish Youth groups, who held conclaves at our camp during Christmas and February school vacations.

Jay went right to work for us on a year round basis. He continued at camp in the summer, first as my administrative assistant and then the next year Jay and his wife Linda ran our Drama program at camp. During our nine month "off season" he did two jobs. He and Linda both worked at camp with other counselors in our environmental education program, but Jay's primary responsibility was in sales. He visited with school principals, and tried to interest them in bringing their fifth or sixth grade students to our camp. Year round camping kept him with us at camp for another two years. But he concluded, and rightly so, that he would never make a real living that way. His conclusion coincided with my decision to give up the environmental program and turn it over to a full time director. So the day of parting came as Jay and Linda both went to work in the outside world. I felt badly that Jay never did go back to school.

I was a little less concerned when he called me that Spring to tell me he had been working at Radio Shack, and had just been promoted to Manager of their Somerville, Massachusetts store. He came to visit the following Winter, and, during the visit, was proud to announce that he was now manager of the Malden Radio Shack. A few months later, he called to tell me he was promoted again, this time to manage their store in Braintree, their busiest store in Eastern Massachusetts. Two years later Jay became New England Regional Manager of Radio Shack. It looked as though the lack of a BA wasn't holding him back.

Jay and I talked on the phone a few times a year. He had been Regional Manager at Radio Shack only a few years when he called me with another surprise.

He invited Judy and me to come and visit them in their new house in Randolph. They had bought the house while Jay worked at the Braintree store.

Jay was still a very young guy. I knew he was doing well, and I knew that Linda had a steady job working for Olivetti. But still I didn't think they would be able to buy a house so soon.

The house was lovely, a typical suburban three bedroom split level with room for family growth. The rooms were still mostly unfurnished, but the large kitchen was warm and very welcoming. As we sat at their kitchen table munching on Danish pastry and coffee, Jay delivered a new surprise and an explanation of their sudden good fortune.

"I retired. I'm not working for Radio Shack anymore. I'm not working for anyone but myself. "I sat speechless and waited. " I cashed in my stock options, and I've made a lot of money in the market. I'm pretty sure I'm on the right track."

"Jay, the stock market doesn't sound like a way to make a living."

"It is if you know what you are doing. I follow an excellent investment letter. So far they haven't been wrong very often. That's why we can afford this house."

When Judy and I left that night, I was excited for them and amazed that Jay could have learned so much so fast. It hardly seemed possible to me that he could be doing so well in the market with such a very few years of financial experience. But he was, and it was great.

A few years passed. Jay called one day and said he and Linda were going to be free next summer. Would we like the two of them to come and be our Drama Counselors. I said we'd love to have them but housing would be a problem.

"We won't need housing in camp. The truth is we just bought some property up in Danbury right near camp, and we're planning to buy a trailer, and live there."

Jay simply wanted to return to a place where he had always felt safe and accepted. So he returned to camp. Jay and Linda successfully worked as a team at camp for four summers in charge of our dramatics program. Several summers later they returned as administrative Assistants to my successor, Scott Brody.

More than a dozen years have passed now since they returned to New Hampshire and made a new life for themselves. They started a small company called "The Computer Doctors", and make their living helping people with programming and hardware issues. Not surprisingly, they also became very active in a number of local theatrical groups, and appear in two or three productions every year. I think Jay and Linda have settled into a relaxed life style that they both enjoy.

19
Sticky Fingers

Stephen was a very conscientious counselor, and he was worried.

"What can I do about it? There's stuff missing from our bunk every day. All the kids in the bunk are upset. The things that have been taken aren't really valuable, but they are to the kids who lost them."

"If nothing of real value has been taken, at least we don't have to consider theft by any of our employees. So, we know it's a camper, and the chances are good that camper is one of the kids in your bunk. It's time for you to do a little detective work."

"I'm willing. Just tell me how to start."

"It's obvious the thefts have to be taking place at one of the times when the bunks are supposed to be empty. That means meal time, free play, and activity periods. When your group comes up to meals or goes out to activities, stay in the area for a minute. See if one of your kids hangs back or goes back into the bunk after everyone else is out. During free play, stay in your area and keep an eye on the door of your bunk. I don't think it will take long for you to discover your thief."

Stephen came back to the office the very next day.

"It's Carl. He takes the things out the back door of the bunk. I followed him. He grabs things, puts them under his shirt, and then rushes out to hide them. There's a big pine tree at the edge of the road, by the girls' ball field. There's a hole in the ground right next to that tree. He brings his treasures there, and buries them. He covers the hole with leaves. He certainly can't make use of anything he's taken. He just enjoys taking them. Maybe he's mad at the bunk. But now I know it's him, I don't know what to do. I don't want to confront him. What's your advice?"

"Maybe you do need to confront him. We can't let him think he's getting away with it."

"But he's so insecure. He hasn't made any friends in the bunk yet. He still feels like an outsider. Three of the other kids in our bunk were together last year. The only other new kid is Sam, and he fit right in. I'm sure Carl considers me his only friend in the bunk. If I catch him in the act he'll be humiliated. I'd hate to do that to him"

We both thought for a few minutes until Stephen came up with an idea.

"How about if I just let him continue to take things for awhile, and I go to his stash when he's not around, and I steal the stuff back little by little, returning the things to the kids who lost them. He'll see they got their things back. So he'll know he isn't getting away with it, but he won't be embarrassed by a confrontation, and maybe he'll just stop."

"Good thought, Steve. Give it a try, but it can't go on too long. Sooner or later one of the other boys will catch on, and if they confront him it will be a lot more damaging than if you do. Let me know what's happening. If your method doesn't work pretty quickly, we'll have to change plans."

Stephen followed through with his plan, an unorthodox but ultimately successful solution. It became a game with the boys in the bunk to see what might disappear each day and which missing items would reappear. After an additional week or so of items being stolen and returned, Carl apparently tired of the game. Things stopped disappearing.

Carl never quite made it as part of the group, but he wasn't picked on or ostracized either. Sometimes we had to take comfort in doing the best we could for a camper, even if it turned out that our best produced only a very modest success.

Theft in camp can be demoralizing and upsetting to a cabin group, an entire age group or even a whole camp. It has been a problem in camps forever, and our camp has not escaped without incidents, small and large. Instances of stealing have run the gamut from missing comic books and "Screaming Yellow Zonkers" (candied popcorn) all the way up to expensive tennis rackets and baseball gloves. Perhaps most upsetting of all was the time two hundred dollars disappeared from the dresser drawer of one of our Evergreen counselors. It was not very smart of her to have that cash sitting in a dresser drawer, and was definitely against camp policy. Nonetheless, it was stolen and she was devastated. Our goal in camp has always been to get the missing items back to the victims rather than to apprehend the culprit. Sometimes it is not possible to accomplish one without the other. Other times neither is possible, and all we can attempt is to prevent a recurrence of the crimes.

20
Camp Detective

We had the kid barricaded in the Camp Evergreen office. He was a skinny kid who looked about fourteen years old. He was defiant and sulky.

"You can't keep me here. I dint do nothin. When my uncle gets here, you'll have to let me go."

We were a sad looking group of jailers. I was exhausted. The seat of my pants was wet from sitting on the dew covered lawn for hours waiting for something to happen. Norm was doing his best to look intimidating. But despite brandishing his trusty night patrol baseball bat he just looked old and tired. Even Phyllis, who had more energy than anybody else I've ever known, looked worn down from our late night activity. The town cop I had called was pathetic. He was the one doing the questioning. He looked half asleep, and clearly couldn't wait to head back to bed. He needed a shave. His eyes were bloodshot. His pajama bottoms stuck out under his unpressed uniform pants. His uniform jacket was not buttoned all the way, and the gray curly hair on his chest protruded where you might have expected to see a shirt. I was sorry I called him. He actually seemed to believe the kid's story.

"I don't see how I can take him in or hold him for anything. From what you've told me, the only thing he did wrong was trespass on your property. He agreed to get out of here, and stay away."

I held my temper. Our town cop was clearly not burdened by an excess of brains. I was glad we had also put in a call to the state police. "The state police should be here any minute. We have to let the trooper question him. If the trooper comes, and you've released the kid, he's gonna be pretty angry. We have to keep him until then. Let the trooper decide whether or not to hold him."

Just then the Trooper made his entrance. It looked as though he had stepped right off a recruiting poster. Everything about him looked sharp. His face was rugged. His features were good, but not quite regular enough to be called handsome. He was tall and had a solid build. His wide brimmed hat was square on his head. His uniform was perfect, without a crease. The belt and holster and the butt of his gun all were polished. Even his boots had a high gloss. I breathed a sigh of relief.

A children's summer camp is a world apart. Our goal is to create the most perfect self contained world we can for seven or eight weeks every year. It is remarkable the extent to which we succeed. We and our campers are so wrapped up in our world that none of us know or much care what is happening outside.

We are independent. We produce our own meals; we bring our drinking water out of the ground; we have fire fighting equipment. We are our own internal police force. But our private world sits just on the edge of civilization. Every now and then the outside world intrudes. It was the summer of 1968, and the outside world was getting more and more difficult to ignore. It kept intruding. For weeks that summer I got emergency calls almost every night. "Arthur, there are prowlers in camp."

Night after night we organized our "Bat patrol", borrowing our most responsible male staff from Kenwood, each equipped with his favorite baseball bat. By the middle of August it was getting to be routine. We were all losing a lot of sleep and accomplishing very little. It was an elusive problem. One night there was knocking on the walls of one of the girls bunks; another night one of the counselors saw some unknown man running in the woods near the bunks. On still another night, a strange guy was seen on the girls' ball field. Were there really prowlers? Or were we chasing ghosts? Was it just that the fears created by one incident fueled another? In each instance, we had to react to the alarm as a real threat.

The night before there had been a real threat. There was a gunshot. It sounded like an explosion in the silence of the night. We all heard it. Counselors came running from every direction. We went running down the paths in the direction of the noise; not sure what we would actually do if we were to confront somebody with a gun. Fortunately we weren't able to catch him. But there was no longer a question that he was real. We found five or six cigarette butts close to the source of the sound. It was a swampy mosquito infested area where counselors would never have congregated to smoke or socialize. Somebody was there, either just to upset us or posing a genuine threat to the safety of our campers.

This night we were on high alert, wanting to confront rather than just react to a new emergency. As soon as Taps had sounded our key people assumed our "battle stations". We were spread on paths leading into camp and nearest to the bunks inhabited by our older girls. At least one of us could see anybody approaching no matter where they came from. We were stationed in heavily shadowed areas; some behind bushes; some lying down in hollows in the grass. We sat and waited

It was 11:30 when Sam came running to my station. He was breathing heavily from the exertion of his run and gasping as he told me what he found. "A truck stopped down by the road leading to the lake. I tried to stay out of sight as I went down to see who it was. By the time I got there the truck was empty. I didn't see where they went, but I think there were two men."

I went down with Norm to see the truck; get the license plate number, and see if we could learn anything. There was nobody around it. I opened the door, and couldn't believe my eyes. Whoever had left the truck left his keys in the ignition. I took the keys, and put them in my pocket. Now we wouldn't have to find him. He would now have to come looking for us or he would be stuck there.

We went back to our original stations, and I sent a messenger to draw our counselors into a tight perimeter around the girls' cabins. We would just have to wait. At 12:45 the kid came sauntering down the lawn in the middle of the camp as though he didn't have a care in the world. "Who stole the keys to my truck?"

"What are you doing here?"

"None of your business. Where are my keys?"

"Are you here alone?"

"Give me the damn keys."

" You know this is private property. You have no right to be here. You'll have to wait here with us until the police come. Maybe you'll get your keys back, and maybe you'll have to leave the truck because you'll be in jail."

That's how we wound up in the Evergreen office. The kid's story was patently ridiculous.

"Some guy we met earlier today owns the land down by the railroad tracks. He asked my uncle to do a lumber survey, and give him a price. We just parked at the nearest turnoff, and it happened to be near your camp."

Since we owned the land by the railroad tracks the story sounded even more far fetched to my ears. it was obvious to anybody that nobody would seriously survey for lumber in a strange place at midnight. It was hard to believe our local cop even listened to this nonsense. The State Trooper laughed out loud when he heard the story.

The kid had just finished telling his story for the second time when there were more footsteps on the office porch. The door opened and we got our first look at "Uncle Jed". He was a grubby looking local tough in his mid-twenties. He had on a ragged tee shirt and chino pants caked with dried mud stains. His work boots were mud covered and unlaced at the top. His face was red, and his voice was belligerent. "Why is my nephew in here? He hasn't done anything wrong. You can't keep him here. Give me back my truck keys. We've had enough of this place."

Then he looked up and saw the Trooper. He stopped almost in mid sentence. It was clear they knew one another. "Well, Jed, we meet again. What are you up to this time? Don't give me any of your crap. Just tell me what you're doing here."

Judd gave him the same story the kid had given us. The Trooper laughed again. "You wait here, Jed. I want to have a little chat with your nephew." He took the boy out of the office, and walked off into the darkness. They were gone a few minutes. When they returned he was prodding the kid ahead of him, and pushed him into the office. The kid's hands were cuffed behind his back. Without a word, the trooper grabbed Jed's arms; twisted them back and put handcuffs on him. We noticed that the trooper had a small gash on the side of his neck, and had blood running down onto his immaculate uniform shirt.

"The little bastard had a knife. I got the whole story from him before he decided he could cut me and run away. He was released a couple of days ago from a Juvenile home in Fitchburg, Massachusetts. Somehow they gave his uncle Jed custody. Jed promised him he'd find him a girl he could screw. They had spent the last couple of days looking for girls. Jed knows about your camp. He lives just down the road in South Danbury. They were planning to grab one of the older girls or a counselor walking alone. They would both do her. He showed me where they were standing looking in the windows of that Red House across the way." It was just then the kid pulled his knife on me.

"I'm taking the two of them to jail in Franklin. They'll be arraigned tomorrow morning. I'll need at least one of you down there at 10:00 AM to file a complaint. If nobody comes the judge will probably just let them go."

I wasn't going to let that happen. "I'll be there." I was in court the next morning at 10:00 AM. The nephew was not in court. The Police had reached the kid's Mother, and released him back to his Mother's custody earlier that morning. The Judge listened to the trooper and listened to me. He also knew Jed from some previous appearance, and he bound him over for three days to find a lawyer, but he would have to sit in jail for those three days. I went back to camp relieved that he was off the streets.

Three days later I was back in court. There was a new Judge. Jed said he hadn't been able to find a lawyer and needed the court to appoint one. The new judge appointed one of the lawyers sitting in the back; gave him a week to prepare defense and, over my objections, released Jed without bail.

One week later I was in court again. So were the judge and the lawyer. But Jed never showed up. At that point I knew that he was never going to go to trial.

Ten days later we read in the local paper that Jed had been arrested for indecent exposure and attempted rape in a parking lot in Concord. He was being held for trial, this time without bail. I lost track of Jed. We never saw him or his nephew again. We never did find out who shot off the gun the previous night. That mystery hung over us the rest of the summer.

21
A Shot in the Dark

April Duncan was a vision. She towered over her Mother, who brought her for the interview. She was lumpy looking, rather like a snow man fashioned out of mashed potatoes by a group of children with good intentions, but a poor sense of proportions. Her face was round with heavily rouged red cheeks. Her stringy hair spilled over her forehead in the front, and burst out in all directions from the loosely tied pig tails in the rear. None of her clothes quite contained her erratic figure. Her legs were encased in knee socks, one blue the other red.

April had come for an interview for a job as a waitress at our camp. I did most of my "waiter & waitress interviews" after supper during work week. As she walked into the dining room, I saw our guys look at her with barely suppressed laughter. I left my meal in mid-stream. I wanted to get her as far from their stares and giggles as possible. I walked with April and her Mother to the far end of the dining room. After about one minute of conversation, it was obvious to me that April was retarded. After a couple of minutes I was ready to say "I'm sorry, but I don't think we have any jobs left open. The last one was filled earlier today."

April's Mother was a very bright woman. She knew what was coming. "Can we talk privately for a minute?" I nodded yes. "Sweety, why don't you go sit at another table for a while. I want to talk to Mr. Sharenow about something." April got up and sat down a few tables away.

"Could you please give her a chance? She has such a hard time getting a job. She's a very hard worker. She would be very dependable. Please can you give her a chance?"

"I would give her a chance, but she could be made miserable here. I'm not sure the kids would give her a chance. The teen-age campers and even some of the younger counselors would pick on her and make her miserable. I would hate to give her a job and see that happen, and I'm not at all sure that I could prevent it."

"I know you're trying to be nice, but look at her. You must realize she has spent her whole life with people teasing and picking on her. It's terrible, but it's normal for her. She's used to it. It's far worse for her to be sitting at home with no real job and nothing to do. I'll make sure she gets here on time every day. She'll do a good job for you. Just give her a chance."

Against my better judgment, I took pity on this worn middle aged woman and her twenty-two year old retarded daughter. After all, if it didn't work out, the worst that would happen would be I would have to send her home.

April worked for us for six summers. She was far and away our most reliable waitress. Yes, the children laughed at her. Yes, some of them teased her. But she was so good humored and so eager to please and so hard working that the teasing stopped after the first few weeks. Each summer it would start again with some new counselors and campers, but it would quickly be brought under control. Most of the counselor staff enjoyed talking about her astonishing use of makeup and laughing about her ever changing and bizarre combinations of clothing. But people were kind to her in person. I heard veteran counselors stifling comments from their campers. It was a job for April and an education for the rest of us. She became part of our camp family.

April wrote to Judy and me every winter to bring us up to date on the rest of her life. One December I received a classic letter from April. I didn't save it, so I can only give it my best recollection.

"Dear Judy and Arthur ... I just sewed a new skirt that I will wear next summer at camp. You will like it. I have to go and feed the 3 cows, and five ducks and Sandy and Rex and the cats there are too many to count. Our well got out of water so I had to do the dishes in the stream behind the house. It's getting cold too. Mama says I should always put on shoes when I go out in the Winter. How is little David? (Our son's name is Robert). I hope he's growing to be a big boy. Henry came to visit. Him and me are getting married soon. I'm moving in his trailer in Penacook. He promises to get me to camp on time every day. Can you come to my marriage day?
Your friend, April Duncan"

We met Henry, a small timid man with some obvious physical problems. He and April made a comical looking couple. In all dimensions she was twice his size. He had a high pitched voice.

"Pleezd ta meecha". I hoped he would be kind to April.

The following Winter we got this letter.

"Dear Judy and Arthur ... I have to live at camp next summer. Is that all right? Henry threw me out of the trailer. I wasn't even dressed. I had some clothes on, but no shoes. Mama says I should always wear shoes in the winter. I didn't have my coat too. It is nine or thirteen miles from Henry's trailer to Mama's house. I walked all night. It was very cold. Mama says I can stay there while it's cold, but have to move out when warm weather comes. She has a new border. He sleeps in my room. I can sleep in the kitchen near the stove. So I'm warm now. Sandy sleeps next to me.
Your friend,
April Duncan"

I was determined to find housing for April but it presented a problem. The "kitchen boys" (ages14-17) lived together in a single camp cabin with no interior partitions. The "dining room girls" commuted from home. That arrangement saved the camp administration from having to deal with potentially difficult social and sexual situations. But April was older, and hardly a social butterfly. She needed a place to live. We converted what had been a storage room under the camp dining room into her summer bedroom. It was bare bones, with a bed a chest of drawers and a lamp. It wasn't much, but she was happy to have a place to live.

One night that next summer Judy and I were in bed when I heard knocking on the door. I quickly put my pants on over my pajamas, and went to the door.

"Arthur, there was a rifle shot in the middle of the camp just a couple of minutes ago."

I would normally have assumed that the "OD" (Counselor On Duty after "Taps") must be mistaken. But that was a summer in which there had been frequent alarms over prowlers, peeping toms and others near our girls' camp. There had never been an issue of prowlers or invaders near the boys' cabins, right in the middle of camp. But there is a first time for everything, and we certainly couldn't ignore any threat.

"I'll be there in two minutes. Have the other ODs check the bunks to make sure everything is normal. I'll meet you by the office door. Make sure everybody has a baseball bat. I got dressed fast and grabbed my favorite bat, which served as my night stick in our war against night prowlers in that era.

We gathered together by the office. One by one the assembled counselors assured me that all was normal in their bunks. The kids were unharmed and sound asleep. I questioned all who had heard the shot, and it was clear that nobody knew exactly where it had come from. We spread out from the center, and searched as far as reason would allow. We never saw or heard anyone. After a couple of hours of fruitless searching, we were convinced that the culprit had just meant to give us a scare, and was long gone from camp. I was still uneasy, but we all went to bed for what was left of the night.

The next morning my office door was open and there was a note on my desk.

"Dear Arthur,

Last night I was lying in bed in my room downstairs under the dining room. I felt like having a cigarette, so I reached for one and put it in my mouth. When I lit it, I heard a sizzle. It was a fire cracker. I was lucky. I threw it out the window before it exploded. It's a good thing the window was open. It made a loud noise. I hope I didn't wake anybody. I'm sorry.

Your friend,

April Duncan"

Postscript

April worked for us for another two summers. Then her Mother, who was getting older and was in poor health, found April "a year round job" in a protected environment, a kind of a half way house in Northern New Hampshire. I was never sure whether she really had a job or was a paying resident. April's last letter to me came about a year after we last saw her. She told me she was happy and was getting married again, this time to a man who lived in the same house. Many years have passed, and we never heard from her again. I hope her second marriage worked out better than the first.

22

Straight Arrow

Harry had been a camper with us for years. Pound for pound he was the best all around athlete in camp. In his younger years he was our best baseball player. As a young Senior he took up tennis, and rapidly developed into our number one tennis player. The summer he returned as a Junior Counselor he took up archery. He spent all of his spare time with our archery instructor. By mid-season, he surpassed his teacher, and was the most skilled archer in camp. Unfortunately, Harry's superior athletic skills were not matched by equally superior power of reason or maturity. Every chance he got he practiced his skills as an archer. One day I got a phone call from a neighbor down the road.

"One of your big kids was out shooting squirrels and chipmunks with a bow and arrow. He was not far from my house. I've got little kids. They play outside. I don't want to have to worry about them getting shot by some crazy kid."

There was no doubt in my mind who he was talking about.

"Harry, my boy, you cannot go out with your bow and arrow, and start shooting. Somebody is going to call the police. In fact, somebody did report you, but they called me rather than the police. If there is a next time I'm sure they will call the police."

"I was just shooting squirrels. I didn't think there was a law against that."

"It doesn't matter whether there is a law or not. Don't do it again. We don't want to upset our neighbors."

"OK, I promise I won't do it again."

That was the end of it, I thought. A few days later Mike Knopke, our rookie Canteen manager came running into the office."

"Arthur, there's an awful stink in the Rec Hall. It smells like a skunk moved in."

"Thanks for telling me, but there's not much we can do. He'll move on if nobody bothers him. Just keep people away from there for now."

Half an hour later Harry came to me with a big smile on his face.

"Arthur, I shot him. I shot that skunk that was hiding under the Rec Hall. He was way back in where the floor almost comes down to the ground." Harry was very proud of himself.

"Harry, do you realize what you've done? We'll never be able to get him out of there. That smell will be with us the rest of the summer." And it was.

23

Neighbors Can Be a Headache

William B. Grant 1960s-1990s

"... I understand you have an interest in my land at the end of Eagle Pond. .... and twenty-five thousand dollars would seem to me a fair price for the land..."

"Ansel, what can you tell me about this William Grant?"

He had no reticence in answering this. "People say he's never done anything but wheel and deal his whole life. Some people think he's not honest. I don't know about that, but I know he's bad news. I'm sorry you'll have to deal with him to buy the land, but I'm pretty sure he just bought it to turn it around and sell it to you. That's the kind of business he does."

We never did get to buy that land, and I was to learn to my sorrow that it would have been worth a great deal more than $25,000 he was asking to not have to deal with William B. Grant as a neighbor.

After receiving Grant's letter asking $25,000 for the land, I at first decided to just ignore it such an outrageous number, but then I decided there was no harm in making a counter offer. But how much can I afford to offer? I vacillated back and forth between four and six thousand dollars, and finally settled on six. . That would give him better than a 100% profit for doing a few hours of strategic paper shuffling. I decided to make a formal offer in writing. We couldn't really afford it, but if he said yes, somehow I would have to find the money.

"Dear Mr. Grant,

Yes, I am very much interested in the land you own at the end of the lake. I hope we can come to an agreement. That land is probably more valuable to me than it is to anybody else, but I truly cannot afford the twenty-five thousand dollars you are asking, or anything close to it. My finances were stretched to the limit when I bought the camp. The amount that I can offer now is $6,000. This is not a negotiating position. It is all that I can afford. I hope you will consider my offer in the spirit in which I make it. If you feel you cannot accept this offer I will understand, and will look forward to having you as a neighbor in the coming years.

Sincerely,

Arthur Sharenow

Not surprisingly Grant rejected the offer, but I soon learned he did not abandon his original plan to sell the land to me at his price. Grant started a kind of public relations war with me.

That very summer, just a few days before Parents Visiting Weekend, we noticed at lot of activity down at Grant's end of the lake. There were bulldozers at work followed by hours of sawing and hammering. He was apparently building a swimming area and a boat dock. His dock was situated in an area not exactly desirable as a swimming area. The water was shallow and swampy, with vegetation creeping in from both sides. Access to this area required users to climb down a very steep hill. We also heard and occasionally saw bulldozers at work on the upper part of his land, property adjacent to our Senior Camp area.

Two days before visiting weekend two large plywood signs went up. One was on Eagle Pond Road, just past the entrance to Sr. Camp, where he had created a gravel driveway onto his property. The other was at the entrance to Eagle Pond Road, where it met Route Four. He positioned his sign to be as visible as possible to our campers' parents, almost all of whom reached camp by car from the South. His sign partially blocked our camp sign from view for parents approaching camp. But that was less disturbing than what was on the sign.

Eagles Nest Camp Ground
Camp sites and trailer park
Swimming and Boating

He had a show of intense activity down at his waterfront that weekend. I don't know where he found all of the people, but they were there in rowboats, canoes and motor boats, zipping around our small lake. One of the talking points of our rather small Eagle Pond was its exclusivity. We didn't actually share its use with anybody. Here he was demonstrating a very different reality to our camp parents. It worked. There were very few camper parents who didn't ask me about the new trailer park next to camp. They were worried about the traffic on the road and even more about the traffic on the lake and the concurrent loss of privacy for the camp.

As soon as Visiting Weekend was over the activity at his waterfront came to an end, and the property seemed quiet and deserted, but the signs stayed up. During the remainder of that summer we had an irregular trickle of innocent strangers driving into camp. They came in their Motor homes and camping vehicles, in complete confusion, looking for the nonexistent trailer park. It was a nuisance but much better than the reality of a trailer park would have been.

But that was just his opening salvo. That summer he wrote me another letter, raising his selling price to $30,000.

"The increase reflects the increased value I have added to the property by constructing a real waterfront where there had previously been just swamp."

The following winter was a severe one in our neck of the woods. In those days we did not plow the interior camp roads. Of course, the town plowed Eagle Pond Road, but the only way to actually get around our campus was to climb the banks along the side of the road and just tramp through the snow. The snow that year piled up early and often. I came up to check on (visit) Ansel who was working in the Red House, which was located just across the road from the main part of our campus. When I arrived I could see he was in an unusually animated state. In short, he was seething with anger.

"They've cut off the tops of your Hemlock trees. I know it was them. I followed their snow shoe prints in and out. Here, I want to show you."

He got out two pair of traditional north country snow shoes, made of bent wood and raw hide webbing. They were like large tennis rackets with leather holster ties to keep your feet on the shoes. I had never used them before, but I thought it would be fun. He showed me how to walk, penguin fashion, feet splayed out at a forty-five degree angle. It was easy enough on Eagle Pond Road, but when we climbed the banks, and down onto the soft snow on campus, I discovered that snow shoeing can be hard work. With every step I sunk in, and occasionally the back of one snowshoe crossed over onto the other. For a while I was falling all over myself until I achieved a certain technique. He led me across the girls' ball field, by Bunk 3, and toward the path that led to the dining room. Walking on top of the snow, I estimated we were five or six feet off the ground. When we came to the scene of the crime I could plainly see that the top six or eight feet had been cut off of three of our fifteen foot Hemlocks. They were cut off right at the snow level, and dragged out. They would certainly make nice Christmas trees for someone. Ansel led me along the tracks in the snow to prove his point that they came from Grant's place. I thought he was probably right, but it was certainly not conclusive that Grant had anything to do with it, and I was not prepared to accuse him of cutting our trees without a lot better evidence. A week later, coincidentally a sign went up at the end of Eagle Pond Road.

Eagles Nest Tree Farm
Christmas Trees For Sale

I have no idea whether some of the trees he offered for sale were those cut on our property. His business was real, but "farm" was a misnomer. He had no plans to plant or grow trees, only to cut them down. After selling as many Christmas trees as he could, he set up a lumbering operation, which eventually cut most of the standing lumber on his eighty acres. Before he started lumbering the land was better than half woodland and the rest animal grazing land. When he was through lumbering a few years later there was only a thin stretch of trees bordering the road. The interior was stripped. I'm sure the work went on spasmodically through the year, but it seemed to me that his major burst of lumbering activity always occurred as our campers arrived at the start of our camp season and just as our Parents arrived for camp Visiting weekend.

Another letter came, another offer to sell. This time the land was going to be put up for public sale at $50,000. "After all," he said, "I've improved the land, clearing it of all those trees. It will make it easier for you to make ball fields and play areas for your campers. Some other buyer might want to make a housing development. There's plenty of room for that. But I'm giving you the right of first refusal."

To me he had depreciated the value of his land rather than improving it. But I was still anxious to buy either for future expansion or as protection against some future detrimental use of that land by Grant. By the mid-1960s when this letter came I felt a little more secure financially, and was able to increase my offer to $8,000. I didn't expert him to accept my offer. On the other hand, I was puzzled because he must have known by then that I could not seriously entertain the price he was asking.

The next chapter in our decades long saga with Bill Grant occurred in 1968. Fourth of July was on a Monday that year. That meant a four day holiday for many people. The Grant family planned a big party to celebrate the Fourth. The vehicles started rolling in Thursday. Over the next five days Eagle Pond Road became a dust bowl, with a constant caravan of motorcycles, beat up cars with moisy mufflers and even a few trailers. Several of them turned into the camp driveway by mistake. After the first couple of days I posted a counselor at the junction of our driveway and the town road to direct newcomers to the Grant's driveway. This worked fine during the day, but I couldn't ask a counselor to sit out there all night ... We became accustomed to the thrum of the motorcycles, as they turned in, came up the hill toward the dining room, realized their mistake and turned back out. This happened many times. Several didn't realize their mistake in time, and drove right down onto the campus and came to a stop in front of our little boys' cabins. But this was far from the worst problem associated with the Grant's Fourth of July House Party.

The incredibly loud music started about eleven o'clock every morning and went on and on through the night into the first light of dawn, day after day after day. I don't know what kind of amplifiers they had, or what speakers, but they created stupendous volume. When it first came on each day, campers and counselors alike were startled by the sheer volume. We got several phone calls that Thursday from angry neighbors, some of whom lived as far from camp as downtown Potter Place. They all assumed the noise was coming from camp because we were the only ones with outdoor speakers. We got the word out that it wasn't ours. It was Grant's. I don't know if anybody followed up with visits to the party site or not, but at least the phone calls stopped by mid-day Friday. By then they all knew where the noise was coming from.

After that first day and night we had to do something. Our Senior boys, closest to the noise, claimed not to have slept at all. Throughout camp, people said they couldn't sleep. Our counselors who were on duty at night said it was impossible to get the kids to bed with that racket. I walked over to try to find my good friend William Grant. I expected to see motorcycles and trailers and broken down wrecks of cars. I expected to see tattooed young men and women, half dressed and probably drunk or stoned. What I didn't realize until I saw with my own eyes the massive number of people, who were now camped out on the property. It looked like hundreds, and this was only Friday. What would those numbers reach by Saturday night? I could see the monster speakers, set up on the peak of the hill above Grant's waterfront. It was clear now why the sound traveled so well. There was nothing immediately in front of those speakers but the lake. The sound could travel uninterrupted through the camp and well beyond.

I looked for Bill Grant, but didn't find him. I did find his son Clyde, who apologized for the volume, and promised to try to keep it down in the future. I watched him go to the amplifiers and turn the volume down. I thanked him and returned to camp. When I got back to camp word had spread that I had stopped the noise, and everybody congratulated me on my successful mission. The congratulations were premature. A few hours later the music was back at full volume. I called our local police chief, and pleaded with him to do something about it.

"Well, you're not the only one to complain. But it is Fourth of July you know. People do make noise when celebrating."

"I know that, but for how many days and how loud?"

Chief Flowers agreed to go and talk to Grant. I was not at all sure that he actually went because there was no appreciable change in the volume of the music. In fact, it was now punctuated by the boom and sizzle of exploding fireworks that exploded at ten or fifteen minute intervals through the day. At night the intervals seemed even shorter. I may not have gotten the results that I wanted from having the police go over there, but I did get a reaction. The reaction came in the form of a visit the next morning from my friend Bill. I saw him pull up in his pickup truck. He leaped out of the truck, slammed the truck door, and bounded up the side steps to my office. For a big guy, who was moving on in years, he was very agile. I met him at the door.

"Sharenow, who the hell do you think you are calling the police to interfere with a patriotic social gathering? If you have a problem with something happening on my property you come talk to me." He was screaming at me. His face was red and spittle was gathering at the corners of his mouth.

I really don't like people screaming at me. "Bill, you better just calm down or get out of here. I won't even talk to you if you come in here raving like a maniac."

"Who you calling names, Mister?" He looked like he was about to take a swing at me. I thought I better diffuse this now or he might actually try to hit me.

"Bill, listen for a minute." He did quiet down. He was still visibly seething, but he, like me, must have realized how close he had come to taking a swing at me. "I went over looking for you. When I couldn't find you I talked to your son Clyde. He promised to lower the noise level. And it did get lower for an hour or so. Then it went right back to full volume. A asked him to tell you I was there looking for you. He said he would."

"Well you should have found me if you came over. Don't ask my kid. Talk to me."

"I guess that was my mistake. I'm sorry I called the police without talking to you first. But I see the police visit didn't have much effect. Bill, I'm asking you to please use your influence with your boys and their friends to hold the noise down. We have a couple of hundred young kids here who need to get some sleep. The noise is annoying during the day, but it is more than annoying at night."

"You people." He spit that phrase out sneeringly. If there was any doubt in my mind who "You people" were, he cleared it up immediately. "You people can celebrate your holidays your way, and we won't interfere. Just let us Americans celebrate our most important holiday without any crap from a ... greedy Jew businessman."

"Bill, get out of here now before I have you thrown out. And remember this, if you or your friends continue to break the law I will call the police. Right now you are breaking the law by creating a nuisance, and if it doesn't improve my next call will be to the state police. You probably don't have any influence with the state troopers like you do with our local cops."

Whatever he thought of me, somehow the noise level was lowered the rest of Friday and Saturday until Saturday night when the booming of music and fireworks were louder than ever. That night I called the state police. Their visit to the Grants had some effect. It quieted down and was quite reasonable all through Sunday and daytime Monday. Monday night, the actual fourth of July they were at full volume again. I decided not to do or say anything further. This, after all, was the holiday, and I assumed the guests would leave the next day and it would be over.

Eventually that night was over, and the huge gang of friends and guests drifted away over the next few days. My relationship with Bill Grant had always been cordial and proper, but never friendly before that party. It now entered a new phase of open hostility that was to last for the next three decades.

Several years after that party I received a letter from our local planning board, inviting me to a hearing involving the land next door. William B. Grant had petitioned the board to allow him to subdivide his property by cutting off two one acre lots adjacent to the road from his eighty acre plot of land, and transferring those lots to his sons. As an abutter I had a right to be heard. I went to the hearing, but voiced no objection. I'm sure Grant was expecting a legal battle from me. I actually had no objection. I thought if anything, with his sons living there, he was less likely to do anything with the property that would cause us grief. Time would prove me wrong. We shook hands at the end of the hearing.

His sons built houses on their lots, and they and their families became good neighbors. Clyde and his wife Martha had the lot closest to camp. Years passed, and their children grew older. One of their daughters applied for a job as a waitress at camp. She was a lovely girl, and was with us for three summers. It was amusing to me that Bill Grant's granddaughter not only came to work as a waitress at our "Jewish" camp, but that she had a close friendship with one of our few black counselors. He happened to be a great kid who had grown up in camp, and was on the way to being an outstanding adult. I couldn't help but chuckle to myself when I thought about how Bill Grant would react to that information if he knew.

The last chapter of the William B. Grant saga with camp was a political battle. He sought permission to turn his once beautiful piece of property into a Sludge Dump. He proposed to make that land into the dumping ground for sewage from the city of Concord, NH and from several manufacturing plants. He had already stripped the land of saleable lumber, sold all of the top soil, and finally converted it into a sand and gravel operation. Other than the two acres he had deeded to his boys, the land had become a barren plot. He had to do something with it, and came up with the idea of making it a place to dump sewage. Since most of his property was in the Town of Danbury, he had to get town approval. We fought the good fight at a special Danbury, New Hampshire Town meeting and won, my most dramatic and important victory ever. Perhaps most important, all of our other neighbors joined with us and voted with us to end this threat.

24
The Peter Principle and the 1967 Season

During the summers of 1967–1969 the Vietnam War was at the peak of its' bloody years. The draft had been revived, and every male college student over the age of eighteen had a draft number. The national mood was a mix of anxiety and anger. In cities all over the country there were anti-war protests. Nowhere was the disruption of normal routine more profound than on college campuses.

College students boycotted classes, took over college buildings, and burned flags. They desecrated once revered symbols of their own institutions. Many College Presidents and Deans resigned during and immediately after this three year period. The educators had originally accepted their highly respected positions with the expectation that they could further lofty philosophical and educational goals. Instead they found themselves in the role of embattled peace keepers, sometime negotiators, and, unfortunately, even policemen.

During the summers of 1967–1969 turmoil in summer camps was also in full bloom. The Vietnam War and student protests were the catalysts for that turmoil. At camp, we had a few Senior Staff, but most of our counselors were college students. The students who chose to come to camp as counselors almost certainly represented the most conservative "Establishment" types. And yet these conservative students had spent their college years surrounded by protest. Protest was a way of life which they carried with them to camp. Those three summers presented a crescendo of difficulties, culminating in the1969 camp season, the most challenging for me and for many other Camp Directors. Many directors retired after that summer. Owners sold their camps. They just could not face another embattled camp season like the one they had just experienced. The thought of quitting never occurred to me. I loved camp too much to consider such a drastic step.

The Peter Principle 1967

Everything that could go wrong did go wrong.

Our1967 staff was filled with memorable counselors. It was the only camp season where I ran a shuttle service to the bus in New London, driving a just fired counselor there and a few minutes later picking up his incoming replacement. But the handwriting was on the wall well before the arrival of the first campers, even before the arrival of the Counselor Orientation Period. Work Week of 1967 was one I will never forget. It was the first clear evidence that 1967 would be a summer in which anything that could go wrong did go wrong. It was almost impossible to find new counselors for that camp season. Our Work Week staff gave me a preview of the camp season ahead. Our slim group of only seven workers included just two returnees and five newcomers. Those five were among the most picturesque of my hiring failures that year.

The Cast: Rich Grollman

Rich Grollman made his debut in Work Week. He was a one man disaster that week. The first afternoon we were carrying rowboats from storage in our Recreation Hall to the girls' waterfront. Rich tripped on the steps to the waterfront, and managed a nice gash in his leg. I dispatched one of our two veteran counselors to take him to the Hospital emergency room in New London. A few stitches and he was back in time for dinner. The next day he insisted he was fit and ready for work, but I thought it best to give him a relatively easy assignment. He spent the day painting, and though he didn't do a wonderful job, he did no harm.

He was back with us the next day. After a forty-five minute course of instruction, Rich's job was to mow the Junior Camp lawn with our Gravely tractor. That is not as easy as it sounds. He did well that morning, and agreed to continue mowing in the afternoon. We never did find out how he lost control of the Gravely, but Rich managed to run it into the corner of one of the boys' cabins. The Gravely was in the repair shop for a week. Ansel and one of his helpers spent the better part of two days repairing the corner of the cabin.

On the afternoon of the final day of work week we had a job I always looked forward to, assembling the Kenwood waterfront. It was a beautiful hot sunny day, perfect weather for positioning and installing docks on the waterfront. I always tried to save that job for hot sunny afternoons, when it would be a welcome relief from working on ball fields and tennis courts.

Our wooden docks were supported by Styrofoam floats. The whole system rode up and down on long poles attached to the dock by metal collars and sunk into the under surface of the lake on either side of the dock. This way when we have a heavy rain, the docks float up as the water level of the lake rises, and during extended dry spells the docks float down. We were not very far into the afternoon when Rich dropped his end of a twenty foot long iron pipe on his big toe. This required his second trip to the emergency room. His broken toe meant that he was on restricted activity at the start of the season. This was not an auspicious debut for Rich, who was slated to be our new key man in camp.

I remembered our first meeting. The man sitting across from me reminded me of a Schmoo. The Schmoo was a post World War II pear shaped cartoon character who could inflate into a balloon or deflate into a door mat. That resemblance struck me when I opened the door and escorted him to our family room. He was there for an interview. I tried to erase that comic image from my mind, but I was not successful. First impressions are not fair, but they are real.

Rich was very heavy without being obscenely fat. He looked like the kind of guy who would always find it easier to plop down rather than to get up. In fairness, he was carefully dressed for the interview, but nothing worked. His sport jacket was a little too tight. His tie was a garish astrological nightmare. His pants were brown and his shoes were black and down at the heels. I tried to ignore the acne on his pasty white face. His strong point was that he was clearly educated and highly articulate.

"I can do it all. I've done it all. I have experience running every activity you have in your program. I've coached baseball. I've coached basketball. I have not actually coached a soccer team, but I've run soccer activities and I know how. My specialty is motivating kids to want to play."

That sounded great. "Tell me about your actual camp experience. I see you were at 'Boys and Girls Club camp' in Sharon last summer. Tell me about your job there, and why you're interested in changing jobs." As I listened to him prattle on about his camp background and a truly astonishing array of talents, I looked at him and had trouble imagining this overweight middle aged man being the dynamo he described. I tried to picture him out on a ball field running from home plate to first base. In my mind's eye he arrived at first base panting and red in the face. I couldn't even imagine him running back and forth on a basketball court or a soccer field. But he continued to talk, and I listened. I asked questions and he answered. All of his answers were right.

Later that day I called Sam Schwartz, the Director of Boys and Girls Camp.

"You say he really was your head athletic man last summer?" ….. "And he was really good working with staff?"

"He's not too much of an athlete, but he does know the sports, and seemed to be able to coach them well enough."

I still didn't really believe it, but, on paper, he was not only the best candidate for Senior Unit Leader, at present he was the only candidate. In our camp the Sr. Unit Leader job is the job with the highest degree of responsibility. The only one which required greater responsibility was the position of Waterfront Director. There is a geographic reason for this. The Boys' Senior Unit is far removed from the rest of the camp. The distance, as the crow flies, may be as little as seventy-five yards. But few camp administrators are crows, and the deep valley between two imposing hills that separates our teen age boys from the rest of camp represented a barrier breached no more than once or twice a day by Head Counselors and Directors. The Senior Unit leader position is crucial, and we didn't have any home grown young man ready to be promoted to that job.

Two weeks later Rich Grollman came for a second interview. With great reluctance, I hired him. I talked myself into believing that he could do the job. I couldn't know then how badly I had blundered or how much it would cost.

Rich's Work Week performance was not confidence inspiring, but, after all, I rationalized, physical labor is not a test of a good camp counselor. Orientation Period, which followed, was uneventful on the Rich Grollman front. There were murmurings of discontent from some of the counselors in Dick's unit, but there were sure to be murmurings about almost any new person in a position of authority. However once the season started there was little doubt that Dick, not only did not relate well to other staff members, but that the kids detested him from the day they arrived in camp. After a very few miserably run activity periods, it was also obvious that his familiarity with baseball, basketball and football coaching was limited to what you could garner by watching "Pride of the Yankees" and the "Knute Rockne Story". My faith in his leadership ability was gone as was any thought that he might be able to coach sports, but I held out the hope that as a responsible adult, he would at least be able to keep the kids and counselors from making any serious or dangerous mistakes.

July 4th comes early in the camp season. Fourth of July is a Holiday celebrated with fervor in New Hampshire. Whatever discontent might have been rearing its head on college campuses across the country in 1967, it was barely noticed in Potter Place, New Hampshire. Fourth of July was a time for pancake breakfasts, flea markets on the school green, square dancing in the street, a band playing from the platform of an open hay truck. It was a time for grandmothers to twirl around with grandchildren, for sweethearts to sneak off into the dark, and for a great fireworks display as the culmination of the night. Surely there are bigger, fancier and more spectacular displays on the Esplanade in Boston or on the shores of Lake Erie or arching over the artificial lakes of Disney World, but nowhere are the fireworks more important than they are in the small towns of New Hampshire on July 4th.

When we were Counselors, Judy and I and as many of our counselor friends as could get off duty, always headed for Andover, the nearest town with fireworks and square dancing. It was a wonderful evening. Though a patriotic celebration, the experience of this small town celebration was as foreign to our sophisticated suburban eyes as a native festival in a foreign land. Shortly after we bought the camp we decided that it was a shame our campers were so close, and yet could not be part of this spectacular event. After all, we were only three miles from Andover.

By 1967 we had already made it a tradition that our Senior boys and girls would go, in separate busses, to Andover with their counselors and be in time for the fireworks. Our campers were not allowed free reign to wander about at night or to take part in any of the other activities. They were there to see the fireworks. They sat together as a group, surrounded by counselors, oohed and ahhed with everyone else, and then piled in their busses to head back to camp. That was the way it had gone for the past few years.

It was about 11:30 at night when I started to worry. The girls' bus had returned to camp by 10:45. The girls were back in their cabins and as quiet as excited teen age girls are likely to be. But there was no sign of the boys' bus. We were discussing sending out a car to see if we could find the bus. It was a straight run down US Route #4 from camp to Andover. We couldn't miss them on the way. I had just about decided to do so when we heard the bus rumbling up the camp road. A few minutes later we heard it leaving, having discharged its load of campers and counselors.

Senior camp was a fair distance from my house where Phyllis, Judy, Norm and I were gathered. I assumed that after Rich and his counselors got the kids into their bunks and quiet, he would come down and let me know how things went, and why they were so late getting back. More time passed than we would have expected, when the knock came on the door. It wasn't Rich Grollman. It was one of his young counselors, a boy who had grown up in camp and who, not very many years before, had been a Senior Camper himself. He was noticeably shaking when he came in.

"Arthur, it was terrible. We didn't know where anybody was. He let the kids off the bus, and just told them to meet back at 11:00. They all disappeared into the crowd. Some of us tried to keep track of our own kids, but it was impossible after he told them they could go. We weren't even sure where they were during the fireworks display. "

"Didn't he ask you to stay together as bunk groups and tent groups?"

"Absolutely not. He just let them loose. It was a mob scene there with lots of drunks. Some of our third year Seniors (15 year old boys) tried to pick up a group of girls. It turned out the girls had boyfriends. There was almost a fight. I got there in time to stop that one. I don't know what else happened. I had to come and tell you. I know Grollman won't. I questioned him when we got back, and he accused me of trying to steal his job. I love working with the Seniors, but if that guy is staying I want to switch to Junior Camp. I don't think I can work with him."

The next morning when I called Rich in to discuss the fireworks outing his response was truly unbelievable to me.

"I left with thirty-three and I came back with thirty-three. That's a successful trip." It was clear that his idea of being accountable and responsible for campers was different than mine.

As the season progressed Rich achieved a certain historical notoriety. He is the only person in camp history to start the camp season as Senior Unit Leader (our largest age group with the most boys and staff); be demoted to Junior Unit Leader (a much smaller unit with fewer boys and counselors); be again demoted to Junior Counselor. Of course we did not call him a Jr. Counselor. He was called a Specialist, but he was relegated to the kinds of jobs usually assigned to seventeen year olds learning how to be counselors. Ultimately he was invited to spend the remainder of his summer back home in Massachusetts well before the end of the camp season. In retrospect, I only wonder that it took me as long as it did to finally send him home.

The Cast: Peter Green

The next character in our Work Week drama was Peter Green. It would be a vast understatement to say Peter was unattractive. His appearance was, in fact, distinctively grotesque. The bright red scar that ran in a jagged diagonal across his forehead almost made his wretchedly reset crooked nose recede in prominence. However, as soon as he opened his mouth it was difficult to notice any of his other features. He was missing several front teeth, but the two prominent upper middle teeth were very much in evidence. One was perfectly positioned, but was encased in a gold crown that seemed to catch and reflect light beams. Its immediate neighbor was discolored and twisted to the side so that its edge faced the outside world like an unlikely offensive weapon.

I was sympathetic to Peter. When I interviewed him for the job It was my assumption that he must have sustained his facial wounds in Vietnam, and was just now starting to get his new life in order. It turned out he had been in the army, but quite a bit earlier, during the Korean War. I didn't want to push when he said he would rather not talk about his experiences in the army. It wasn't until much later that I learned his years in the service had little to do with his ghastly appearance. It seemed that a year or so before he first arrived at camp he had been at a party where there was a lot of heavy drinking. He had gotten so drunk that he accepted a dare to dive, fully dressed, into the host's backyard swimming pool. He failed to notice that the pool was empty. He told this story to one of the counselors, who promptly began circulating it. By the time it made its way around camp and got to me I wasn't even surprised. By then campers and counselors alike referred to Peter as Snaggle-Tooth.

I had hired Peter, with great misgivings, as our riflery instructor. When I reached my decision to hire him I know I was overly influenced by the childhood admonition "You can't tell a book by its cover." In Peter's case the cover was a fair representation of the book.

As soon as the third day of Work Week I came to regret my choice. I had just gotten out of the shower in my cabin late in the afternoon, when I heard a knock on the door. I yelled "come in" while I slipped on a tee shirt and pair of chinos. I came out of my room and Bill Gold was standing in the hall. Bill was one of our two returnees.

"Arthur, I don't want to sound like a tattle-tale, but Peter may turn out to be a problem."

"Tell me what's wrong." He hesitated. "Don't be nervous."

"I know you don't want any drinking in camp, even before camp. Well he brought two six packs of Schlitz into the bunk. He handed each of us a can of beer. Dick Hunter, Patrick and I turned him down. I told him it wasn't allowed, and he laughed." He said the trunk of his car was full of beer, enough for the whole staff when they get here.

"That doesn't sound good. I'll have a talk with him. Thanks for telling me."

"That's not all."

"Okay what else?"

"You remember he asked if he could try out the rifle range yesterday?" I nodded yes. "Well, I went down with him to unlock the rifles, show him where things were and to make sure he had everything he needed. He asked me to stay and I did. He said he didn"t want to bother with targets. He started by shooting beer cans, but then some Canadian geese flew by. He stood up and started popping at them. He's a good shot. He got two of them."

"Thanks again, Billy. I'll take care of it from here."

This was irresponsible and dangerous behavior. Shooting birds meant he was shooting into the air. Our rifle range was located in a safe place for the kind of prone target shooting we did. But if somebody was standing and shooting at birds you could never tell where the bullets might go. It was possible he could hit a car on the camp road or even one of the Grant's kids in their yard next door. He knew better. We had discussed safety rules exhaustively during his interview and again when I told him he could use the range during Work Week.

I talked with Peter after supper that night. He appeared properly ashamed of himself, and agreed he would never do it again. Then I turned to the beer issue.

"Look, you're an adult, and you can do whatever you want on your time off away from camp, but most of our counselors can't drink legally in this state or in Massachusetts. I have to be able to count on you older guys to set a good example for them. If you offer them beer now it sends a very bad message."

"I'm sorry, I thought it would be okay before the kids get here, but I get it. No more beer in camp, and I won't give it out either."

I wanted to believe him. I hoped he meant what he said. I think he kept his word, but from that day on, I was never completely sure I could trust him.

The Cast: Tom Albany

When I interviewed Tom Albany at our house in Lexington, I could see that he was ill at ease. I quickly learned he was a city boy who had never ventured very far from his home base in South Boston. I don't think I intimidated him, nor did our house. But he was clearly very ill at ease. It was the density of trees in our neighborhood. Tom had never spent any time in the country. In fact, he had never been away from home. He had no camp experience, not even day camp. How could I have even considered him?

In my defense, he did play sports, baseball and basketball, but that was not the answer. The answer was 1967.

Tom wanted to get away from the city. He wanted to escape from school with its constant anti-war protests, sit-ins and general turmoil. He was a student at Boston University, one of the least troubled college campuses, but still, it was too much for him. He just wanted to escape for the summer. I could appreciate his emotional reaction. I might well have felt the same had I been a student at that time. My only qualm when I hired Tom had to do with his apparent fear of being in the country. He assured me he could adjust.

The first night of Work Week I invited the boys to come down to my cabin. I didn't often feel the need to do this, but with only two returning counselors in the group, I wanted to give the five new guys something to do and some place to go their first night in a brand new place. I had brought down whatever snack food I could scrounge from the camp kitchen, where pickings were slim on the first night in camp. The group stayed for about an hour, chatting and eating. I did most of the talking, filling them in on camp history, and telling them some of the funny things that happened the summer before.

Tom asked if he could use my phone to call home. We had a long cord on our phone so he was able to take the phone into the bedroom, close to door, and give himself the illusion of privacy. We were not trying to listen to his conversation, but the door was very thin and we heard his side of the conversation clearly.

"Ma, it's so dark here. .... No, there are no street lights. The forest is all around us, and its spooky. .... I heard all sorts of noises outside the bunk. I'm pretty sure there's some animal living under our cabin. .... I know I won't sleep at all tonight. .... I'll try, Ma. I"ll try. .... Yes, I know I have a contract. .... I'll call you tomorrow night if I can get to the phone again. .... Bye, Ma. "

We all pretended not to have heard, and resumed a desultory conversation with renewed energy. I felt embarrassed for him and also worried about him from what I heard.

Right after breakfast the next morning I asked Tom to join me in the office for a private chat. I told him we had overheard his conversation with his Mother.

"Are they all going to start making fun of me?"

"Nobody is going to make fun of you. We all felt badly that you were so scared. Nobody teased you about it last night did they?"

"Nope."

"They're not going to. Don't worry about that. What we have to concentrate on right now is just getting you through these next few nights. "I know it's very dark and it can be scary at night. But things will pick up when Orientation starts. All of these bunks will have people in them, and there will be lights on all over the place. I think you'll be so busy making friends and doing activities that you won't have so much time to worry. You just have to make it through these next few days, and you"ll be fine." He sat and listened. I don't know whether he believed me or not, but he did stay.

Tom survived Work Week. He was not a great worker, but he tried hard. Most important, he was able to hold his night fears at bay. When the rest of the staff arrived for Orientation he perked up, as I hoped he would. After a week of orientation, he was ready for opening day, ready to become a camp counselor. Though he was far from a ball of fire, he was a sensitive counselor, who cared about his campers and worked hard at activities.

The Cast: Patrick O'Neil

I was perhaps more surprised and disappointed by the failure of Patrick O'Neil than by any other in that awful hiring year. Patrick was a good looking young man, neatly dressed, conservative and very polite. Usually I am suspicious of young men who appear to be overly polite, but he won me over with ease in the course of a two hour visit. He seemed just the kind of young man we needed as a counselor. He had a great attitude about camp and about life in general. He knew the difference between right and wrong. This was an increasingly rare trait, I thought, in college age students during that troubled period.

Patrick had spent the last twelve summers of his life as a camper and later as a staff member at Camp Sunshine. Sunshine was a Religious camp sponsored by the Catholic Archdiocese of Boston. Ours was a private Jewish camp where religion played a minimal role. But I had no doubt he would make the adjustment from one culture to another and prove to be a positive force in camp.

"But why are you leaving that wonderful camp now after so many years?"

"I spent my whole life thinking I was going to be a Priest, studying to be a Priest, and working to become a Priest. The last few years I've come to doubt that I have the calling. Just a few weeks ago I got my courage up, and went to the Bishop to tell him I was leaving the seminary. We talked for hours. He was the one who made me realize that if I was going to make a break, it had to be a complete break. If I went back to Camp Sunshine again it would be too easy for me to slip back into that life I know so well. The Bishop was right. I need to put some distance between my past and my future. I think your camp will be just the right place for me."

Patrick joined us for Work Week. He worked hard and well, and never complained about anything. He made it through Orientation Period, and seemed popular with the rest of the staff, but the night before the campers were due to arrive he came to visit me in my office.

"Arthur, I just can't stay. I don't have a problem with anybody, and I liked working with you. It has nothing to do with any individual. But the culture is just so different here, It is too much for me to absorb. I feel like I'm in a foreign country where I don't know the language and can't even read the maps."

"I understand how this is all new to you, but don't you think you should give it more time before making the decision to leave?"

"I think it is best that I leave before any campers arrive. I know I won't change my mind, and I wouldn't want any of them to think they were responsible in any way for my decision. I guess I just need to take some time out to figure out where I am going with my life.'" His mind was made up. I didn't try to dissuade him.

The remaining two counselor spots in our Work Week cast that summer were two entirely normal returnees, Bill Gold and Dick Hunter. Bill had a positive attitude about everything. Dick was somewhat more problematic. Though he was a very good counselor working with campers, he enjoyed an inflated sense of his own intellect, and had a condescending attitude toward any contemporaries who didn't measure up to his lofty standards. Needless to say, none of our newcomers measured up, and he provided broad signals to them of their intellectual inferiority. His presence did not help morale that week.

Our work group totaled eight including me, but with our cast of characters it was not surprising that we were well behind schedule by Friday. This was the last day of Work Week, and we still hadn't set up the Evergreen waterfront. Very early in that afternoon activity Rich Grollman broke his toe, and we were down to seven. Putting those docks in place was a complicated business that always took as many people as we had available. Weather conditions were perfect when we started, a hot sunny afternoon with no wind or current. But the job took us several hours and weather conditions deteriorated steadily through the afternoon. By the time we were in the final crucial stages, the day had turned cloudy and cold. The stiff breeze had churned up the water and there were now small white caps.

It didn't go well. While we tried laboriously to set the deepest section of dock in place catastrophe struck. We lost our grip on one of our twenty foot iron poles while is was partially in one of the collars that attached to the dock. The pole tipped over and into the water, the dock section broke in half. Those of us working on that end wound up in the water, luckily avoiding being hit on the head by the heavy iron pole. We were all shaken up, and called it a day. It was a fitting end to that work week.

A Sad Case: Robert Carlton

If Rich Grollman was our most important failure, Robert Carlton was our most notorious of that ill fated season. The camp season was already underway when he first appeared on the scene. I was on the Senior tennis courts assisting with tennis instruction, when I first spotted a vision walking my way. The Senior Tennis courts are at the far end of the Senior Ball field. After the first few seconds of disbelief I quickly understood that I was looking at Robert Carlton, the new counselor I had hired after a lengthy telephone interview the day before.

Robert was extraordinarily tall. I knew from the telephone interview that he was six foot four. He was dramatically pale. His arms and legs, neck, and face were a ghostly white. But his most striking feature was his head. It was a strange tall head. It started wide at the jaw line and got narrower and narrower as it proceeded upward to a distinct cone, similar to the top of Mount Fuji. At the very top of his head was a small patch of orange hair. His appearance was not striking. It was alarming.

My first thoughts were very unkind. "Where can I hide him? My God, I don't know what the kids will think if they see him." I dropped my racket, and headed across the ball field to intercept him. We met in the outfield. We shook hands.

I said "Let's go back to the office. We can chat for a while. And you must be thirsty after your long ride. We can get you a nice cold drink." I took his arm, and led him off the ball field and toward the office.

His response was completely normal. "Yes, that would be nice." As we walked back toward the office I was thankful that most of the camp was at the waterfront, and wouldn't have to see him until I had a little time to absorb his appearance and figure out what I was going to do.

Safely ensconced in my office, far from the prying eyes of the camp world, we sat and talked. Matty, our office boy, brought ice coffee from the kitchen for both of us. I felt guilty about my reaction and a little ashamed of myself. Robert was clearly nervous and a little disoriented, but he sounded just as normal talking in the privacy of the office as he had in our telephone interview the day before. We were really short on staff, and I had offered him a job as a cabin counselor with our Seniors. He was here now, having driven ten hours from Buffalo, New York.

I talked to Robert on one track while my mind raced on a different track, trying to figure out what to do. "I can't just turn him around and send him home. That would really be unfair. I'm going to have to introduce him to the camp at assembly tonight, and we"ll see what happens. He may be dynamite with the kids. Despite his appearance, he could be just the guy the kids in Hut three need. I didn't really believe it, but I was hoping. But I'd better not actually assign him to the bunk. I'll just turn him over to Bill Gold, and let him report back to me."

I paged Bill Gold to the office. He came from the waterfront with his bathing suit still dripping on the office floor. I could see the astonished look on his face as he caught sight of my visitor. But I have to give Bill credit; he recovered quickly and gave Robert the same kind of welcome he would have given any other new counselor.

"Bill, I'd like you to meet Robert Carlton. He's the young man I told you about last night. The plan is for him to work with you in the Senior unit. But for now, I'd just like you to bring Robert up to Senior Camp, meet the boys, and generally get a sense of where he is."

I turned next to Robert. "Bill is Senior Unit Leader. He'll take care of you, and I'll see you back up here at supper time."

"What should I do about my stuff? Everything's in my car."

"For now, why don't you just take out what you need for overnight since I'm not sure yet where you'll be living?" I'd hate to have you unpack and then ask you to move again in a day or two." Actually I was pretty sure where he would be living. It would most likely be in Buffalo, New York. But he seemed to accept my statement at face value. He and Bill left the office and I was left with a dilemma.

When the Seniors came to the Assembly area that night, Robert was with them, walking along with some of the counselors just behind the boys. He towered over all of the Seniors and most of the staff. Nobody in camp missed Robert's most impressive physical characteristic. As the camp slowly came to order and lined up, I could hear giggles everywhere. For most of the campers and staff this was their first Robert Carlton sighting. I hoped Robert would think the giggles were a normal part of Evening Assembly.

Later that night, just before the sounding of Taps I went up to Senior Camp to find and talk to Bill. "Well, what do you think? Is he going to make it?"

Bill looked at me. "No way! He's already a target. It doesn't really matter what he does or doesn't do. The kids will never give him a chance."

"You're probably right, but I think we've got to bend over backward to see if it can work. If you're going out tonight I'd like you to take Robert with you."

"Yes, a group of us are going to the Gray House." The Gray House was a favorite meeting place for counselors from all of the surrounding camps. There they sat, flirted, and gorged themselves on Brownie Nut Sundaes and Hamburgers.

"Tomorrow morning please give me your impression of how he communicates with other people in an informal setting. See if he can make it with the other guys." I could see Bill was not thrilled with the prospect. After all, it was his time off, and I knew he wouldn't look forward to shepherding our newest arrival into the great social world of the Gray House. But he was a good kid, and agreed to do his best.

His morning report was bleak. He reported that Robert's head was instantly the center of attention. He didn't slip into Gray House unnoticed. But then, after things calmed down, he had nothing to say to anybody. "We tried to bring him into the conversation, but all he did was answer in monosyllables. And he seemed to mumble a lot." Bill summed up the situation. "Nobody really wanted to talk to him, but you could see they were dying to talk about him."

That was it. I realized my decision had already been made. I had just wanted Bill to reinforce it. Robert would have to go. I felt terrible and cruel, but I knew I had to do it.

"Robert, I feel terrible, but it just isn't going to work out for you here."

"I know. I knew last night when you told me not to unpack. It's the same everywhere. It never does seem to work out for me anywhere."

I paid him for his travel expenses and half of the salary he would have earned had he stayed, and Robert was gone. This was a sad chapter. His final words "It never does seem to work out for me anywhere" have remained with me.

Robert was at Camp less than twenty-four hours, but he became an instant legend. The joke that immediately made the rounds of the counselors was that I was going to have to add a new line to my staff application. Henceforth there would have to be a line for "Hat size". The day after he left camp there was Robert Carlton graffiti everywhere. "Robert Carlton slept here" was on the wall over his cot. "Robert Carlton sat here" in a toilet stall in Senior Camp. "Robert Carlton tripped here" proclaimed a small sign next to a tree root on the path to Sr. Camp. Robert Carlton was the comic hit of Song & Cheer Contests for Maroon and Grey (our boys color teams) and for Green and Gold (Evergreen's teams). To this day, forty years later, there are still people at camp who claim to have been the first to see Robert Carlton when he arrived at camp. Many making the claim had not yet been born.

The French Chef

It was a Wednesday in mid-July. Two days earlier I had sent Robert Carlton back to Buffalo. Earlier on that Wednesday morning I had fired the twelfth of the seventeen counselors I would be relieving of their duties that camp season. The counselor staff was a mess. Things were not going well at all. But by day, my job was to appear confident, happy, dynamic and very much in charge. Both the campers and the counselors needed to see me looking like everything was on course. Then they would be free to enjoy themselves. If either the counselors or the campers saw me in a panic, it could be contagious.

My optimistic mask slipped from my face when I made it back to our cabin at night, where I felt free to give way to the gloom I felt. My wife Judy's job was to buoy up my sinking spirits and tell me that everything was going to be all right. She was very good at it.

"Count your blessings. Think about all of the things that are going right. You don't have to worry about maintenance. Ansel takes care of everything even before you tell him. With Edna in charge, the laundry is certainly in good hands. You don't even have to worry about the kitchen or dining room. With Jack and Anna in charge, nothing will ever go really wrong."

Just as she completed my list of blessings the intercom rang.

"Ring...ring...ring...ring...ring...ring..."" That was the house ring on our ancient intercom system.

The call was from the camp nurse.

"Hello, Arthur, this is Miss Morley. I'm afraid I have some bad news for you. "I laughed a rueful chuckle. I sat down to prepare myself.

"That's just what I don't need."

"Well, there's no help for it. I've just sent your chef Jack Beyea to the hospital. Anna is driving him. He has a very severe cough. His lungs don't sound good. It is a serious bronchial condition, and I think it is probably pneumonia."

"Oh, my God!" It took me a minute to absorb what she said. "Thank you, Miss Morley. Please keep checking with the hospital, and let me know what the doctors there think." There was no doubt in my mind that if Miss Morley thought it was pneumonia, it would assuredly be pneumonia. Miss Morley was another of my blessings.

"Well Judy, that took care of one of my blessings. What you don't know is that Jack fired his second cook yesterday. There's nobody in the kitchen who knows anything."

Have you ever made chicken fricassee? I never had until that day. Of course Miss Morley was right. Jack did have pneumonia. I placed an SOS call to our old reliable, my ancient friend Churchill Brown, who promised he would arrive at camp that night. In the meantime, I had to figure out lunch and dinner. The lunch menue called for cold cuts and tuna salad. With the help of the kitchen boys, that was easy enough. But dinner was a different story. The dinner menu called for Chicken fricassee. There was no alternative in sight. We were at the end of the meat delivery cycle. We were due for a delivery early the next morning. For now what we had on hand was a tub full of pulled fowl. Jack's last job before he succumbed to his "bad cold" was to strip the fowl of their meat in anticipation of making fricassee the next day. There was nothing else we could do with chunks of raw fowl.

I consulted with Judy, who had never made a fricassee. I checked with every woman in camp. They were all almost, but not quite, as ignorant as I. Finally, I had no recourse but to call Jack. Sick or not, he knew how to make Fricassee. They put me through to his room.

"Jack, what do I do with this stuff?" I felt mildly guilty as I heard him alternately coughing and gasping on the other end while he gave me step by step instructions. I thanked him profusely, wished him a speedy recovery, and went to work.

The stock pots he told me to use looked about nine feet tall and as wide across as a small pond. Once they were lifted onto the range the top of the pot was higher than I was tall. Though I had never seen Jack use a stool, I found one and climbed up so that I was now taller than the pots again. As instructed, I turned the faucet for the water tap that was situated over the Garland Gas Range. A steaming hot waterfall of Niagara proportions cascaded down into the monstrous stock pot. I jumped back off the stool to keep from being scalded. I fell back against the Chef's bench, and dislodged two of the pots that hung over the bench. Luckily they missed my head on their way down. Jack had neglected to tell me that the tap was hot water. Probably he thought I knew. Eventually I was able to turn the water off with the aid of a long handled pipe wrench.

The chicken came next. I was back up on my stool, feeding chicken into the caldron. On the other side of the range was the equally imposing pot for the fricassee sauce. I was ready to mix according to Jack's directions when I came upon another omission in his instructions. None of the utensils I found could possibly stir anything in a pot as deep as the one I was using. One of the kitchen boys, seeing my puzzlement, went into a corner and came out with a sawed off canoe paddle.

"I've seen Jack use this paddle when he uses those pots."

He was right. It worked like a charm. I was able to stir just like a professional chef. Then came that awesome moment when the chicken was to be united with its sauce for the remainder of the cook time. With the help of three strong boys we got the enormous pot with the chicken off the range and down to the floor. The best part was that none of us got burned. The chicken was now in position. I plucked it out of its hot tub, and transferred it little by little into the sauce mixture on the left hand side of the range.

Jack had said to keep stirring it every so often. I tried, but the total mixture was so heavy that my canoe paddle felt like I was paddling a canoe upstream against an impossibly strong current. The goopy combination wouldn't move. I was ready to cry. Jack had told me if I didn't keep stirring all of the chicken and sauce would stick to the bottom of the pot and burn.

I called Jack at the the hospital again. I described my problem. The answer was to add liquid from the stock pot that was furthest in the back and apparently a permanent resident on the range. I ladled it out until finally I was able to move the mass with my paddle.

An hour later, shortly before dinner, I asked for volunteers, kitchen workers brave enough to taste what I had made. One after another they tasted it, and proclaimed it delicious. It was a triumph! My day was made! The only problem was it didn't look like Chicken fricassee or chicken anything at all. It looked like oatmeal.

At assembly that night, I asked Stu, our Assistant Director, to make the announcements. I didn't dare leave the kitchen or face the campers. Stu announced

"Today we were honored by a visit from a famous French chef. He prepared one of his specialties for us. He said it was his contribution to the good will and harmony that exists in relations between our two countries. Unfortunately, he was called away just a few minutes ago so I will not be able to introduce him to you. But I am sure we are in for a real treat. The campers and counselors enjoyed his speech. They laughed and clapped. Unfortunately, when they saw the chicken, they stopped laughing. The verdict was almost universal. It looked disgusting. Only the bravest would even bring it close to their mouths. We used a huge amount of peanut butter and jelly that night and an even greater quantity of cold cereal.

I was sad when I saw all of that yummy fricassee coming back untouched from the dining room and being dumped into the garbage barrels. At least the pig farmer down the road would be happy when he saw the huge bonus his prize animals were going to enjoy. My spirits lifted again when I saw Churchill Brown come through the back door into the kitchen. Churchill would take care of the cooking until Jack was back on his feet.

25
The Summer Of '69

A lot of years have passed, and yet I still have trouble coming to grips with the reality of the awful 1969 camp season. My memories are fragmentary. I hope the reader will forgive any lapses.

I looked forward to the camp season enthusiastically, without a clue that a personal nightmare would unfold. To be sure we would be operating Camp Evergreen without Phyllis, our sparkling head counselor, who I had insisted take a summer off to get to know her first child, who was born in February. I tried to locate Pauline, Phyllis's immediate predecessor, but was unsuccessful. But I thought we had that base satisfactorily covered when we went further back in time and coaxed an old Evergreen head counselor out of retirement to rejoin us for the 69 season. She had last worked at camp in the mid 1950s, under Bernice Huberman as her Camp Director. My wife, Judy, had been a counselor that summer, and thought her friend and one time boss Susan would be great.

Camp Kenwood looked solid. Joel Wolfson was returning, and bringing with him the scarcest of commodities in that troubled era, young men who he assured me would be fine camp counselors. Joel had joined us the summer before, replacing the departed Stuart Goldberg, both as Head Counselor and as our Camp Representative on Long Island. In his first summer with us Joel had brought a few strong young male counselors with him, and I had every reason to believe that the additional counselors he recommended for this summer's staff would prove to be equally good. Joel had been their high school football coach, and had great confidence in each of his former players

So how did it all go wrong? I can blame much of it on the era, and I would be right. This was the summer of Woodstock. The Woodstock Festival was not in itself a cause, but it was a reflection of the prevailing mood of the times for college students. It was the summer of "Make love not war," "never trust anyone over thirty," and "down with the establishment." There were many problems, some very real administrative issues, and some just plain bad luck. But the main cause for the most disagreeable summer I ever experienced as a camp director was a counselor staff made up of college students who arrived at camp looking for a continuation of the conflict that had been raging in universities the entire academic year.

I can blame some of our problems on Joel, our Kenwood Head Counselor/ Assistant Director, who seemed to favor the counselors he brought to camp. He helped to create a degree of dissension among our more traditional Kenwood counselors. He tended to devalue our former campers because they lacked the athletic skills and experience of "his boys." Some of "my boys" came to me to complain about unfair treatment relatively early in the summer. Fred Wasserman was one who hesitantly brought the subject up with me. By nature he was not a complainer.

"Whenever anything goes wrong" he said "he blames Dan Budd or one of us. He lets his guys get away with everything." I knew who he meant by "us" and certainly by "his guys."

I can blame a portion of our problems on Susan, our newly retread Evergreen Head Counselor, who seemed better suited to the 1950s than she did to the late 1960s. She seemed disoriented and disorganized, and finally became demoralized by the unexpected demands put upon her by an inexperienced counselor staff that really needed strong leadership. On her staff were three "new girls" whose boyfriends were the leaders of what became the Kenwood staff rebellion. Though not nearly as strident as the boys, the girls too took up the revolutionary causes espoused by them.

I can certainly assign a large part of the blame to myself for devoting so much of my time to Evergreen and leaving Kenwood almost totally in Joel's hands. Was I hiding out in Evergreen or was I justified in spending virtually all of my time there? Evergreen was in plenty of trouble with inexperienced counselors and weak female leadership. Judy was not available except for consultations. She was busy taking care of our own children who were too young to be campers. It seemed to me there was nobody else available to run that show. Was I really spending most of my time there because I was needed there? Or was it because I liked working with the girls better than the boys? Or was I trying to avoid a confrontation with Joel? Many times as I walked through Kenwood I saw Joel initiating activities (like Johnny on A Pony) that were more rough and tumble than the kinds of things we usually promoted or even allowed in Kenwood. Probably all of those factors came into play. The result was that I distanced myself physically and emotionally from the Kenwood staff and Kenwood senior Campers, groups with whom I had always enjoyed a solid relationship. I came to be looked upon in Kenwood as one of "them" and not one of us. It is far easier to rebel against somebody identified as "them."

Surely the awful weather we experienced can be assigned a significant portion of blame. In that era our camp season was fifty-six days. During that camp season it rained some part of twenty-eight of those fifty-six days. On many of those days it rained all day, hard, bone chilling rains. On more than a few days the rains were positively torrential. For much of the summer our clay tennis courts, soccer fields. outdoor basketball courts and baseball fields were unplayable. Our waterfront was literally a mess, with debris constantly coming in from the banks of the lake. Boats broke away from shore, and had to be chased all over the lake on an almost daily basis. Through the long summer, there were very few warm sunny days when campers would actually want to go swimming. Our Senior boys who were housed in tents, suffered most. By mid-season all of their tents had sprung leaks. Both the boys and their clothing were getting damp and depressed.

The heaviest rain that summer waited for the two most crucial days of the camp season, Visitors weekend. Over those two days the parents and their children trekked back and forth through muddy paths and fields between the camper cabins and our gym, which was the only place in camp where physical activities could function. But for the parents of our senior boys their time watching activities in the gym was a distinct improvement over the hours they sat with their sons in their soggy tents. Not surprisingly, we received more than a few complaints about the weather from camper parents after that season, as though we could have planned it differently.

"Arthur, you have a very nice camp, but _____ won't be returning next summer. You never told me your camp was in the rain belt."

The following summer we switched to one day of visiting rather than a weekend. We also replaced our long cherished tents with cabins for our oldest Senior boys.

There were times that summer that I felt like the little Dutch boy with his finger in the dike. No matter how fast I moved, more leaks sprung, and I didn't have enough fingers to plug all of the holes. Unfortunately only a small portion of the leaks were related to the rain.

So what did go wrong? What were those awful things too painful for me to remember? I am left with some indelible impressions. My most prominent impression was that of constant grumbling by the counselors. Our young men and women seemed dissatisfied no matter what program we ran; no matter what policy; no matter what tradition. The grumbling started with the Kenwood counselors, spread to our oldest boys, and then eventually into every part of our camp world. A few examples provide some insight into the kind of mood I faced increasingly as the summer lurched along on its eight week course.

One Thursday morning I came into my office, and found an oversized envelope sitting squarely in the middle of my desk. On it were the words "Demands and Requests."

What now, I thought. This is not a good start to the day. I went into the kitchen to get my wakeup cup of coffee, and came back to the office, closed the door, and, with some trepidation, opened the envelope. It was neatly done, a numbered list.

1. We demand an end to ceremonial flag raising and lowering. If you feel you must fly the flag, there is no need to require the entire camp to stand at

attention, while a bugle call sends the flag up in the morning and down at night. Our country is engaged in an immoral war, and we no longer feel we owe its flag our allegiance or respect.

2. We demand an end to the singing of grace in the dining room. The singing of grace is an exercise of religion, and many of us do not believe in any organized religion. We strenuously object to being forced to participate in a religious exercise.

3. We demand a twenty-four hour day off every week. You have given us enormous responsibility for the welfare of your campers. We accept that responsibility, but for the good of the campers they deserve a well rested staff. A twenty-four hour weekly time away is necessary for us to recharge our batteries, and serve the camp and our campers as well as they deserve.

4. We request that the Senior campers be allowed to have coed free play after supper. It is important for our older campers to get to know one another in a relaxed and unstructured environment, the kind of environment that exists at this camp only during free play periods. It is necessary for their sound emotional development.

5. We request that trip days, overnight hikes and canoe trips be scheduled on a coed rather than a single sex basis. There is no rational reason that trips out of camp should not be scheduled on a coed basis. These are non-competitive activities, and we know they would be more popular with both the campers and staff if you change this policy.   There was no signature... no list of names.

I wondered who made up the list and how many were in on it. It was well done, and it couldn't be ignored, but it took me most of that day to decide how and when to answer it. Finally I decided to address it at our regular Sunday night staff meeting.

I waited through Thursday, Friday and Saturday for the other shoe to drop. Surely, I thought, they wouldn't be able to contain themselves. The authors would have to talk about it. They would have to give themselves away. If nothing else, they must be wondering when or how I would respond. But the other shoe never did drop. Sunday came, and finally Sunday night.

That Sunday night, I replied to their concerns. There had been no discussion by anyone about the paper I was addressing. It was as though it never exisited. Nobody had stepped forward to claim they were the authors. I decided that it was best not to make reference to the word "Demands." Demands require either agreement or denial, and immediately formalizes a battlefield. Addressing concerns, however, is conciliatory. And I couldn't be sure who or how many of the counselors were even aware of that paper?

Toward the end of the meeting I started to address the Demands letter. "I am aware that some members of the staff have been concerned about certain issues, and I would like to address those issues now." Then I went on to discuss them one by one.

As to the first concern, I replied "I have sympathy with your upset at the Vietnam War. I too wish it was over, and think we have no business staying there. But our country has survived a major crisis in virtually every generation, and it will survive this one too. When we honor the flag we are not saluting the present administration in Washington. We are saluting and paying respect to the best ideals of our country and its wonderful people. We are showing respect to all of those who died fighting for our flag and our country."

The second demand related to our singing grace in the dining room. During lunch and dinner we had traditionally started the meal with the singing of grace. The kids enjoyed this tradition. The songs were fun, and it was something of a unifying event twice a day. I couldn't believe that any of the counselors could be seriously exercised about this. I was reasonably sure it was just there to pad their list.

I thought my response was quite reasonable. "I don't consider *Johnny Appleseed*[1] or *Noon Time Is Here*[2] or *Hark To The Chimes*[3] religious songs, at least not songs belonging to any organized religion I know and I don't think the kids do either. They are fun songs. But if it troubles you to sing them, you don't have to sing. Just stand quietly and respect the rights of those who do want to join us in grace." They seemed to accept this without comment.

Their third demand was a 24 hour day off. This was kind of a counselor wish list item, which I understood. I think they knew my response before I gave it. I explained to them that this was impossible. Practically speaking, the issue was an overnight day off. This would mean we would have cabins with sleeping campers and no counselors in the cabins in case of emergency. They understood my concerns. They knew we didn't have enough counselors to make this a practical reality. But they wanted it anyway. Finally a compromise was reached on this item. They agreed that it was not possible for us to do it all of the time. We agreed to allow twenty-four hour days off whenever we had enough staff to safely cover all of the cabins. That almost never happened.

Number four was the request for coed free play. This was not exactly a novel issue. Free play was unscheduled time after supper when the boys and girls could do whatever activities they wanted and they were also free to read a book or do nothing at all if that was what they wanted. The girls' free play area was on the girls' campus, and one or two nights a week they had exclusive access to the field we called The Hollow. The boys had the Hollow the rest of the nights.

Coed free play would allow both the counselors and the older campers to socialize in the Hollow every night after supper and before formal evening activities. Male counselors had forever wanted better access to the female staff, and this would assure plenty of time for them to arrange their dates and plans for their approaching days off. Senior campers too, boys and girls, for a long time had felt restricted by our Free Play policy. But, as an issue, this was new in one important respect. It had been spread by the counselors to our older boys so that they too were agitating for coed free play, more than in the past.

Number five had been for coed trips, overnight hikes, etc. In that era of Love, the counselors, particularly the male counselors, wanted every possible opportunity to exercise the new prevailing college freedoms. They wanted this freedom for themselves and they projected their needs onto the needs of the campers. Of course, in arguing their case they used a different language. They argued against the unnatural restrictions that we placed upon our campers. They would damage them psychologically. We didn't know what damage we were doing. We didn't understand. We didn't have sensitivity. In fact, our minds and morals were stuck in a different century.

I didn't know whether any of them seriously believed that we could agree with this request, but I was certain this was an area in which I would never compromise. Our camps were "brother-sister" camps, rather than coed. Historically, Kenwood came first, twenty years before Evergreen. When Ken and Bernice Huberman started Evergreen they were careful to reassure the parents of the boys, most of whose children had been coming to an all boys camp for years, that the addition of girls would have little impact on their boys' summer camp experience. Though time had passed and we now did some special activities on a coed basis, much of the original separation and separate identities of the two camps had been maintained. We had rather strict guidelines on how the girls could walk to the dining room and other commonly used facilities, which were largely located on the Kenwood campus. To maintain gender privacy, boys were not allowed on the girls' campus at all. Girls' boundaries, when walking in Kenwood, kept them far from the boys living areas. I was always careful to explain to parents of prospective campers, the distinct personalities of the two camps.

"Gentlemen, you all know that we run this camp as brother-sister and not coed. We have essentially contracted with the parents of our campers that this is the way the camp will be run, and we intend to keep faith with our word. You all really understood this when you signed your contracts, and agreed to come as counselors. You knew the camp rules and policies when you signed them. None of our policies came as a surprise to you. These are the contracts you signed. But, if you can't live with them we cannot hold you to them. You are free to leave. I personally hope that you all do understand, and that you all will elect to stay. Most of you are or can be very good camp counselors. I would hate to see you leave. If you do we will have trouble replacing you. But, if you do stay, please don't bring these same issue up again. It's not fair to me, to the camp or to your kids."

As it turned out nobody took up my invitation to leave.. After the fact, I wondered if we would have had a better camp season had a few of the principal gripers departed that morning. They stayed, and they lived with the camp policies, but always in a grudging way.

The individual incidents were less important than the prevailing mood of hostility and the sense of an adversarial relationship that solidified and grew more pronounced during the course of the season.

There were a few distressing incidents worth nothing. One had little to do with camp other than camp being the locus of the activity. It was brought to my attention that one of our counselors, a graduate student, ran a late night class in our dining room explaining (or perhaps tutoring) a group of younger counselors how to make bombs. After I heard about it and called him on it, he agreed it probably wasn't the best time and place for such lessons, and agreed to stop. I think he did stop. What could ever have possessed a serious student who came to camp to be a camp counselor to be teaching bomb making? Was he trying to inspire actual violent activity or just pursuing an intellectual exercise? I'll never know.

The next was far more important in strictly camp terms. For the overwhelming majority of our campers our late season color competition was the premier and most popular event of the camp season. "Let it rain. Let it pour. All we want is Color War." We heard that all summer long, with the dining room chants escalating in a rising crescendo as we approached the actual surprise starting days. During their separate color wars the boys (Maroon and Grey) in Kenwood and the girls (Green and Gold) in Evergreen operated in a fever pitch of excitement as they competed in all aspects of camp activity. It finally culminating the last night in a song and cheer contest. Through the whole year that followed, whenever a group of campers got together they relived color war and sang their color war songs that were imprinted on their minds and in their hearts. That's the way it usually went. That's the way it is supposed to go. In the summer of '69 it didn't go quite that way.

"One two three four, we don't want no color war....One two three four... We don't want no color war." The chant started early in the season with the Senior boys. Kids were reciting the chant, kids who had been in camp before and had loved color war in past summers, even kids who had never been in camp before, and had no idea what it was all about. The idea had been planted in their impressionable minds by our anti-war counselors. Equating camp Color War with the War in Vietnam was protest for the sake of protesting, trouble making whose only goal was the making of trouble. They knew that kids cheering enthusiastically for their team in basketball or singing fight songs in the dining room were not activities remotely analogous to a shooting war in Vietnam. But they tried to equate the two..

We were not about to abandon the camps' very best activity because of a protest. This was too important. We won. Or did we? Before it even started there was trouble. Counselors who usually vie for the role of "Head Coaches" turned down the honor and asked instead to be judges (Neutrals). We were left with the choice of younger leaders, who had less automatic respect from the campers and other counselors. Maroon and Grey got under way, and the difference in attitude was apparent immediately. The counselors who acted as coaches took a low key attitude toward the activities, treating them exactly as they had through the summer. There was less cheering, less singing, less enthusiasm. The prevailing attitude that was sold to the kids was "It doesn't really matter much who wins." By the end of the week one team had pulled way ahead.

The last two events of Maroon and Grey, are always an afternoon swim meet and the evening Song & Cheer contest. Almost always teams remained in mathematical contention until Song and Cheer. Unluckily in that year the winning team clinched a win early in the swim meet. The other team was mathematically eliminated even if they swept Song and Cheer that night. They stopped trying. Some of their kids refused to swim in events for which they were scheduled. The Senior boys on both teams became rowdy and unruly. After the final swimming event they chased the judges off the docks with the goal of throwing them in the lake. The Head Coaches did nothing to stop them.

After the swim meet and before dinner I called a meeting with all of the coaches for both teams, and told them how important it was for them to bring their teams to the Song and Cheer contests with enthusiasm as though both teams still had a chance to win. I think they really tried, but it was too late. The emotional damage was done. The boys on the losing team felt like losers and the boys on the winning team acted as though it was all a big joke.

When the singing was over, we, the administration and the counselors designated as Judges left the Recreation Hall and went to the dining room to vote on winners of each song. While we were discussing the event in the dining room things apparently got out of control in the Recreation Hall. By the time we returned to announce the winners several benches had been broken, banners and plaques were stripped from the walls and little kids on both teams were crying. It was an awful scene. They grew very quiet when we reappeared. We announced the results, sang Taps, and sent everybody back to their cabins. I know I was upset, but I didn't realize I had showed my degree of upset until Bob Kramer (our August camp doctor) came over to me and offered to get me a tranquilizer. I turned him down. I'm not sure I should have. I didn't sleep much that night.

With only two days left to the summer it was almost not worth calling the counselors who had acted as coaches for a conference. But I couldn't resist. I wanted them to understand and admit their responsibility for the mayhem and acknowledge that the situation was physically dangerous for their campers.

We just had to get through the two days, and start the following year with an entirely new counselor staff. Nothing more could go wrong, I thought. I couldn't wait for it to be over. But it wasn't quite over yet. The last night of camp is always problematic after the evening program comes to an end. Boy friends and Girl friends always want that one more opportunity to get together. We usually clamped down on the Senior boys. All counselors were on duty. None were to leave the area. If the counselors were alert, no campers coujld sneak out… There would be no clandestine meetings. The same was true for the Senior girls. The entire staff was on duty. The girls couldn't possibly get out.

Not surprisingly on that summer's last night both the boys and girls managed to evade their counselors, some of whom must have been intentionally looking the other way. They got out, and they met behind the gym or on the waterfront or in the woods. When I awoke at 5:00 AM I heard and then saw them running all over camp. When they saw me they ran back to their cabins.

That was the last unruly gasp of a summer I have wanted to forget. In subsequent camp seasons we experienced several truly heart wrenching events. The worst of these were summers with automobile accidents in which counselors died. We had at least two seasons when police arrived in camp intending to arrest counselors. Those were upsetting and harrowing events, which I remember with painful clarity. We had a few camp seasons with contagious illnesses which effected large numbers of campers. I remember every step we took. But I have preferred to bury and hoped to forget the details of the summer of 69. I do remember after it was over wondering whether I was any capable of running a camp in this new era.

My spirits were revived at the Fall Conference of the American Camping Association, where I heard many nightmare stories from the summer of 69 from other camp directors. I was told later that 20% of all of the camp directors in the country retired after that fateful season. I have no idea whether this statistic is true or not, but I found it believable then and still do.

It is interesting to reflect so many years after the summer of 69 that two of the counselor "demands" of that year evolved into changes in camp policy over the next two decades. Now our campers do have coed free play after supper. The "free play" areas are confined to the gym and the Hollow, both of which are supervised by counselors from both camps. Counselors now get a twenty-four hour day off, starting before supper and ending after supper the next day. This later change, instituted by my successor, Scott Brody, was made possible by increasing the size of the staff to assure at least two counselors live in each cabin so that there can be no lapse in coverage for the campers. Apparently the new policy, though it creates logistical problems, is very popular with the staff.

Notes to Chapter
Summer Of '69

1. *Johnny Appleseed.*
    The Lord is good to me,
    and so I thank the Lord
    for giving me the things I need,
    the sun, the rain and the apple seed.
    The Lord is good to me.

2. *Noon Time Is Here.*
    Noon time is here.
    The board is spread.
    Thanks be to God who gives us bread.
    Thank God for bread.

3. *Hark To The Chimes.*
    Hark to the chimes.
    Come bow your head.
    We thank thee Lord
    who gives us bread.

26
Night Shock

Camp was pitch black. It was an overcast night, with clouds obscuring the moon and stars. My family and I were the only ones living in camp. The last of the counselors had left a week earlier. It was eerie walking around our empty camp at night, hearing the strange scurrying sounds, as the animals ventured back in, cautiously reclaiming the domain we had appropriated for the summer.

I was working in the Evergreen office when I heard a car drive onto the camp road. The car stopped. Its door opened and closed. Through the trees I could barely see the dimly lit car interior. The car was on the road by the girls' ball field. I opened and closed my screen door quietly, going onto the porch to wait and listen. I thought any proper visitor would see the office lights and come my way. I waited to see a flashlight beam, but I saw nothing and heard nothing, not a sound. I waited, but still nothing. The silence did not bode well. Then I heard the car door open and close again. The engine started. I breathed a sigh of relief as I heard the car move away from the ball field and up the road.

There had been a lot of trouble throughout the country that summer, and we at camp had had our share from the outside world. We had caught and jailed one pair of intruders, who had come to camp intent on rape, but night after night prowlers, ranging from peeping toms to teen-agers stealing athletic equipment, had been a constant source of anxiety and lost sleep through the summer. Now that the camp season was over and all of our girls had gone home I assumed there would be no more night prowlers, but I was still concerned enough to remain alert.

I listened as the car drove slowly up the dirt road. Somewhere off in the distance I heard it stop again. This time two doors opened and closed. It sounded as though they were in the Senior Camp area. There'd be no legitimate reason for anyone to park there. I listened for a while longer and heard nothing but silence.

I went back into the office, and picked up the intercom. I called Judy who was down at our house. Our house was located just above the Evergreen waterfront and was surrounded by trees. It was invisible from the camp road. The office was about half way between the house and the camp road.

"Judy, check the door. Make sure it's locked. I think we've got company."

"You're calling to tell me that? Come down here right now! You can't leave us alone if you think there are people prowling around camp."

"Honey, I'm calling the police now. I have to be somewhere where they can find me when they come. If I'm down at the house with you, they'll drive in, see nobody, and leave."

"Oh, that's good. I'm so glad you'll be there to show the police the way. What about us? What about the guy wandering about camp? What if he knows the camp paths, and comes up from the back of the house?"

"Don't worry. Whoever it is, they can't move that fast in the dark. They're parked up in Senior Camp. Even if they're headed down here it will take them a while to get here. I'll keep an eye on the house while I wait for the police. I'm calling the state troopers, not the local cop. I have to be out here when they come."

I called the highway patrol office in Concord. The dispatcher was reluctant to send a unit without better evidence of a problem, but then I gave him a run down on all of the problems we had that summer. He finally agreed he would send the closest unit.

"Please let the officers know not to come in with sirens screaming and lights blazing. I want to catch whoever it is, not just scare them away. If we just scare them away, they'll be back. " I stationed myself half way between the office and the road. From where I stood I could still see the front of our house. I waited just a few minutes and was relieved when I saw the beam from the trooper's headlights before I saw the car itself. I ran out to the road to intercept them. I was very happy to see the man who climbed out of the driver's seat. It was Jim Brown, my favorite state trooper. He had come several times that summer. One of those times we actually caught two would be rapists. He was the one who made the arrests. The two of us were in court together the next day testifying. I got to know him pretty well, and I thought he knew me well enough to know I wouldn't bring him out for nothing.

"Hi, Arthur, what have you got for us this time?"

"I'm not sure, but there is someone in camp who doesn't belong here. I think there must be two of them." Jim introduced me to his partner, and then we worked out a plan to encircle the intruders. Jim would continue up by the road, on foot. His partner, Andy, would come with me across junior ball field, up the hill, and toward the senior tennis courts, where I estimated they must have stopped the car. Jim was taking a more circuitous route so we gave him a few minutes head start.

As soon as Andy and I climbed over the hill and onto the senior plateau, I could see the outline of the car silhouetted against the sky. It was just about where I thought it would be. We started right toward it. I could see Jim's shadowy figure approaching from the other side. We arrived within seconds of one another. Jim and Andy had both drawn their guns and were ready for anything. I too was ready. I held my favorite night stick, a small baseball bat that was kept in the Evergreen office for just such occasions.

We all turned our flashlights on as we surrounded the car. It was empty. We swung our light beams in a wider circle around the car, and lit up two distinct lumps on the ground just about where the right fielder would be stationed if there was a ball game going on. We approached the lumps, which looked more and more like sleeping bodies the closer we came. That's what they were, a young guy and a girl in sleeping bags. It was obvious to me that the sleeping bodies lying in front of us posed no danger. Nevertheless, Andy continued to shine his light in their faces, and yelled at them.

"What are you two doing here? Get up. You don't belong here." Both sleeping bags seemed to jump in fright. Then faces emerged from the sleeping bags, startled, scared faces. They sat up, and their eyes widened as they saw two guns pointed right at them. They looked about twenty, a bearded boy and a girl with long stringy hair.

"Arthur, it's me. Tell them who I am. You know me." I didn't actually recognize him, but something about him seemed familiar. "I worked here last year as a counselor. "It's me, Steve Schwartz. I was the counselor in Bunk Two last summer."

I looked again. Now I recognized him even though his scraggly beard had given his face a totally different look from the clean shaven young man he had been the summer before. The troopers holstered their guns. I apologized for bringing them out for what turned out to be nothing. I was very thankful they came. "I can't tell you what it meant to me in peace of mind when I knew you were coming." Jim handed me a blank report form, and asked me to fill it out and mail it back to him the next day. As they walked away grumbling, I got the feeling they were perfectly happy that there wasn't a real emergency.

"My God, Steve, you scared the life out of me." They were both standing by now. He had his arm protectively around her shoulders. She had tears in her eyes. He was visibly shaking.

"I scared you? How do you think we felt waking up, staring at guns in our faces?" He introduced me to Jodi, and the three of us walked down to the house to reassure Judy. I knew she'd be sitting there worried until I got back. She was very relieved to see us and listened attentively as both sides told their story. She put up water for tea and we all sat together having tea and cookies while Steve and Jodi slowly recovered from their shock.

"Steve, when you stopped near the Evergreen ball field, why didn't you walk over the office to say hello?"

"I was planning to find you, and ask permission to camp out, but the whole camp was dark, and I didn't want to wake you. I saw the light in the girls' office, but I didn't think anyone was there. I remember last summer that light was on all the time. So I stood and listened for a while just to make sure. I didn't hear a sound so I assumed you were back in your cabin asleep. I decided I wouldn't wake you. I didn't think you'd mind if we camped out in our sleeping bags overnight."

Steve and Jodi slept the rest of that night in one of the senior camp huts. In the morning I found a thank you note tacked on to our screen door.

"Dear Arthur & Judy, Thanks for the hospitality. But, if we come back next year I hope you'll have a different welcoming committee

It was a night to remember, and one I'm sure Steve and Jodi will never forget.

Part Four
The 1970s

27
A New And Better World

I was never certain why 1970 marked such a positive change at camp. The war was still creating daily scenes of death and destruction and they were all brought vividly home to us in living color on our nightly newscasts. Protests were becoming more aggressive. Police reacted to protestors with greater determination, and sometimes violence. Student protesters were shot at Kent State University in the spring of 1970. After the fact, I reasoned that perhaps that was a turning point. Perhaps moderate students simply had enough, and realized that, however righteous their cause, protest could lead to tragic consequences.

Whatever the reason, our college student counselors came to camp in 1970 looking for fun not trouble. Perhaps it all comes down to luck. We were just lucky in 1970. We had a wonderful cadre of young men and women, many of whom had grown up in camp and were just coming of age to be counselors. These were joined that summer by several extraordinarily gifted newcomers, many of whom stayed in school for years, working toward advanced degrees, which left them free to keep returning to camp over a multi-year period.

We had some exceptional counselors before and since, but never such a confluence of maturity, talent, spirit and creativity in one counselor staff.

With such a wonderful staff the 1970s should have been a period of real growth and financial stability for us and for all camps. But that is not what happened, at least not in the early seventies. What happened instead was that there was a dearth of camper age children. Consequently schools were being shuttered all over the country, and camps were being forced to close their doors. In the 1960s we lost a whole generation of young men and women who should have been going through college, getting started on careers, marrying and having children. Instead many of them were in the service for crucial years, and their schooling was delayed. Others were protesting more than studying in the late1960s, and their student years stretched on almost endlessly. It was this long interruption in the normal student progression that led both to a drastic reduction in the number of children available for camps and a bonanza of more mature young men and women available as camp counselors.

To us it meant that I had to get better at enrolling campers, and I did. Many times when I went to visit a family and show my slides I discovered that I was one of several camp directors the family was planning to see before making a decision. During that decade I enrolled about eighty percent of the prospective new campers I visited. It also meant that we had to have a wonderfully high percentage of returning campers year after year, and we did. Many of those years, mainly because of our superior counselors staff, our return percentage was 90% or higher. While we experienced a period of slow but steady growth, I watched as camps all around us closed.

Every winter I attended several sad auctions at camps, and felt like a scavenger as I bid on the dying camp's equipment and supplies. Over the years I bought beds and bats and balls at these auctions, a curtain for our theater, a walk-in refrigerator, rowboats and canoes, silverware and pots and pans. It was fun to master the bidding game and buy things we could use at bargain prices, but it was also sad. Invariably the owners of the defunct camps were in attendance. I saw their pain as they watched their camps being dismantled and sold off piece by piece. I vowed it would never happen to us.

28
Still Running

We inherited Phyllis Margill. She came with the camp. She was fifteen when we took over as directors. Ken Huberman, my predecessor. alerted me that Phyllis was a very powerful personality, and the leader of our oldest group of Senior girls. "If you're going to work with those Senior girls, you have to get Phyllis on your side. If you want them to do something, Phyllis is the one you have to convince. It doesn't matter much who their counselor is, she'll set the mood for the group."

I thought he was overstating the case. Her brother had been one of my campers when I was a counselor and he was a rambunctious fifteen year old. I had gotten warnings about him too. "He and his friend Richie are trouble makers" I was told. He turned out to be a nice kid, easy to deal with as long as he was either playing baseball or discussing it. I had no trouble relating to that.

It turned out Ken was right about Phyllis. But he understated the case. If the Senior girls planned any sort of mischief, she was the instigator and chief perpetrator. I remember intercepting Phyllis and her Red House girls noisily making their way through the woods on their way to raid Kenwood's Senior Camp. Many years after the fact, she claimed she and her friends had succeeded many times.

As a camper Phyllis was irrepressible. She had a bubbly personality, and seemed to have an energy level that was totally at odds with the normal lethargy of teen-agers. She was not the number one female tennis player in camp, but she could and did beat the number one player during Green & Gold, when the match was important to her. She was pitcher on "My" softball team. She was at the center of a large group of boys and girls at every "senior social". She always tried out for and usually got a lead in the Senior show. She jumped up to lead singing in the dining room. She was a bundle of energy, enthusiasm, and fun.

Imagine all of that energy and all of that talent channeled into a leadership role as a counselor. Her first year as a counselor she was already the best activity leader, best cheerleader, best motivator, and was absolutely adored by her girls. Her second summer as a counselor she was the youngest unit leader in camp history. Nevertheless I gave her the responsibility of leading our senior girls' canoe trip. Of course, we had to have a twenty-one year old with proper credentials along too, but Phyllis was the actual trip leader. She led those trips for many years, even after becoming Head Counselor. Our long canoe trips in the 1960s and early 1970s were on the placid Connecticut River. Usually the biggest challenge on that river was overcoming the boredom of paddling on and on with no end in sight. On many of Phyllis' trips, she and her girls ran into dramatic storms with thunder, lightning, and heavy rain, the kind that makes you get off the river and as far away as possible from your aluminum canoes.

Through the years, rain caused us to abort many multi-day hikes and canoe trips. We had to do emergency pick ups day and night. Typically, the counselor in charge searched for and found a telephone. He or she called camp; told us that the kids were wet, that their sleeping bags were soaked, and that everybody was miserable. We got in our vans, and picked them up. We never received calls like that from Phyllis. No matter what the circumstances, her girls came back laughing and ecstatic and always with a group song they had composed while sleeping in a pig farmer's barn or under a bridge or while paddling along the rural stretches of the river, literally Singing in the Rain.

During her college years she had a different boy friend every summer. Sometimes she would "draft" a boyfriend as a camp counselor to try him out in her summer home. If he didn't seem to love camp, he didn't make the cut, the romance was over. By the next summer Phyllis always came with a new candidate for Mr. Evergreen. Finally along came Mickey Dank, and we knew Phyllis had hit it right. That first summer Mickey came early to join me for Work Week. By the time the week was over, I knew he was a winner. He was so pleasant and agreeable under all circumstances I thought there must be something wrong with him; but no he was just that kind of guy. He also proved to be a hard worker. He was a big hit with me and the rest of the staff during Counselor Orientation Period. Once the campers arrived at camp he was a natural working with kids. He loved camp; loved working with kids; and seemed to be able to make his own special place in camp without feeling threatened by Phyllis' seniority and her well established camp status.

Their engagement announcements did not come as a surprise. Once they were married, Mickey became part of our permanent camp family. While he was in school he came to camp each summer, but when he graduated from law school and became a full fledged lawyer, he could no longer take summers off so he came up every weekend. Some of his weekends had a way of stretching from Thursday night until Tuesday morning. In his many years as a weekend volunteer, Mickey did everything from teaching swimming, and umpiring ball games to taking out the garbage.

In 1966 Phyllis became a wife and a Head Counselor. She had been Miss Evergreen. She was now also Mrs. Dank. She adjusted to the role of wife without missing a beat. In the Head Counselor department she was dynamite. She bubbled over with a sense of high energy and fun. It seemed nothing could dampen her effervescent spirit. That's why I was so shocked to hear a piercing scream coming from her cabin late one afternoon. I couldn't imagine what kind of catastrophe had struck. Phyllis was not easily frightened. As I ran to her cabin, the door swung open, and Mickey was standing in the doorway.

"Don't come in. Don't come in. Everything is all right." Well, it wasn't quite all right. Phyllis had been helping her blond hair with a rinse. That afternoon, after her run, she had showered and then rinsed her hair. It seemed the rinse bottle was mislabeled. It was black instead of blond. Phyllis missed supper that night and did not emerge for the evening program. The next morning she came to assembly with black hair and a big smile on her face. It took the campers and counselors a while to recognize her. Her black hair became the subject of every comic song that summer, but after that first horrified scream when she realized what had happened, nobody could tell by her demeanor that she was anything but delighted to become a sudden brunette.

We were near the end of the 1968 camp season when Phyllis confided to us that she was pregnant, and the baby was due the following February. By then she was the key leader in Evergreen. Judy and I discussed the situation, and decided that it would not be fair to Phyllis to have her return as Head Counselor with an infant. The head counselor job was and is enormously time consuming. She would need time to bond with her baby and learn what it was to be a parent. She disagreed, She was sure she could be a new mother and a head counselor without a problem. We were firm. Phyllis stayed home with her new baby the next summer.

That was one of the worst decisions we ever made in our years running camp. Phyllis was right. She would have had a ball at camp with her baby son Bryan. She proved that a few years later with her infant daughter Randy. For us at camp, the summer of 1969, was the worst and most agonizing summer ever. Though our most serious difficulties involved the Kenwood staff, dissension and unhappiness are contagious. They did infect Evergreen counselors as well. Had Phyllis been with us, no matter what the mood of the Kenwood counselors, Evergreen would have been dominated by her personality, and our girls' staff would have become an asset rather than an additional source of problems. That was her one summer off. She returned for the 1970 camp season, and we never let her get away again.

Phyllis never learned how to walk. At camp she only knew how to run, from one activity to another. Now in her sixties, she is still a dynamo whose battery never seems to wear down. She runs, she skis, she plays tennis. At camp she still referees soccer games and she stilll goes jogging every afternoon at 4:30. After her run and a quick shower, she starts moving again, running evening activities; taking kids out for treats at night, having conferences with counselors, doing up the daily schedule or planning sensational new surprise "Breaks" for "Green and Gold". . She usually calls it a day around 1:00 AM, and lolls around in bed until 7:30 the next morning.

One of Phyllis' annual high points is the start of Green & Gold, our Color War. Our Green team plays against our Golds in every conceivable activity, and even some that might seem inconceivable to the uninitiated. The tradition of Color War is that when it will start and how it starts must be a surprise. It usually starts with a "Break-out", a dramatic surprise. Phyllis takes the need for a dramatic surprise opening very seriously. She probably loses sleep over the next summer's color war break as early as the first snow of winter.

One summer in the late 1980s, Phyllis and Mickey were on a Day off from camp. They were driving and heard a helicopter over-head. Phyllis looked up and saw that the helicopter was painted green on the top and Gold or a reasonable facsimile thereof on the bottom. Whichever way the helicopter went, Mickey had to follow, until they got to a wide enough clearing for Phyllis to catch the registration numbers. She cut short her day off; returned to camp; and made phone calls tracking down the helicopter for use for a Green & Gold Break. It took many phone calls, but she found it. One night, as we were finishing supper, we all heard a helicopter hovering over the dining room. The entire camp abandoned their tables and raced outside, knowing that something spectacular was about to happen. The green and gold helicopter slowly descended onto the field just below the dining room. When it landed, the head coaches from each team leaped out of the cabin, appropriately dressed in unmistakable green and gold outfits. The girls screamed and cheered their excitement, and then raced back to their cabins where experience from past years had taught them the green and gold team lists would be posted and waiting. It was one of the best Green and Gold break outs of all time. Nobody was more excited that Phyllis.

That was Phyllis. Her first summer as a camper was 1951. It is now 2012, and Phyllis will be returning to camp for her sixtieth camp season. As I write this, eight years into my retirement from camp, Phyllis is still dashing from place to place, and still helping to make Camp Evergreen a very special place in the hearts of its' campers and counselors.

29
Stormin Norman

When we last visited Norm and Shirlee in Florida, Norm seemed to have shrunk. His voice was soft. His movements were slow and hesitant. He was reluctant to express opinions. He had retired from teaching several years earlier. His job as Head Counselor was a receding memory. This man, who had oozed power, now looked powerless. All of his status was gone. An athletic man all of his life, he could no longer afford to play tennis or golf at "the Club" because his teacher's pension didn't keep up with the escalating fees. He was a shadow going through the courtesy rituals he practiced as a man. We did not know then we would never see Norm again.

"Stormin Norman" was a nickname given to a hurricane a few years ago. It was also the name ascribed to General Norman Schwartzkoff during the Persian Gulf War. We at camp had our own Stormin Norman. It was 1963 when I hired Norm as waterfront Director we were both thirty years old. Norm was a fixture in camp through the 1998 season, his final summer at camp.

Norm was dubbed Stormin Norman almost immediately. The nickname was inspired by both his booming voice and a very short fuse on his temper. Norm was a big strong guy, well over six feet, broad and muscular. When he chose to yell, the sound rumbled around inside his large frame, seeming to start at his feet and gather strength all the way up through the body and out his mouth. No drama coach ever had to tell Norm to project. When he was on the waterfront, and yelled " ALL BOATS IN," everybody in camp heard it. It was even rumored that skippers of boats on lakes and ponds all over Merrimac County immediately brought their ships in to shore, and stood awaiting further instructions.

Reinforcing his image was the sheer physical power he exhibited. When it was time to install or even repair waterfront docks, Norm took charge. Usually, it took four very strong young men or six normal counselors to lift and carry one of our dock sections. When Norm was part of the crew, he lifted and carried one end, while three of us carried the other end. Once, when we were moving a former ice fishing shack into position to be used as an equipment shed on the waterfront, the final operation required one side of the building to be jacked up, while we placed cement blocks underneath for support. Norm held up the side of the building for several minutes while several of us positioned the blocks.

When Norm's anger was directed at somebody I have seen them cower as far away as possible to escape the full fury of the storm. Fortunately this did not happen very often. But, when it did, it became part of his legend. He was tough, but he was a good waterfront director. He knew how to run a waterfront. Swim instruction was well organized and well taught. General Swim was safe. When Norm yelled "Buddy Up", there was no question about it. The buddies got together, raised their hands high in the air and called out their numbers. If he told a counselor on lifeguard duty to keep his eyes on the water, the chastened lifeguard was all attention the remainder of the swim. It was a safe place, a tight ship and kids were learning how to swim. As explosive as Norm could be in situations which caused his anger to ignite, he was inspiring as a swim instructor, particularly for little boys with a fear of the water. He worked effectively with his assistants, who usually started the season a little afraid of him. But soon learned that his loud reactions were frequently followed by a calmer almost apologetic mood. Despite his temper and his sometimes scary voice, Norm was a first class waterfront director, a position he held right through the 1970 camp season.

Norm wanted the newly vacant Head Counselor job for the 1968 camp season. I felt I couldn't give him serious consideration because of his temper. In addition, it was clear to me that the next Kenwood Head Counselor would have to be someone who could also enroll campers. He agreed he was not that person. So I was able to avoid any discussion of his qualifications. I hired Joel Wolfson to take on that dual role

When Joel and I agreed to part after the disastrous 1969 season, it was again time for a new Head Counselor. Once again, Norm applied for the job. Once again I had to pass him by. During the 69 season the staff had been so negative, particularly in Kenwood, that I decided to take on the Head Counselor role myself, hoping to restore positive attitudes. I was concerned that Norm would not be able to create the necessary change in attitudes, but I truly valued him in camp and didn't want to lose him. Norm remained Head of the Kenwood Waterfront, and took on additional duties as an Assistant Head Counselor. It turned out to be a good solution for both of us. There were many occasions when my Head Counselor duties would be in conflict with my duties as Camp Director. Norm frequently pinch hit for me as Head Counselor, and did the job well.

His method of dealing with situations on the waterfront had always been to shout first and ask questions later. This was understandable on a waterfront, where danger always had to be forestalled and there might not be time for polite correction. However, I feared that if he dealt with situations that way as

Head Counselor, he would immediately antagonize the whole staff.

In 1971, with many reservations, and after lengthy discussions with him about "anger management", (In those, days, we called it "controlling your temper,"), I gave him the job of Kenwood Head Counselor. It worked out pretty well. He fulfilled that role in camp through the 1997 camp season. Surprisingly, he was able to rein in his temper, and achieved a degree of flexibility I would not have believed possible.

Norm grew up as a kid in the war years. Though he and I were too late to be soldiers in World War Two, we were shaped and influenced by those years. Our heroes were strong men who knew right from wrong. They were tough. They brooked no nonsense. We saw them lead men into battle in a hundred movies. They always came out unscathed because they stood for what was right and decent and The American Way. Norm was a product of this childhood education. He was a perfect exemplar of the "Warrior Generation" without ever having been a warrior. He was strong, positive and intelligent. But he lacked patience with people who didn't quite measure up to his standards. In quiet moments, and when he had time to reflect, he understood nuances, but when he was excited or upset, he simply reacted and usually at a high decibel level. . He rarely saw things in shades of gray. When he decided a counselor was a great guy, it would take have taken some pretty terrible behavior to change his mind. Conversely, if he started off with a negative impression of a counselor, that person was unlikely to ever to do anything right in his eyes. Through the years I had to smooth a lot of ruffled feathers.

He was a strong athletic man; a man of few words; a man with a powerful sense of discipline and positive feelings of right and wrong. It would be easy to write him off this way, and ridicule his foibles. But he was much more than that to camp. Norm was smart, hard working, well organized and loyal, all attributes I valued. He made things happen, and they happened on time and they happened as they were supposed to happen. Groups always knew where they were supposed to be, and there was almost never any confusion. Norm was particularly good at saying "NO". He was unafraid to be the bad guy and he always insisted that staff members obey the camp rules. Every organization needs a person who is good at saying "NO". Norm was our "No" man for years.

In his later years at camp they still called him Stormin Norman, but it was mostly tradition. He mellowed over the years. When he became Head Counselor he was not a "complete" Head Counselor in the sense that Phyllis was, but he provided important organizational strength. First, I knew he was one hundred percent reliable. If I asked him to do something I knew it would be done. Second, he was a wonderful quartermaster, not only making sure that program areas had the supplies they needed, but that the counselors to whom they were delivered knew how to use them. Third, whenever there was any kind of physical set up for program, I knew Norm would be the man to make sure it was done correctly. On weekends, with special events activities, I could count on Norm to organize large group activities no matter how complicated they might be.

Norm and I complemented one another's strengths and weaknesses well. With all of his vocal power, he was very shy with people; nervous about speaking before assembled groups; lacked the confidence to lead singing; did not tell bed time stories and was no good at all in providing the kind of soothing conversational support frequently needed by counselors and even more often by campers. He lacked either the desire or the creative bent to run most evening activities and special events. Phyllis did most of those things as part of being Head Counselor at Evergreen. I enjoyed playing some of those Head Counselor roles in Kenwood.

When I think about Norm it makes me sad. After his many years at camp, it is sad to think how badly it all ended. Norm thought he had a lifetime job as Head Counselor, and perhaps he would have, had I never sold the camp. He didn't believe that the change in ownership and administration meant new people and a new approach. We had many discussions on the subject, but he didn't really believe my warnings. It didn't matter that Scott, the new owner, had been his friend or that he was formerly Scott's boss. He had to adjust, but he didn't. He took it as a blow when Scott wanted a vigorous younger man as his Head Counselor. Scott gave Norm a chance to stay on in the newly created position of athletic director, but Norm looked at it as a demotion, and made a half-hearted attempt to satisfy the job description. The termination, the anger, the recriminations, and the age discrimination law suit that followed, had an effect on all of us. Most of all, it devastated Norm. He never recovered from this blow to his self-image.

30
A Paratrooper Drops In

Bob Christie: Master Chef

Bob Christie was the man Jack brought to camp as his replacement. Bob was great. An ex-paratrooper, he loved working in the kitchen. He did all the ordering; paid attention to the budget; and was also a very good cook. He made wonderful soups. They were so good that Judy asked him to bottle some for us to take home. He did this for us at the end of each of his summers at camp. We enjoyed his soups all winter long. He was honest, honorable and an incredibly hard worker. He didn't care how long he had to work as long as the food came out right. What more could I ask? He even sang while he worked. He organized the kitchen boys into a singing group.

"Can we be in the Counselor show opening night?"

"Well, I'm sure you'll be through work, but the boys are going to have a lot of dishes to wash. It's always slow getting things organized at the beginning."

"Don't worry about a thing. By the time the campers come these guys will know their jobs so well they will be able to do them in their sleep."

During his first few summers at camp Bob was like a miracle worker with those kids. I would walk into the kitchen and everybody was smiling. The kitchen looked spotless. They were all singing. They were chopping vegetables, polishing the refrigerator door and washing the floor. It reminded me of that wonderful Texaco television commercial from the Milton Berle Show. A car would drive up to the station, and one bright shining attendant would start pumping gas, while an equally smiling guy wiped the windows and a third checked the tire pressure. "Those were the days, my friends", and I was witnessing the camp kitchen version of it. Too bad it had to come to a crashing halt. After Bob's era in our kitchen I went on a long Safari into kitchen "Never Never Land".

Bob was with us at camp over a twenty year span, but unfortunately not twenty consecutive years. He and his wife Mildred had been with us for seven or eight years when Bob heard of a "can't miss" opportunity to buy his own restaurant in Wyoming. I pleaded with him not to do it. I quoted restaurant failure statistics to him. I told him he and Mildred would work themselves to death at a 24 hour a day restaurant, which was what they were buying. He couldn't resist the temptation that has been the downfall of so many wonderful cooks. They went to Wyoming. I think the restaurant blossomed for a time under his management. I don't recall how many years passed before the inevitable bankruptcy. When he came back to us quite a few years had passed, and Bob was emotionally defeated and physically worn out.

In the interim period when Bob went to Wyoming his place was taken by Harvey.

Harvey was a big blustery guy who knew everything about everything. It was his view that Bob was nothing but an enthusiastic amateur.

"Bob doesn't really know anything about cooking. He can't even make decent hamburgers. His chicken is awful. And his soups are disgusting."

I replied "I think Bob's a good cook. Admittedly his hamburgers are not wonderful, but it's hard to turn out hamburgers for three hundred fifty people who all want them at the same time. I think everything else he made was very good. I hope you will do as well as he's done"

"Don't worry," Harvey said. "I'll show you how a professional chef cooks and runs a kitchen."

He showed me all right. The first time he showed me was the night we had flank steak. The wall behind our electric grills caught fire and we had to call the fire department. The kitchen and dining room were so filled with smoke that the camp had to eat out-of-doors the next day. But we did manage to salvage a few of the steaks.

I wasn't in the kitchen the first night Harvey made hamburgers, but I must say, he turned them out. They were good and there were enough. I could smell the smoke from my seat in the dining room, but a little smoke is a small price to pay for really good hamburgers. I went into the kitchen to congratulate him and ask how he did it. My mouth dropped open when I went through those swinging doors. Harvey's back was to me. He was standing over the big gas range. His kitchen whites were covered in soot. So was everything else. The kitchen ceiling near the chef's area was black. The chef's table was black. The floors were black and greasy. Instead of using the grills he was using the top of the huge gas range as his grill. We had to dispose of those ranges and get new ones after that summer. Harvey made it though the camp season, his only camp season.

Through the years of Bob's absence many other chefs came and went. Some were with us for a summer; others not quite that long.

Amos was one of the brief encounters. Famous Amos was the name we gave to our new chef. "Famous Amos" was a popular cookie brand of that era. The packaging of those cookies showed a smiling black man holding an inviting looking chocolate chip cookie. Our Famous Amos was about twenty years older, but otherwise could have posed for those packages. He had the most wonderful smile and a disposition to match. It was a pleasure just looking at him. He was such a wonderful agreeable guy with a wealth of experience. He was an Executive Chef at a well known university. Surely he knew his stuff.

During our staff Orientation period Amos' food was wonderful. I thought I had finally struck gold. In those days, we were feeding just over a hundred people during Orientation. That week meals came out of the kitchen flawlessly, but I knew that Orientation Week is often the honeymoon period for new chefs. The real test comes when the campers arrive at camp and our population more than triples from a little over one hundred to about three hundred fifty.

I had cause for worry the night the campers arrived. The dining room was filled with noisy happy kids, waiting for their food. "Waiting" was the crucial word. The meal was already fifteen minutes old and only about a quarter of the tables had received any food. The dining room was getting noisier as our impatient teen age boys grew more and more hostile with the delay. I looked up and there was Amos, standing outside the kitchen doors surveying the dining room. He smiled benignly at the campers, counselors and waiters. He was meeting and greeting newcomers, and being as agreeable and pleasant as I knew him to be.

"My God, what's he doing out here? No wonder so many tables don't have food."

The operative word that I learned I must avoid in the future was the word "Executive." When hiring chefs in the future I kept in mind that the word "Executive" in front of the word "Chef" on an application meant "I no longer do the work. I only supervise." In our kitchen the Chef had to be the number one cook. We didn't have the luxury of an Executive. When Amos and I parted company at the end of the second week of camp, we were both smiling and cordial. He really was a very nice man. And we were once again in big trouble in the kitchen.

I promoted Denis, our second cook. Things went well for a few days. However, it took less than a week from the time Denis had been promoted for me to recognize that we had a serious problem. It was my habit to be the first person other than the cooks to be up in the morning. I would come in, draw my first of many cups of coffee, and check with the chef to see if there were any problems he wanted to tell me about. One day I came to the kitchen door, and it was locked from the dining room side. I didn't see any lights in back. No lights meant no cooks. I went outside around to the back and unlocked the door. I turned on the coffee maker and then I went to Denis' cabin. My knock on his door produced no response. There was an unmistakable smell of liquor oozing out from the cracks beneath and around his door. I knocked. I hammered. I yelled, risking waking the whole camp an hour too early. Finally I got an answer.

"Go away. Don't bother me."

"Denis, it's me, Arthur. You have to get up."

"I can't get up. I'm sick."

It was clear enough that his sickness came from a bottle. I woke our second cook, and he got up to start breakfast. The second cook, who had been originally hired as a prep cook, was a very young man just learning. He didn't really have much experience. I suspected we could manage breakfast together with the help of some of our kitchen boys, but what would happen with the meals that required actual cooking? I helped out in the kitchen, and somehow breakfast was ready on time. Mid-morning I went back to Denis' cabin, hoping that he had slept it off by then. His door was locked, and I got no answer at all. We got through lunch with cold cut sandwiches, salads and Jello that was already in the refrigerator. I pounded on his door again mid-afternoon, and again got no response. I tried the door. It was latched from the inside. He was in there all right.

I went back to my office, and phoned in "Camp Chef Wanted" ads in three newspapers, the *Globe* and *Herald* in Boston along with the *Manchester Union Leader*. The ads would run the next day. The next thing I did was write a note to Denis telling him he was fired, and that I would have his final check ready for him before supper. I slipped it under his door.

I made an "emergency" call to one of camp's most reliable friends, Churchill Brown. Churchill was now quite an old man. He had first arrived at camp in the late 1930s as a member of a chef's crew. By the time I arrived at Kenwood as a young camper in 1942 the chef with whom Churchill had come to camp had long since disappeared from the camp scene; but Churchill was already a fixture. He was the camp's cleaning man. I loved Churchill. When Judy and I bought the camp, Churchill, like Jack, was part of the package.

This was Churchill's summer home. He always seemed to be grousing about something, but somehow he managed to pull it off without ever being in a bad mood. There was always a wisp of smile behind his complaints. Churchill was not only a meticulous and hard working cleaning man, but he was also our pre camp cook every summer, cooking for the small group of counselors who came for work week. In early June I would pick him up outside his Cambridge apartment, where I would find him sitting on the curb in front of the building, his meager baggage sitting next to him. We became great working friends, but he never invited me inside his apartment. We drove to camp together. He and I preceded any formal kitchen crew or even the counselors who were coming early to help me open camp. He got the kitchen in working order, and cooked for the next week for our "work week" crew. He was a good cook and a great breakfast man. In recent years he had "retired" from full time camp work, and just came up to help us open.

I could always count on Churchill. "I'll catch the 4:00 bus out of Boston. Don't forget to have somebody meet me now."

"Don't worry. It will be somebody you know."

Denis was still in his cabin at supper time. After supper I went and pounded on his door again.

"What do you want?"

"Denis, I want you to pack up and leave. We'll get you to the bus or even into Concord if that's where you want to go."

"I'm not leaving. I like it here."

"Denis, I want you out. You are no longer welcome here. I have your final salary check in an envelope. I'll slip it under the door. There are a few dollars in cash in the envelope too."

"You can't make me go."

"Actually, I can. If you don't come out on your own I'll call the police. They'll get you out."

Judy went to New London to meet Churchill's bus. It was due in New London at 7:30.

It was getting dark when the police cruiser pulled up next to the kitchen. After a few minutes of persuasive threats by the police, Denis came out of the cabin, screaming and swearing at me, at the camp, at our stoves, at everything he could think of. He finally got in the back of the cruiser. As it pulled out of the driveway, Denis had one more message for me.

"You better not plan to sleep at night, Sharenow. I'll be back one night, and I'll burn your whole camp down."

Churchill managed for us for a couple of days until the new cook I had hired from an ad arrived at camp.

Harold came from Florida. There are a lot of cooks, chefs and kitchen people from Florida who come to New England in the summer as the Southern country clubs and restaurants start laying people off until fall. Harold had good experience and even references we were able to reach and talk to on the phone. Harold hit camp like a whirlwind. He really did know his stuff and he wasn't afraid of work. We had also hired another young cook who had answered our local ad. Churchill stayed for a few days until Harold got his bearings, and then he headed back home."

"You don't need me. I think this fella can cook. If I'm wrong, you know where to reach me"

Harold stayed sober until the last night of the camp season. The morning the campers were to leave Ansel, our head maintenance man, informed me that I shouldn't expect Harold in to work that day. His car was teetering on a stone wall just outside the Red House. Harold was in the driver's seat, his head slumped over the steering wheel, apparently out cold.

Ansel was worried that he might get killed.

"If he moves the wrong way that car could tip over with him in it."

We called a wrecker, and I didn't worry too much more about Harold. We could and did live without him for that last breakfast. All of our campers safely boarded the homebound busses headed for Boston and New York. We said goodbye to Harold later that day. I considered us very lucky Harold had enough self control to wait until the very last night of camp to lose it.

The next year I hired "Big Al". Big Al was the camp's first and only Jewish Chef. It was clear when he came for his interview that he liked to eat. If his size was any indication I reasoned that his food must be wonderful. He was enormous. I speculated that with his weight he would not prove to be too energetic. He was probably not going to be a dynamo, but he did have good experience. He had worked at a camp before, and he had good references. In the face of that evidence, his weight was only a small obstacle.

Like so many others, Big Al seemed to know what he was doing.

"Yes, I've placed the opening order. There's nothing for you to worry about."

It didn't take long for me to discover that his assertion was not precisely true. Our camp dining room had been built many years earlier, and it grew as the camp grew. In all there had been eight additions to the original building through the years. One of those additions was a major excavation under the kitchen to create storage space for groceries and extra refrigeration. When Al came to camp I showed him around the camp and the kitchen just mentioning the storage down below. It seemed that by the time he placed his order, he had never ventured down the back staircase to review the downstairs storage area.

The meat truck arrived and backed in next to the kitchen. Ansel and his helper were unloading the truck when I came on the scene.

Ansel said "I don't know where we're going to put all of this meat?

"What do you mean? Al told me he just placed an opening order?"

"Take a look at the slip." I didn't believe what was on that slip. Al had ordered meat for the entire camp season. Upstairs we had a walk-in refrigerator and a small freezer. Down below we had another freezer and another smaller walk-in refrigerator. We had enough refrigeration space for one week of food. Our chef had ordered eight weeks worth.

"Don't unload another thing. Where's Al?"

Just then I saw Al lumbering my way. He had heard the truck, and had hauled himself up the hill from his cabin. He was gasping for breath by the time he reached us. I felt bad for him, but I had to ask.

"Didn't you ever look downstairs before you ordered?" The answer was obvious.

I told him to go over the delivery slip, and pick out what we needed for the week. I called the meat company, and asked them to take back the rest, explaining what had happened. Fortunately, it was a company we had been doing business with for years, and they agreed to take back the ninety percent of the merchandise we didn't need just then.

After Al's grand opening I didn't know what to expect. He actually wasn't bad. Things were sometimes a little slow. The kitchen was sometimes a little sloppy. The food was sometimes not wonderful, but it was usually acceptable. Al made it though the summer.

I had enough. It was time to resort to a food service. All of my troubles would be over. They were pros, and had an inexhaustible supply of cooks and kitchen workers. I would never have to worry about mid season replacements again. They would manage food costs and their own staff discipline. Marriott had an institutional food management business. They certainly had a well known name, and a reputation for quality. I had confidence they would come through for me.

George was our new "Chef/Manager". He worked for Marriott year round. He brought with him a second cook, a prep man, and four dish washers, all part of the package. George actually was a good manager. He ran his crew well. He organized well. He did all of the ordering. The kitchen was always clean. There was only one small problem. The entire camp was starving after the first few days. The fact that the food was bland and uninteresting was less important.

I called Marriott, and demanded a conference. Their regional food director came the next day. He and George sat down with Judy and me for several hours. All of their food was "portion controlled". I knew that. I knew nothing was fresh, and that everything was coming from the freezer or from packages. I said I didn't mind that, but either the portions had to be larger or there had to be more of them. Our kids and counselors were getting very frustrated and so was I. They agreed to increase the portions by twenty percent.

It was only when George and company started to turn out enough food that we were able to focus on the fact that the food really was totally uninviting. However, the commitment was made, and Marriott was with us for the summer. Our kids grew hungry for fresh vegetables, recognizable fruit, meat that was hot and flavorful, and deserts that weren't all scooped out of cartons. We supplemented with numerous trips to the local Pizza restaurants, ice cream parlors and hamburger joints to try to fill some of the aching empty stomachs of our deprived teen age campers.

As it happened, that summer was cool and rainy. My wife Judy, who was the menu planner for camp, kept putting soup on the menu. Somehow the soup never appeared. There was always some lame reason for the omission. Finally, a week before the end of the camp season, Judy called George aside, and said

"We have to have chicken soup at the Boy's banquet the last night of camp. It's a tradition." George promised her he would come through for her that night.

We had visions of Bob's delicious soups in mind. The night of the boys' banquet, George came up to Judy to assure her that we would be having chicken soup. Before the meal I went into the kitchen to get a tasting. When I saw the pile of empty cans of Campbell's chicken noodle soup, I almost cried. It wasn't that important. But why, if they were just going to open cans, couldn't they have done the same on some of those cold rainy nights?

Through the years there were more chefs and more stories, but I think this will give the reader a taste.

31
The Great Flood of 1971

Our 1971 Camp Season started with an unremarkable Work Week. The only notable day of work week was the last. That was the day it started to rain. The next day was the opening of Counselor Orientation, one of the most crucial weeks of the camp season. It is often the week that sets the atmosphere and mood for the summer as new staff members become integrated with old. Former campers, recently elevated to the status of Junior Counselors, try on their new roles as staff members. It is also a week in which to complete the physical set up of camp.

Counselors arriving for Orientation were greeted by a heavy unrelenting downpour as they emerged from their vehicles. They slogged through high wet grass and occasional short patches of mud as they found their way to their cabins, doing their best to keep clothes and other possessions shielded from the rain. By mid-afternoon, an amoeba like lake had already formed in the low spot in front of Bunk 2. This was a spot that normally filled with water during heavy rains, but on this day it had spilled over its normal shoreline, with the excess rolling unimpeded onto the not quite ready for play tennis courts below. The three courts would soon become a small pond.

The whole staff assembled in good humor and anticipation for our evening meal. This was followed by the official opening program of Orientation. Everybody was welcomed and introduced; ice breakers were played; opening talks were given; the program for Orientation was laid out for them; and snacks were served. Even the least religious among us prayed that we would awaken to sunshine the next day.

Our prayers fell on deaf ears. The rain was relentless. If anything, it was harder than the day before. At breakfast, I was surrounded by counselors reporting leaks in their cabins. These had to be noted, but not much could be done to seal them until the rain stopped. Mitch Kaplan, Kenwood's waterfront director, warned that the water in the lake was rising precipitously, and that the docks we had laboriously installed during work week were in danger of floating away.

Norm Laakso, who was beginning his first summer as Kenwood Head Counselor, had been our waterfront director for several years, and knew our lake better than anybody. His assessment didn't cheer me up. "If it stops raining right now, the water will continue to rise for another 24 hours. We can put row boats on the docks, and let them fill with water. That may hold the docks down if the lake doesn't go too high. If it keeps raining much longer we are going to have to pull the pipes, and tie the docks to the shore."

Our lake is like a big sixty-five acre bath tub except that it has three water sources, and only one outgoing stream. The practical implication of that three to one ratio is that when we have a heavy rainfall, water rushes into the Lake much faster than it can possibly escape. It is not unusual after a heavy rain for the water level in the lake to rise as much as three or four feet. After the rain ends the water level continues to rise for several hours before it begins to recede.

One of the first physical changes I had made a couple of years after we bought the camp was the installation of a floating dock system. The dock sections were mounted on Styrofoam floats, and bolted together. The intact system then rides up and down on steel pipes that go through iron collars attached to the dock sections. The docks can ride up quickly with the water level, and lower slowly with the water level as it goes down. The pipes that the docks ride up and down on are different lengths according to their relative position from the shore line. The longest of the pipes is twenty feet. The system works well under all but extraordinary circumstances. But it too has limitations. When we install these during Work week, the pipes set in the deepest part of the swim area are about three or four feet into the bottom of the lake, and go through a depth of eight or nine feet of water, leaving five or six feet of pipe sticking up next to the docks. The water level can rise that five or six feet, and the dock system remains secure. If it goes higher than that we have problems. What Mitch told me that morning was that we were already on the far edge of normal and that we might be on the way to losing all of our docks.

I was in our house exchanging my soaked work shoes for dry ones. There was a knock on our door. One of our new Evergreen counselors stood there. I knew her name, Cindy Reinhart, and a little about her, but I didn't really know her. What I saw was a very wet girl close to tears. Her hair plastered in strips down her face, her windbreaker looked as though it could be wrung out. Her blue jeans were soaked and her sneakers were encased in oozing mud. A pool formed at her feet as she stood in the doorway. Though she was a college Sophomore, she looked discouraged and dejected like a little girl who needed to be comforted by her Mommy.

"I'm not going to be able to stay here in camp. I'm just too cold and too wet. I don't have enough clothes and I don't have any dry shoes. I want to call my parents and see if one of them can pick me up this afternoon. I'm awfully sorry, and I hate to do this. But I just can't stand it."

Judy and I got her into the living room, and had her sit in front of the fireplace, which was crackling with heat and radiating good feeling. Judy got her a towel and helped her dry her head. We listened as she poured out her litany of woes. She cried some more and we consoled. She was new, lonely and wet. She was already out of dry shoes and clothing. We fixed her up with a rain slicker, rain hat and a couple of spare sweat shirts and a sweater. Shoes presented a problem. We needed all of ours. The solution was comical, a pair of old golf cleats that my Father had left in my camp closet. Cindy left her shoes to dry out by our fireplace. She clogged out of the house, still wet and unsure of herself, but feeling a whole lot better than when she came in. She agreed to try camp for a few more days.

I'm not sure how we got through that Orientation. It rained for five consecutive days. Occasionally it let up a little, and then it would start again with renewed vigor. It was really depressing. People were soaked and they were discouraged, and we were constantly forced to revise the orientation program to keep people invested and busy with indoor activities. But the onslaught of the water produced a continuous series of unusual crises.

The first and most dramatic was at our two waterfronts. The water level, which eventually rose twelve feet, defied every effort to keep the docks sitting on their poles. They rode up; floated off the poles and swirled rapidly down toward the outlet stream at the Southern end of the lake. Since the dock sections were all bolted together, we knew they wouldn't be flushed out of the lake and get lost down stream, but there was a serious danger that they might be broken apart by the swift moving water. The tops of the poles, to which the docks had been tethered, were now completely under water. Those of us working to save the waterfronts devised a method of tying large plastic bottles with long ropes to the tops of the poles so that when the water did recede, we might be able to float the docks back into place and have them settle on the posts that were now submerged. The poles were totally out of sight and our waterfront counselors actually had to dive down to locate and secure the ropes with the plastic bottles attached.

Ironically, the next even more serious threat was to our drinking water system. Our drinking water was pumped from a shallow well and from there up to large storage tanks under the kitchen. It was distributed around camp from there in underground pipes. Our old wooden pump house, which housed the vital pumps, was located close to the lake and well below the level of the dining room. The actual capped wells were even lower than the pump house. As the lake water rose above the level of the wells, we could only hope that the cement covers would keep out any of the lake water that was full of all sorts of floating debris. But the truly serious threat was to the pumps themselves. If the water level got high enough, the water would short circuit the pumps and they would stop working. We could find ourselves surrounded by water but without any to drink. Fortunately, though the water rose above the cement covered wells, and lapped against the bottom of the pump house, it didn't quite make it to the pumps.

The third threat was to the camp road, our lifeline to the outside world. Our camps are laid out in an irregular crescent shape along the western side of the lake. Coming from the Blacktop (boringly referred to on maps as Route 4) onto the dirt road into camp, it was necessary to cross two bridges that had been built in the horse and buggy era. They were wooden bridges with plank tops spanning a substructure of irregularly shaped granite boulders, "pointed" with mud and smaller rocks. We jokingly referred to these bridges as our early warning system. Cars and trucks coming over the larger of the two bridges, invariably lifted the ends of the tread boards and slapped them back down as they passed; the larger the vehicle the louder the rumble as they crossed the bridge into camp territory.

After the first two days of torrential downpour, I checked out the bridges. I wanted to be reassured that they would not collapse. As I stood on the larger of the two bridges, I looked down at the water rushing just inches below the boards. It was not a reassuring sight. Two days later the water had risen above the level of both bridges, and cars could no longer come in or out of camp. When the rain finally stopped the day before the campers were to arrive, I eagerly walked down the dirt road toward the bridges. I couldn't get close. The water was now six feet over the bridge and was working its way up the dirt road.

That afternoon, I was not sure how or if we would be able to get our campers into camp. Our dirt road starts close to Route Four, goes well beyond camp, and connects with a network of other dirt roads which eventually connect to blacktop highways. Though it is a much longer ride into camp, we had used this circuitous route in the past when bus loads of campers were coming back from long tiring trips late at night. Normally we had the busses come in directly from Route Four. Since we never trusted those bridges entirely, it was our policy to have the campers get off and reload after the busses successfully crossed both of our ancient bridges.

After supper I took a ride out the back road to see if that would be a viable alternative. I wanted to have company on what could become a treacherous ride. I asked Brenda if she would like to come. She was our girls' waterfront director and definitely the adventurous type. She was delighted. Brenda had been doing yeoman work the past few days, and I thought she would enjoy the diversion of looking at something other than her own disastrously flooded waterfront. Riding away from camp on the back road we saw evidence everywhere of the enormous amount of damage that the rainfall had wrought in the surrounding area.

We started out on a compromised road that threatened to become a quagmire. I was driving our Chevy Impala Station Wagon. The drainage ditches on either side of the road were like small rivers. At dips in the road we frequently went though standing water more than a foot deep. I could tell as much by the lapping sound on the floorboards of the car than by any visual measurement. Brenda enjoyed the ride. She was upbeat and chirping away in her high pitched voice. I enjoyed it too. It was an adventure. Not only was I not sure we could make our way to actual paved roads this way, but I wasn't at all sure that we would be able to find a place to turn around if, at some point ahead, we were unable to continue.

Finally we made it through to the blacktop. Better still, we made it back to camp. I was elated. The rain had stopped, and the odds were good that our campers could be brought into camp the back way. Other alternatives would be much worse. The most likely alternate plan had the busses drive the incoming campers as far as they could on the camp road, and then we would walk them to the edge of the swollen lake, and shuttle them into camp in row boats and canoes. This plan had a kind of romantic feel to it, but it would take a very long time. Just shuttling the campers by row boat would take hours rather than minutes, but campers do not come to camp empty handed. In those days they shipped their heavier luggage by Railway Express, but they still all came with hand luggage. There were always a few who arrived with heavy duffel bags and trunks which had been packed too late to be shipped ahead.

The other alternative was too horribly complicated to contemplate. It was the logistical nightmare that we would create if we decided to postpone camp opening a day or even two. It would mean not only making alternate plans with the bus companies, but also calling and reaching the parents of every camper, and they all had their plans, based on our scheduled opening day.. Happily, once the rain actually stopped falling we were able to discard that alternative.

Early in the morning on Opening Day the water started to recede. Campers were not due until mid-afternoon. We watched as the level went down, and by early afternoon water was again lapping at the undersides of the wooden bridges. At 3:30 that afternoon the first busses cautiously edged onto our muddy dirt road. The drivers felt they had traction, and continued as close as they dared to the edge of the first bridge. There we emptied the busses and the campers walked across the bridge, a few at a time, and walked into camp. Our junior counselors and maintenance staff carried all of the hand luggage across the bridges and into pickup trucks and cars waiting on the camp side of the bridges. We didn't trust those bridges to carry even empty vehicles at that point. There was no way to know to what extent they had been undermined by the flood. But we were happy. Our campers arrived safely in camp. The sun came out that day, and we had good weather through most of that camp season.

32
The Mill Stream

"Down by the old mill stream,
  Where I first met you. With your eyes so blue,
  Dressed in gingham too, It was then I knew,
  That you loved me too;
  You were sixteen, My village queen.
  Down By the old ... mill stream."

That mill stream was ours. As a kid, I thought somebody had written the song about our very own mill stream. The stream was a wonderful glacial gash in the landscape about two miles down the dirt road from our camp property. When I first saw it I was twelve years old. The first sighting of the stream came at the end of a hot, dusty, thirsty hike from camp along a seemingly endless road. There was little on that road but a few shabby, dilapidated farm houses. The only pause and relief along the way had been a stop at an ancient well, where we lowered a bucket to refill our canteens.

We came upon the stream after a bend in the road. It brought us surprisingly onto a narrow wooden bridge, whose top planks groaned in protest under our collective weight. We were so hot and tired, when we looked down it was like seeing an oasis on a desert. The water gushed and cascaded from a rocky horizon far above and to our left to a much lower and softer horizon of Pine trees and Hemlocks, where it disappeared to our right.

What an adventure! What a great day! Our counselor, Judge Goldblatt, who wasn't really a judge at all, led us on a secret path through the woods, to the very edge of the stream. In those days the decrepit old mill still perched on the side of the stream. The paddle wheel was gone, and the decaying building leaned dangerously toward the beckoning waters below. We were to strip, and enter the icy water just where the paddle wheel had once powered long forgotten machinery.

"OK, boys, we can jump in here. It's plenty deep enough. Then after we take a swim, we'll have our lunch. After that we'll spend the afternoon climbing up through the stream. Let's see how far we can go. I want to set a new camp record." Judge always wanted to set new records everywhere we went. "Just one warning, nobody climbs up into that mill. It's going to fall over one of these days, and I don't want any of you in it when it happens." Of course, that was an invitation, and he must have known it.

We plunged into the shockingly cold water with screams. We took delight in splashing the few who stood on the edge trying to summon up the courage to jump in. Finally we were all in, and the water seemed to warm up around us. One counselor stood, as our lifeguard, on the rocky ledge just above the water. He stood there naked as we were. The other two counselors, including Judge, were stretched out on a flat rock, relaxing and working their tans.

Arnie Rubin was the first to swim under the over-hanging mill. "Hey, there's a hole in the floor. I bet we can climb right into it." Donny Aronson and Henry Elkins swam to his side. I was just behind them when Arnie started to climb. He pulled himself up through the hole, and five or six of us started to follow. Just then our not too alert lifeguard figured out what was going on and started to yell for us to get down. Judge stood up, and, when he yelled, we listened. He had just been discharged from the Marines, and he had a strong commanding top sergeant voice. We scrambled out of that old mill as fast as we could. I was happy enough to get out of there. It was a scary place. The boards creaked at our every movement, and it even felt like the whole building was starting to move. We made it out a side window and onto the rocky ledge.

After lunch, we climbed and climbed. Our first stop on the stream was at a small waterfall, where it was possible to go through and behind the falls to look out and wave at our friends on the outside. That was exciting. There was only room for one at a time, but we all did it, over and over again. Judge was in the water with us, and held onto us as we ducked behind the small but thundering falls. When we had our fill we came out of the water shaking with cold. We stretched out of flat rocks to dry off before continuing up through and around the stream.

Further up stream there was another place where we could actually swim a little. We continued beyond the swimming hole. We were tired by then. Finally Judge announced. "We've done it. We've set the new camp record for distance and speed. We can head back to camp now." He led us out of the stream, up an embankment and onto a road which had been invisibl;e to us from the stream. We walked back to "our dirt road" and the long road back to camp. We arrived hot and tired, but all agreed it was the very best day of the camp season.

By the time Judy and I bought the camp in 1960, the mill stream had disappeared from the camp memory. Campers and counselors didn't go there any more. I dug out the camp's old hiking map from its hiding place in the back of an office closet. There it was. The map was where it belonged, and the Mill Stream was right where I remembered it. In the intervening years, the once-a-week "Hike Day" I remembered from childhood had disappeared and been replaced by "Trip Day". Trips Day meant busses, formal destinations, admission charges, boardwalks and guides. In the years between my years as a camper and our return as Directors, camp had entered a new and more sophisticated era. Of course I had observed some of this evolution during my years as a counselor, but it was only when it became truly my camp that I became aware something valuable had been lost along the way.

That very day I got in my car, and drove to the mill stream. The path below the bridge was overgrown, but it was still there. The stream was just as I remembered it, but the mill had been torn down and carted away in the interim. The existence of an actual mill I remembered so vividly would only be a story to the generations of campers I was to lead up and through that stream in the decades that followed.

Through the years I rewarded myself with many dozens of Mill Stream trips. They were a joyful interruption of my hours spent in the office working on programs. What a pleasure to be actually out with kids, introducing them to an adventure and an activity I knew they would remember all of their lives. I got to feel very close to them as I stood shivering in the ice cold water, while helping them get in and out from under the waterfall. The joy in their faces was my payoff. What a pleasure for me to be the one to show them how and where to begin their slide down the slippery ledge and into the whirlpool. This was even further upstream than Judge Goldblatt had taken us so many years earlier. I came to know every rock and crevice along that stream. There was that wonderful slippery moss covered rock, where the kids could feel they were skating as they slid back and forth. They loved the sliding and were happy to have somebody holding their arms to keep them from falling.

On these newer Mill Stream treks there were compromises involved. We no longer hiked the hot dusty road on an all day outing. This became an afternoon outing for me with a small group of campers and counselors. I couldn't afford the time away from "real work" for an entire day. We piled the kids into vans, and shuttled over to the start of the path. The dusty dirt road of my childhood was now a thin ribbon of bumpy asphalt; there were a few new houses; and the once deserted farms now looked occupied and prosperous. These new signs of encroaching civilization, plus the newly coed nature of the camp, meant the end of skinny dipping.

I sometimes took boys' groups, but more often I went with groups of girls. I showed our Kenwood counselors the points of interest, fun, and lurking danger, and I had a high degree of confidence that the male counselors were strong enough to handle whatever help their campers might need. I had less confidence that our Evergreen counselors would have the physical strength to assist kids in trouble, particularly on days when the current was strong. That is the logical reason for me going more frequently with the girls than the boys, but, when all is said and done, I enjoyed taking the girls more than the boys. They were less likely to run ahead and get into trouble. They were more likely to admit to being afraid or needing help. They were also far more enthusiastic and vocal in their joy and their thanks. That made it more fun for me! I even got used to the inevitable "First shower", "Second shower", "Third shower" that rang out as soon as we got in the van to return to camp.

Every so often, whenever I felt I could spare the time, I would take a run over to the mill stream to check the water level. That would determine what age group could go that afternoon. If there had been a lot of rain, and the water was too high, it could be dangerous for any but our oldest campers. If it was a dry summer, and there had been no recent rain, I could only go with younger campers. Without the challenge of high water and some current, our older campers would find it a good deal less exciting. Despite my morning reconnaissance, there were times I was fooled.

It was a July day in 1970. We had a lot of rain that summer. The water in Mill Stream was high. My morning inspection told me that the current was strong, but we had a strong group of senior girls, and I was going to have lots of good help with me. Brenda Lichtman, our waterfront director, was coming along as my assistant along with Susan Poster and Lydia Walshin. There would be four of us, and only sixteen girls.

We left our towels, flip flops and sweat shirts hanging from jutting rocks on what had been the back wall of the Mill. The flat rocks where we usually left them were under water. Instead of jumping down into the water, we just stepped off into the paddle wheel area. I was surprised to find myself in chest deep water right from the start. We held hands as we crossed the deep water to the natural rock staircase on the far side. The current was strong, and we had to pull and haul some of the smaller girls across. Brenda brought up the rear. Lydia was next to me, assisting and Susan was in the middle. By the time I got to the far side, I knew I had miscalculated. The current was far stronger than I ever remembered it. But I wasn't going to risk crossing again at this point. I knew that if we could get a little further upstream, it would be narrower and less deep.

These were all good kids. They knew it had been a battle across, and some of them had been scared, but they trusted me to find a safe way out of the stream. They might have felt less confidant if they knew how worried I was. We were on the left side of the stream, and there was a steep granite wall to our left. We would have to cross to the right side to get out of the stream. Once I was sure we had all completed the first crossing, we started our climb upstream against the current. I felt sure it would be safer to climb up than re-cross. Our natural stone staircase, which I usually loved to point out to the kids, was now totally submerged, and I could only describe it to them. Once they felt it under their feet, the campers felt better and started climbing behind me. At the top of those few steps was an enormous flat ledge, where we sometimes sat and rested waiting for the slowest ones in the group to catch up. There was no sitting down this day. The ledge was three feet under water, and the current seemed even stronger there than it had been in the paddle-wheel pool below. This flat ledge was just a few yards downstream from that nice little waterfall where I usually helped kids through and behind the falls. It was not a nice little waterfall that day. It was a raging torrent.

With our outstretched arms around them, we corralled the girls against the stone wall side on the left, out of the strongest current. We had to get out of this somehow. I had to cross it myself and figure out how we should do it. As I started across, the current was so strong it almost knocked me off my feet. Had it succeeded, I would have been thrown down a ten or twelve foot waterfall over jagged rocks and back into the big paddle wheel pool. But I managed to grab a boulder. Putting the boulder between me and the potential falls, I managed my way through the swiftest water, and latched onto an even larger boulder on the far side. It wouldn't be easy, but I was sure we could get the girls across.

I very carefully retraced my steps to join the girls on the other side. I explained my plan to the girls. Then we started. Brenda and I crossed together to the middle boulder. We rested there briefly, and then fought our way to the boulder on the mill side of the stream. Our plan of attack was to have me stationed in the middle of the stream, with my back against the middle boulder. Susan and Lydia, the other two counselors, would alternate edging out into the stream, accompanying campers toward my outpost. I would grab the camper's arm and then pass her along to Brenda, who would grab her outstretched arm on the other side. The girls who crossed would be safe behind the large boulder on the mill side. We had no problem crossing the first three girls. Wendy, Nancy, and Robin were all tall athletic girls. Next in line was Beth Fields, our smallest senior girl. Beth was a wonderfully coordinated girl, and one of our best swimmers. But she was tiny, and had very short arms. Lydia started to help her across. Beth's arm slipped out of Lydia's hands well short of reaching me. I left my rock and reached Beth in time to grab the back of her bathing suit just before she would have been caught by the current and perhaps be swept over the falls. When I got her safely back behind my boulder she was shaking and looked as though she wanted to cry. I didn't dare pass her to Brenda. Holding her tight, we made it across the gap to the right side. Once all of the girls were safely with us on the mill side, we slowly climbed the embankment and reached the safety of the road.

That was the closest call I ever came to losing a camper in an accident, at the mill stream or anywhere else. On my future reconnaissance trips to Mill Stream, if the water looked high, I wasn't satisfied until I tested the current by getting into the water. I was glad I led the group that day. It was my misjudgment that got us into trouble, but I was almost certainly the only one who knew mill stream well enough to have gotten us out unscathed.

Most trips to Mill stream were far more like the ones I experienced as a camper. But, whether they were difficult or easy, the campers never forgot their mill stream walk. For almost every camper, they later marked it as the best thing they did that summer. As for Beth Fields, she came back to camp for years as a campers, later as a counselor and still later as a camp parent when her two boys became campers. In one of my last summers at camp it was my pleasure to have Beth's son Michael, by then all grown up and a fine counselor, join me as my number one assistant on a Mill Stream excursion.

P.S. I showed this story to Beth recently, and she certainly remembered the incident but said "that's not quite the way I remember it." I'm sure her perspective at the time was far different than my own.

33
Accidents Will Happen

We were very safety conscious at camp. We took every imaginable precaution, but, in an environment filled with athletic and adventurous activities, accidents will and do happen. Rarely did a day go by without at least a few cuts, bangs and bruises. I doubt if we ever went through an entire camp season without at least one or two broken arms or legs. Occasionally we had frightening and dramatic accidents. But we had two nurses and an aide staffing our infirmary. They never complained of boredom. In addition, we had a doctor on staff. That was for my peace of mind. The doctors considered it a vacation with pay. (In the majority of cases the pay was tuition scholarships for their camp age children). For me, their presence represented a personal security blanket, but there were many times when they played a far more important role.

Julie T.

It was seven forty-five at night. All of Camp Evergreen was in the gym, playing Human Anagrams. (a game with two or more teams in which every member of the team wears a letter of the alphabet. Each team has a complete alphabet of players, who are seated in order on team benches. Questions are asked, and the first team whose players line up spelling the correct answer wins a point.)

All of the girls were keyed up and excited, less by the human anagrams game than by the expectation that Green and Gold (Color War) could break out any minute. The boys' color war had started that morning. Since the boys' break out the older girls were at a fever pitch of excitement, ready to scream and jump with joy at the very first indication that their anticipated moment had arrived.

Phyllis stood on a chair, megaphone in one hand, clipboard in the other. She was in that position to be seen easily by the players while she judged Human Anagrams. Suddenly the big garage doors at the end of the gym opened. An ice cream truck came partially into the gym, creating an immediate sensation. There was laughter in Phyllis' voice as she announced an ice cream treat for the camp. The youngest girls, easily fooled, started lining up for ice cream. The Seniors, with years of camp experience, were not fooled for a second. As soon as the truck entered, they started screaming and jumping up and down on their benches. The two color war head coaches emerged from the ice cream truck, dressed in their Green and Gold team regalia, and it was official, color war at last!

Julie T., a Juniper Lodge Girl (our oldest cabin of girls), and destined to be a team captain, leaped from her team's anagram bench and came down with her foot twisted at an impossible angle. She collapsed sobbing on the floor. The other campers were so excited by the dramatic start of Green & Gold, nobody noticed poor Julie, writhing in pain on the gym floor.

Finally they saw her, first two or three close friends from her lodge, and then by a growing number. While concerned campers and counselors gathered around her, the Green and Gold team Head Coaches, oblivious to the injury, continued to read the names of the girls on their respective teams. They started with the Senior Team Captains. When Julie's name was announced as captain, the cheering was louder than ever. The tears streaming down Julie's face were caused both by the pain from her fall and the realization that she was going to be a team captain in this, her fifth and last summer as a camper. She didn't know yet that her ankle was broken, that she would spend the entire four days of Green and Gold hobbled by crutches.

Julie was a terrific kid, full of enthusiasm and energy. She soon mastered her crutches, and, though she could not play any of the sports, was out in front of her team on every possible occasion, leading them in songs and cheers and exhorting them to greater and greater effort. Unless you looked down, you would never know that she was handicapped, even a little.

During Green and Gold the girls line up by teams in front of Spruce Lodge before each meal. Then they advance full speed ahead to the dining room, singing and cheering all along the way. Julie, crutches and all, insisted on leading her team in their morale boosting charge to the dining room. On the final day of Green and Gold, rain had put a damper on the morning activities, but it had partially cleared, and the two most important events of the competition were still ahead, the afternoon swim meet and the final song and cheer contest at night.

At lunch time Julie sped ahead of her team to lead them into the dining room. As she raced onto the wet dining room porch, one of her crutches slid out from under her, and she went down with a cry. Her wounded left leg, encased in a cast, was not re-injured by the fall, but she had excruciating pain in her right shin. Her counselors, Leslie and Barbara, carried her to the infirmary. After a thirty second examination, Dr. Siegel, certain she had a break, lifted her into his car, and drove her to the New London Hospital.

They returned to camp mid-afternoon. I knew the result before they returned. Dr. Siegel had called me from the emergency room. I, in turn, had already called her parents.

"Mrs. T., I'm afraid I have some more bad news for you. Julie slipped and fell again." There was silence on the other end. I waited for a question. When none came, I went on. "She has a small crack in the tibia of her right leg." Again there was silence as Mrs. T. absorbed this news.

"How will she get along at camp? She won't be able to use crutches."

"You're right" I said. "She can't get along at camp. We have only three days left in the camp season. It would be very hard for us to carry her around for three days, and we certainly can't put her on the camp bus to go home. I think you and Mr. T. should plan to drive up here, and take her home."

"She'll be distraught if she has to go home."

"I know, but there's really no choice."

"I don't think we can make it all the way to camp to pick her up tonight. We'll start as soon as we can pack a few things, drive as far as we can tonight, and be there first thing tomorrow morning. Will you be able to manage with her tonight?"

"Of course. When she gets back from the hospital, we'll put her in the infirmary, and she'll be safe."

When Julie came back to camp, she had her own ideas. First, she was determined to lead her team in their songs and cheers that night. She was equally determined to stay to the end of the camp season. For the climatic night of Green and Gold we carried her to the Rec Hall, and propped her up on a chair on stage. All of her team-mates were in formations on the floor of the Rec hall. From her perch on stage, she led her team's songs. She didn't miss a beat.

The next morning she begged her parents to let her stay. Finally we reached an agreement. They would remain in the area at a nearby motel, and, if we couldn't manage, or if she had a change of heart, they would pick her up. Otherwise they would wait for the final day, and let her complete her final summer as a camper.

We spent the next three days with various staff members taking turns carrying Julie, from her bunk to the dining room, from the infirmary to the rec hall, and back to the bunk again. I remember giving Julie a piggy back ride down to her bunk, hoping that I would not trip. This poor girl had been through enough.

I imagined myself in her parents' shoes, thinking

"We sent a perfectly healthy young girl to camp for a wonderful healthy summer, and we will be bringing home a cripple. She'll be in a wheelchair for weeks."

Jill A.

I led a group of senior girls on a walk up the Old Mill Stream, a glacial gorge with small waterfalls, areas featuring natural flat stone slides, and an occasional swimming hole. The Mill stream can be a dangerous place. That's why I always brought a lot of help along, including as many of the strongest counselors we could spare from the camp program. It was fortunate that on this trip I had Brenda Lichtman with me. Not only was she strong and very good in the water, but she was fully capable of taking charge of any situation.

We were in the part of the stream where partially submerged rocks were strewn about here and there, as though by a careless giant in a playful mood. I carefully picked our path from rock to rock, as we made our way up stream, and the girls followed single file behind me. Jill, a twelve year old camper, was two places behind me. She started to slip, lost her balance, and fell. She was able to get her hands out in front of her to partially break her fall. With a little luck, she might have just gotten wet, cut a hand, or perhaps sprained a wrist. However, when her hands went down, they partially landed on and then slipped off two wet rocks and down onto the bed of the stream. Her chin met an irregularly angled rock on its sharpest edge.

According to Brenda who was just behind Jill:

"She just fell down and got up. She didn't scream or cry or anything until she saw blood dripping down from her chin. Then she let out a howl, and broke into tears."

I sent a counselor back to the van for the first aid kit. We wiped the blood away, and I was able to look at her wound. It was an ugly jagged gash. There was no question in my mind that she would need stitches. We put on a temporary dressing to stop the frightening flow of blood.

"Jill, I think you and I are going to take a ride to the hospital."

That set her off crying again. She was so scared!

I left Brenda in charge. She would lead the group the rest of the way up the stream without me. Fortunately, we had come to the starting point in two vans, and Brenda would be able to shuttle the girls back to camp in one van when they were through climbing, sliding and swimming.

Jill's counselor, Susan, came with me on the ride to the hospital to comfort Jill along the way. Jill certainly knew her a lot better than she knew me. The New London Hospital was a warm friendly hospital, small enough so that I had come to know most of the doctors who were on staff. The emergency room nurses helped Jill onto a gurney, and wheeled her into a small operating room.

I asked "Can we come in with you when you examine her?

"You can." Then she turned to Susan.

"Young Lady, how old are you?"

"Eighteen."

"I think it will be best if you wait in the waiting room. We'll get word to you as soon as you can rejoin us."

I asked "Is Dr. Clough here today?" Young Dr. Clough was the current Chief of Staff. His father, old Dr. Clough, had taken care of my wounds many years earlier when I was a camper.

"No, but I'll call him. He's in his office, right next door."

The Doctor joined us within ten minutes. He always looked crisp and efficient. His appearance and manner were confidence inspiring.

"Stitches for sure, maybe eight or ten, but I don't want to stitch the face of a twelve year old girl without authorization from her parents. I know their preference will be for a plastic surgeon. You know we don't have one here. The nearest plastic surgeons are in Hanover or Concord. Jill's Mom may want to have the work done in one of those."

I was able to reach Jill's mother. Dr. Clough got on the phone, and apparently convinced her that he was capable of doing a good job. He agreed to go ahead, without written authorization, based on the phone call.

I stood next to the gurney, holding Jill's hand. I don't remember my words, but I was doing my best to distract Jill and myself from the needle that was weaving in and out of Jill's jaw. Dr. Clough's hand moved hardly at all, but the needle moved in and out, in and out, in and out.

I must not have watched very long. The next thing I knew I was on a gurney. I sat up, wondering how I got there. I was in a different room. Jill and the doctor were gone. A nurse came in. I was embarrassed to discover that I was now an emergency room patient, having fainted in the operating room. When I recovered from my chagrin, I remembered Jill.

"How is she?"

"Your little girl is fine. She's sleeping down the hall. As soon as you're able to get up, and feel steady, you can take her back to camp. Dr. Clough finished quite a while ago. He's back in his office now, but he left you a note." She handed me a folded piece of paper.

"Mr. Sharenow, please do not plan to assist in any of our treatment rooms ever again. We can do the job fine without your help."

Jill recovered nicely. Her parents did take her to see a plastic surgeon in New Jersey after the camp season. He was apparently satisfied with Dr. Clough's stitching, and nothing further was done.

Chris S.

Chris, one of our more competitive Kenwood campers, slid into second base on the senior ball field, dislodged the base with his slide, and impaled his leg on the base spike. These base spikes were about a foot long, pointed on the end that goes in the ground and molded into a triangle on the top to fit into a sleeve in the base. About half of the spike had gone clean through his leg. The other half was still attached to the base. His leg looked so awful it was hard to even look at it.

When I heard the news, I drove up to the field with our station wagon. Several counselors helped me lift Chris and the base to which his leg was attached into the wagon. He didn't cry or groan, even when we hit a bump. We lifted him out of the wagon, and carried him into the infirmary. Ben Siegel took one look, and knew He could not do anything except stabilize the leg for a ride to the hospital.

Fortunately the base spike went right through the fleshy part of his calf and did not hit any bones. At the hospital, they were able to remove the spike without any serious damage to his leg. Of course, he had stitches on both sides of his calf, and was well bandaged when he returned to camp. He was a rare boy, wanting to make as little of his mishap as possible. Almost immediately he started playing again, whatever activities the doctors would allow.

From Chris' accident, we learned a new safety lesson. By the following summer we had bases which were secured on sleeves cemented into the ground.

Double Trouble

One summer I received an early evening call from the leader of a hike group that was camping overnight on Mt. Cardigan. Mt. Cardigan was in the town of Canaan, about thirty miles from camp. This was an era before cell phones and light weight Walkie-talkies. There were a few houses on the side of the mountain. In order to make her call, our counselor who called camp had to walk half way down the mountain to one of those houses and then back up to the camp site. Emergency calls from Cardigan were never made casually. One of the Evergreen counselors had badly burned her left hand, while cooking with a hand held grill over an open fire.

I received the call and made the forty-five minute drive to Mt. Cardigan State Park to pick up the injured counselor. She was a twenty year old "veteran" counselor, but during our ride back to camp she was a wounded little girl, whimpering in pain.

I drove her back to camp, and right to the infirmary. While she was being treated, we received another call from the same hike group. Another of the counselors had an allergic reaction to a bee sting. They had treated her with Benadryl, but she was swelling up. I ran into our treatment room where our Camp Doctor, Ben Siegel, was taking care of the girl with the burn.

His first reaction was "I'll go." Then he thought better of it. "If she has a severe reaction, I won't get there in time. She'll need a shot as soon as possible. See what you can do on the phone."

Canaan did not have a hospital. Nor did it have town offices or a regular police force. I called information. Fortunately, the Information Operator lived in Canaan, and knew a local doctor. He agreed to drive to the state park camp site and give the girl a shot if needed.

Meantime, Norm (Kenwood Head Counselor) volunteered to drive to Mt. Cardigan with a replacement Evergreen counselor. When he arrived the local doctor was there and had given the counselor the necessary shot. He was monitoring her recovery, as her swelling went down and her breathing returned to normal. Despite her obvious recovery, she was very happy to call it a day and take the ride back to camp with Norm.

From that point on, not only did our first aid kits have bee sting kits, but prior to any trip leaving camp, the trip leader was instructed in its use, giving practice shots to oranges in the camp infirmary.

Accidents were not our only medical concerns. We also dealt with illness on a regular basis. Most illnesses were not serious, but sometimes they also produced a crisis of sorts. There was the year a boy came up to camp on the New York bus with a case of Chicken Pox. Ten days later we had a busload of boys with chicken pox. Several days after, that one third of the camp was in itchy agony. We had so many kids in the infirmary with chicken pox that when the photographer came to take our once a year all camp picture, we also had him take a separate all infirmary picture. Perhaps the most dramatic of our illnesses through the years was caused by a visit from Sam and Ella.

Sam & Ella
"I'm feeling fine, Mom. I'm fine. Yes, we know all about it. Dr. Ben explained it to the whole camp yesterday. I'll tell you what he said. He told us "Sam and Ella came to camp, and made everyone have to poop alot and throw up. He said if we are careful and wash our hands every time we go to the bathroom Sam and Ella will go away, and leave us alone. I hate it when I feel like throwing up so I'm washing my hands every chance I get."

It was all my Father's fault. I didn't really want to hear about what Camp Woodlands fed their campers' parents on their Visiting Weekend. I was tired of hearing about Camp Woodlands and Camp Brunonia and Camp Kohut, and every other camp where he knew the directors. I knew he was only trying to help, but sometimes his help was annoying. He knew that Woodlands was a more expensive camp than ours. They charged almost a thousand dollars. Our tuition was six hundred. They could afford to be generous.

It was Visitor's Sunday, 1960, my first summer as a camp director. Ken Huberman, from whom I had bought the camp, was still with me as my guide and mentor. That first summer we did everything just about the way he had always done it. My Dad had come to camp to share our first Visitors' Weekend experience with Judy and me as directors. Afternoon activities were about to start, and a couple of hundred wilted parents came staggering out of the sweltering hot dining room, having just consumed an enormous roast beef dinner. They waddled off in the direction of their camper's next scheduled activity.

"Arthur, it's not a matter of generosity, its good public relations. The Parents go home from their visiting days raving about Woodlands and their wonderful director. Just listen for a minute. Let me tell you what they do. Instead of charging the parents for a big sit down roast beef dinner, they give them a box lunch with fried chicken, fruit, rolls, a tomato and a hard boiled egg. The families take their box lunches, and the whole family has a picnic lunch together. They sit at the waterfront or under a big tree, and they have a lovely time. Then the kids go back to their bunks for rest periods, and the parents go to the dining room for coffee or cold drinks. Think about it!

I did think about it, and after one more summer with overheated parents paying for a sit down three course roast beef dinner, I made the switch. He was right. We gave them a fried chicken box lunch, and they loved it. There were some logistical rough spots the first summer or two after we made the switch, but when we perfected the system, I was sure we had solved the issue of lunch on Visitors Day forever. For years we had our fried chicken box lunches, and for years they helped to create a warm and friendly atmosphere on Visitors Day. And then one sunny Sunday in the early 1980s Sam and Ella came for a visit.

Preparing fried chicken for dinner as a regular part of our camp menu was relatively simple in the 1960s. After all, we were only feeding a hundred fifty campers and another seventy-five or so staff members. It presented a larger challenge for our kitchen staff on Visitors Day. On that day three hundred parents came to visit our one hundred fifty campers. So, instead of preparing chicken for two hundred twenty-five or two hundred fifty people, our chef and kitchen staff had to manufacture that same meal for five hundred fifty people. They couldn't do the whole job by only preparing on Sunday morning. The chicken had to be cleaned, cut into quarters, set out on baking trays and refrigerated awaiting the great Sunday morning assembly line. Days had been spent folding boxes and assembling the other ingredients. But Sunday was chicken day. Tray after tray of cut up chickens emerged from our jam packed refrigerators, waited as briefly as possible on racks, went into the fryalators, next into cake boxes, and then back in the refrigerator, awaiting the noon time invasion of hungry campers, parents and counselors.

As our camper population slowly grew over the two hundred mark, our staff numbers increased disproportionately, and by the late seventies we were feeding three hundred fifty people every meal. When we added six hundred parents, grand parents, aunts and uncles on visiting day, our kitchen now needed to turn out about a thousand perfect fried chicken box lunches. They all had to be ready and picked up within a one half hour time span.

When and how did salmonella infect our food? It was very hot that Sunday morning. Our kitchen must have been like an oven. Did it happen while the chicken was being cut up a couple of days earlier? Or was the raw chicken allowed to sit out too long on Sunday morning before they went into the fryalators? Or perhaps they sat out too long after they were fried. Or were they just not cooked enough in the rush to get them all prepared? Or had we received a shipment of tainted chicken from our meat supplier? I'll never know.

Visitors Day started beautifully that day. We were in the midst of an outstanding camp season, with relatively few serious camper problems, many exceptional counselors and a long helpful run of good weather. All I heard from the parents that morning in my walks around camp were rave reviews and congratulations on the wonderful camp I ran. Lunch was a big success. It was followed by more happy comments. At four thirty we started saying goodbye to our visiting parents, and by five o'clock the camp belonged to the campers and staff once again. As always, when I said goodbye to the last set of parents, I breathed a sigh of relief. I didn't have an inkling of the storm to follow.

"Arthur, Mrs. Green's on the phone. She's calling from the hospital in Concord. She sounds very upset." I went into my inner office, and picked up my phone.

"Hello, Mrs. Green, what can I do for you? Is anything wrong?"

"I'm sick. My husband is sick. We're both throwing up. Before it hit us, I saw other campers' parents pulled over on the side of the highway throwing up. The doctor here says it must be Salmonella. It had to be that fried chicken. I have to go now. I think I'm about to vomit again."

That was the beginning. A few minutes later I got a call from our nurse.

"Arthur, I've got fifteen or so kids here, all throwing up, and feeling very sick."

"Ingrid, it sounds like we have a major problem. Be prepared. There'll be more. Is Ben up there yet?"

"No, I haven't seen him since after lunch."

Visitors Day was also our doctor changeover day, when we said goodbye to our July doctor, and welcomed our August doctor. Ben and his family were probably unpacking, and getting settled in their cabin, Ben Siegel was head of pediatrics at Boston City Hospital and was our August doctor from 1970 through 1994. We were blessed to have him at camp. He helped us through several difficult times over that long time span. The salmonella crisis, in the mid 1980s, was one of those time, and, if there was anyone I could rely upon in such a crisis, it was our Dr. Ben.

We kept getting calls from parents all through that late afternoon and evening. The calls resumed the next morning. The infirmary was bombarded with sick campers and counselors coming in through the night. After a while, despite constant floor mopping and bathroom cleanups, the smell was pretty disgusting in there. Dr. Ben served as telephone liaison with sick parents, helped me frame a letter to all of our camper parents, and, with our nurses, helped set up a viable system for dealing with the growing numbers of sick kids. It was that Monday afternoon that we called an all-camp meeting, and Dr. Ben briefed the campers and counselors on our salmonella related illness, and how to deal with it. This was the meeting that introduced the campers to "Sam and Ella." Despite the seriousness of the occasion, there were some good laugh lines during Dr. Ben's discussion of "poop" and "puke," and the importance of prevention.

He was also the one who informed me that, by law, we were required to notify the New Hampshire Health Department. The Health Department inspectors came in on Tuesday, inspected our kitchen, and gave us a list of things to correct. In fact, as part of the camp licensing procedures, we were inspected annually by the state health department. They never had found anything wrong in our kitchen before or since, but that day, the very same inspector who had told me the previous year that we had one of the very best camp kitchens, now found a dozen things that needed correcting, things that were exactly as they had been when he inspected us the previous summer. I'm not sure what caused the salmonella outbreak, but I'm reasonably sure it was none of the items we were told to correct. We had a two week deadline in which to make the required physical changes. They were completed in less than forty-eight hours.

Our camp gastrointestinal issues seemed to be contagious, and bounced back and forth around camp during the final three weeks of the season. Fortunately, none of our campers or staff members was sick for more than a few days. That was the good news. The bad news, other than people getting sick, was the public relations disaster. It is always bad from a public relations standpoint when anything bad happens at camp. Visitors Day is the time when anything and everything that does happen at camp is subject to parental microscopes. That is when we are on higher state of alert to make sure that nothing goes wrong. Our entire staff is thoroughly briefed before the weekend and presumably at their very best. Bad things are not supposed to happen then. Not only did we have a bad happening, but we had a health issue that impacted many parents directly. I don't know how many parents got sick that day and in the days that followed, but it was a significant number. Most were only mildly ill, but a few became sick enough to require short hospital stays.

As soon as we realized we had such a calamity on our hands, I sent out a letter to all of the parents, telling them what happened, and outlining the steps we were taking to care for their children. After the letter was sent we received a new round of phone calls, this time from parents who were feeling fine and hadn't had a clue that there was a problem.

Almost everything at camp eventually makes its way into our end of the season Color War comic songs. Our counselor song writers had a ball with this one. However, their song writing time period came before the most bizarre post salmonella scene. The last night of camp we have our annual boys' banquet. By that time we still had lots of kids with residual stomach upsets. But everyone made it to the banquet, even our sickies.

Our final banquet usually has the a time sequence that goes like this: Assembly and flag lowering is followed by dinner, and then we take a brief break so that the tables can be cleared. After that we all return to the dining room for speeches, awards, songs and cheers. On that summer there was one slight alteration. After dinner, rather than the usual break, we had what came to be known as a "Barfarama." I told everyone who was feeling ill to go outside, get some air and do what they had to do. Our semi-circular assembly area, which was right outside the dining room, was surrounded by a waist high railing. When I went out to see what was going on, the scene that greeted me was a well populated semi-circle of boys leaning over the railing, ridding themselves of their entire dinner. After the break we all went back into the dining room, and completed the banquet program. That night will be remembered by all who attended as the Barfarama banquet.

34
Underdogs

In 1970 Camp Winaukee was the athletic powerhouse among the boys' camps in the area, as it had been for the past decade and would continue to be for decades to come. From the perspective of Camp Kenwood, with our eighty-eight boys, Winaukee, with more than three hundred campers, appeared as a colossus. Through the years we had a friendly working arrangement with the Winaukee administration, our boys playing against theirs in a variety of sports in most age groups. We would play our best athletes in each sport and Winaukee would get the chance to give their less skilled athletes some intercamp competition. Our arrangement served both camps well.

But, when it came time for The Dartmouth Tournament, all bets were off. Regardless of camp size, each camp presented its very best softball team of thirteen to fifteen year old boys. This was one of the highlights of the season for the oldest boys in all of the camps involved.

The tournament, jointly sponsored by Dartmouth College, the Hanover, NH Chamber of Commerce and the participating camps, had originally been played on the town green in the middle of Hanover. Somehow it added to the challenge and romance of the tournament to play on fields set among birch, oak and maple trees. It worked well in the earliest years with only a few camps participating, and one game being played at a time. But by 1970, with sixteen camps in a double elimination tournament, and the need to play three or four games at a time, the games had long since moved to the more professional expanse of the Dartmouth College athletic fields.

We actually had a good little senior softball team that year, and they surprised me, their coaches and even themselves by getting through three rounds, and making it to the semi-finals. Our opponent in the semi-finals was Camp Winaukee. All eighteen of our Senior boys were there to cheer on the team. A few Kenwood and Evergreen counselors on days off had also trekked north to Hanover to watch the second and final day of the tournament. As it happened that week was Visiting Week at Winaukee, and the parents of many of the boys on their team, came to watch the games. In addition to the boys on their team, Winaukee brought an additional hundred campers and it seemed at least that many parents to watch the games. Their parents came with lawn chairs and blankets, setting up impromptu cheering sections along both base lines and even right behind our team bench. They were the only team with an actual cheering section.

Our boys were very nervous, but tried hard not to show it. The Winaukee team got on the field for practice first. I watched them warm up. They looked great. They were all big, between five foot seven and five foot ten, dressed in blue and gold softball uniforms. Their practice was snappy and flawless.

When our boys ran onto the field for their brief practice several badly mannered Winaukee parents snickered and made audible and disparaging comments to one another about our kids. Our boys were small and seemed even smaller in comparison with the Winaukee players who had just left the field. Only Tommy Lakaso, a draftee from our Junior unit and our only long ball hitter, was near the size of any of their kids. On our team we had Mark Teschner playing second base. Mark had been born with a congenital hip problem, and walked and ran with a lopsided uneven gait. It was tempting to look at Mark, and wonder how he could play at all. What didn't show on the outside was his indomitable spirit. Nor could a first look give the viewer a clue as to the hours, days and weeks of effort it had taken Mark to develop compensating athletic skills. Tommy and Jimmy Reigart, both infielders, were tiny for their ages. Bobby Terk, our catcher, another highly motivated and determined kid, was not much bigger than the Reigarts. Danny Sommer at third base and Alan Herscott who played left field were normal size for their age, but would have looked small on the Winaukee team. It didn't look like a fair match. It looked like our boys playing against their men.

Before the start of the game some of their parents were joking in stage whispers among themselves on the final score of the mis-match to come. I heard them and so did our kids. Their most "generous" estimate was 7-0, but I heard scores ranging as high as 17-2. The Winaukee fans were still chuckling when our kids came up to bat in the first inning. The first inning didn't go quite the way they thought it would. Our leadoff batter beat out a bunt, went to third on an infield out and scored on a sacrifice bunt. Their boys went down one, two, three. At the end of one inning it was 1-0 Kenwood. The score remained that way until the fifth inning. Their boys were hitting the ball hard, but our kids were playing the game of their lives in the field, making plays they had never made before. Nobody was laughing any more. The Winaukee players were shocked at their inability to break the game open. Their parents looked on with disbelief in their eyes. Winaukee tied the game in the last of the fith. The score stood 1-1 through the sixth. In the last of the seventh, Winakuee pushed across a final run, and won the game 2-1.

After the game the two teams, following tradition, cheered one another. But then the Winaukee boys came over to shake our boys hands, and tell them what a wonderful game they played. It was a rare and tender moment for the boys on both teams.

After playing us, the Winaukee team went on to win the championship, battering another camp team, one a little closer to its own size, by a score of fifteen to two.

Our boys were knocked out of the tournament, but they were so proud of themselves. For those boys, it was a day to remember, and I'm sure they do, all of these years later. It wasn't until the late 1970's that Kenwood was able to produce an honestly competitive team that could play Winaukee or anyone else on even terms. But the memory of that undersized 1970 team has a special place in my heart.

35
Tantrums

Isaac was quite a difficult camper, contentious in every phase of camp life. His counselors could never assume that Isaac would go along with a proposed activity, unless it was baseball. He was also hot headed, argumentative, and, seethed with barely restrained violence. Normally he would have been a candidate for an early ticket home. Perhaps this would have been the case had his father not been dying of cancer. A promise had been made to his mother that he would stay in camp for the summer.

We knew that Isaac would present challenges before he ever arrived at camp. His mother warned us about his moods and his tantrums. In a misguided attempt to do the best we could for him, we assigned Dick R. as his bunk's counselor. Dick was a Psychology major at an Ivy League school. He understood the circumstances, and was eager to help this troubled boy whose family was experiencing such pain.

One day we inexplicably lost water pressure all over camp. It was free play time, and there was no extra usage to explain the pressure loss. Several of us took a quick tour of camp, looking for a telltale puddle which might signal a break in an underground water pipe. None appeared. The answer was found just outside the pump house. The plastic pipe that came out of the back of the building was cleanly cut. Ansel, our maintenance man, had gone home for the day, but came right back when I called. In short order he was able to splice in a new pipe, and we were back in business. That line did not just break. It had been cut by somebody who lived in camp. Isaac immediately became our number one suspect. We questioned him, and he professed total ignorance. We're not sure how he ever got possession of one of the knives from the camp kitchen, but, several days later, during a "Camper Hunt", one of those knives was found by a camper hiding under Isaac's bunk.

I watched Isaac at activities. It was not unusual to see him slam his tennis racket onto the court after a missed shot or, become so frustrated that he smacked the ball over the fence and into the lake. Nor was it surprising to see and hear him explode into profanity at a partner's missed shot. I saw him rage in tetherball games, kick shins rather than the ball in soccer, and whip the ball at opponents' heads in Bombardment. Very frequently his counselor Dick would have to remove him from activities to give him time to cool off. I'd see the two of them sitting in a shady place discussing the behavior that had caused his current removal. Sometimes, after a short time, he was allowed to rejoin the activity.

Isaac was a very good baseball player, and would have happily played ball all day long had he been given the opportunity. Though he was only in the Intermediate unit, he tried out for and made our Little League Team. He was the only one in his age group to make that team. That being the case, he was playing with an older group whose boys didn't know him well, and with counselors who knew of Issac by reputation, but had never had to deal directly with his tantrums. It didn't take the Junior Unit counselors who worked with the team long to understand and appreciate the stories they had heard. But he was not denied a place on the team. He had earned it though his play. He was one of the best ball players in Junior Camp.

One day, mid-season, our Little League team was playing Camp Tomahawk. Isaac was pitching for Kenwood. The Tomahawk kids couldn't catch up with his fastball, but he constantly had runners on base. They reached base through walks. Isaac was getting more and more upset with our counselor/umpire.

"That was a strike...What was wrong with that one...You're so busy being fair to them that you're not being fair to me." On and on it went. Finally the umpire had enough of Isaac's scowls and complaints. He went out to the mound.

"Kid, you do the pitching. I'll do the umpiring. Your pitches are not always perfect, and my umpiring may not be perfect either, but, just like you, I'm doing the best I can. So stop complaining. If you don't stop complaining, I'm going to have to remove you from of the game. Do you understand?"

Isaac grunted, but nodded yes.

The next batter bunted toward first base. The first baseman went for the ball, and Isaac ran over to cover the base, but stopped just short of first. When the runner came down the baseline, Isaac stuck his foot out, and tripped him. The Tomahawk kid fell, Isaac covered first, took the throw and the runner was out. But everybody who was there saw the trip. The umpire yelled "Safe". He then walked out to the mound, and told Isaac he was out of the game.

Isaac threw his glove down on the mound, ran off the field, out the path that formed the entrance into the field, up the main camp driveway, across Eagle Pond Road, and into the woods on the other side of the road. As it happened, Isaac's counselor and whole bunk were there to see his explosion. Dick had brought them over to see Isaac pitch. He wanted them to see their bunk-mate, Isaac, in a positive role since he was so often just a pain in the rear as far as the other kids were concerned. Obviously things didn't work quite the way Dick planned. But it was fortunate that he was there.

Dick turned his boys over to another counselor and chased Issac out the ball field path and up the camp road. When he got to the top of the camp road, he could see Isaac in the woods on the far side of Eagle Pond Road, and called to him.

"Isaac, stop running. I want to talk to you."

"I don't wanna talk to anyone. That umpire stinks. It's not fair."

"It doesn't matter if the umpire stinks or not. You shouldn't have tripped that kid."

"I didn't trip him. He just fell over to get me in trouble.

"Isaac, I saw you trip him."

"He fell."

They were yelling back and forth across the road when I came on the scene. As soon as he saw me, Isaac retreated further into the woods.

"Isaac, you don't have to keep running. We're not going to chase you in there."

He stopped again, listening for what I would say. But I had nothing further to say to him. It was his counselor I had to talk to. Dick filled me in on the crisis that precipitated Isaac's run.

"Don't follow him into the woods. Go sit on one of those boulders by the edge of the road. Then he'll understand that you have no intention of chasing him. Just keep him talking. He'll eventually calm down. After a while, see if you can talk him back across the road. Assure him that nobody's angry with him, and that he won't be punished. Meanwhile I'll send one of the JCs (Junior Counselors) up here to stand by in case he decides to run down the road. If he does that, we have no choice. We have to chase him and stop him. We can't let him run into danger.

Isaac and Dick sat on opposite sides of the road for a long time. The game against Tomahawk ended. The visiting team went home and ours went down to the waterfront for a quick swim. Isaac and Dick sat, occasionally talking, but mostly just sitting. The bugle call sounded. It was time for dinner. We assembled for flag lowering. From the assembly area at the top of the hill, I could barely see Isaac and Dick, still sitting on opposite sides of the road. The camp went in for dinner. A Junior Counselor delivered plates of food to the road. Dick gobbled his food down. Isaac's plate was placed on a boulder at the edge of the far side of the road. Eventually he came forward through the woods, picked up his plate, and started to eat.

Dick called out again.

"Isaac. Come on over here, and we can eat together. I'm not mad at you. Nobody's mad at you."

Isaac brought his plate over, and they sat eating quietly. After they finished the food, Dick put his arm around Isaac's shoulder, and they walked back to the bunk together. This crisis was over.

There were several more incidents before the end of the camp season, but somehow we and Isaac managed to get through the summer. Ultimately, the only victim was his counselor Dick, who left camp a week before the end of the season. His nerves were shot, and he felt he just had to get away or he might snap and do something we would all regret

Isaac's Father died a few weeks after the end of the camp season.

36
Disappearing Act

I referred to my map. I read my directions over for the third time. Puzzled, I pulled over to the side of the road. I knew this was the third time I had come to the very same rotary. The Schwartz house was simply not where Mrs. Schwartz's directions indicated. I was sweating with anxiety. I've always been compulsive about time, and our appointed time had come and gone five minutes earlier. I would have been a little early had I had found her house. There was a big old resort Hotel standing where I thought her house should be. It was one of those wonderful rambling old places with a wrap around front porch complete with a series of rocking chairs.

"I'll just have to drive up to the hotel and ask. Somebody around here must know where they live."

It seemed unusually quiet as I walked up the wooden staircase and onto the porch. There were plenty of lights on inside, but no sounds of movement. I listened at the door for a moment, and then pushed the doorbell. I heard the chimes inside. Almost immediately the door opened and a woman stood there, a broad smile on her face, beckoning me to come in. It was then I realized I had arrived. I knew they were rich, but I couldn't believe anybody actually lived in a place that big.

"Welcome, Mr. Sharenow, I'm Zelda Schwartz. I'm glad you found us. You're very prompt. Some people seem to have an awful time finding us since we moved here from Radnor. I can't think why. The directions are as clear as I can make them."

"It would have been a little clearer had you mentioned that your house was the size of a Hotel." That's what I thought. What I said was "I did go by the house once, but as soon as I came to the rotary, I knew I must have just missed your driveway." The interior was intimidating not only because of its vastness, but because it was spectacular. I felt as though I was entering a museum. Mrs. Schwartz led me into a rather normal size room, filled with normal children and a rather normal looking husband.

After that it was quite a positive camp interview. The two little girls, Sarah and Julie, seemed very well behaved and unusually polite. They were enthusiastic about everything. They said they loved every activity slide I showed them.

They were excited when they recognized their cousins at play in some of my pictures. Their little sister Doris wanted to come too, but she was younger than our youngest campers. Her mother told her she would have to wait at least one more year. The parents, Conrad and Zelda, seemed pre-sold. Their relatives had been sending their children to our camp for years, and were so enthusiastic that the only thing I could possibly do there that night was kill a sale. Happily I didn't.

After refreshments were served, and the children were whisked off to bed by Zelda, I learned a lot more about the Schwartz family. Conrad was the owner of the largest Cadillac Dealership in the Philadelphia area. He had season box seats for all of the Phillies' games and two floor seats for the Seventy-Sixers. He and older two girls had been to a World Series, the NBA playoffs and every other prime sporting event in Philadelphia for the past three years. It was clear to me he was boasting a little, but I was impressed.

Before our formal goodbyes Conrad took me on a tour of the house. It was not our typical camper's home. Beyond the Den, he took me through the living room, the kind of room I didn't think existed anywhere but in the movies. My quick impression was of acres of a plush green carpet, several conversational groupings of solid looking furniture and huge oil paintings on the walls, the kind that looked like old masters.

On the far side of the living room he swung open double doors, and turned on the lights. Down three steps and we walked into a truly grand ball room, complete with crystal chandeliers, wall sconces and a raised platform at one end for the musicians. I felt like a tourist visiting a strange new planet. I almost expected to see the Von Trapp family suddenly appear.

"Would you like to see the pool?"

"Yes, of course." I think my mouth must have dropped open. We took the elevator down, and there it was, the first pool I had ever seen inside a private home.

"Wow, that's incredible! Your kids must be great swimmers."

"Yes, they are all quite good. They should be. They've been in the pool since they were practically babies."

I was properly impressed. I wondered how their children would make out in our rather rustic camp. When Sarah and Julie came to camp that summer they didn't appear to be spoiled at all. They were good kids, cooperative and enthusiastic about everything. Their third summer, they were joined in camp by little sister Doris. She too fit right in, and was a very happy addition to camp.

The call came a few days before camp was due to open. The counselors were arriving that day for the start of Orientation Period. The caller had an upper class British accent.

"Mr. Sharenow, my name is Cynthia Breen, I'm calling for Mr. Conrad Schwartz."

"Yes, is everything all right?" I was immediately concerned that one of the children was sick or had broken an arm or leg and wouldn't be coming to camp.

"Everything is fine, Sir. I'm just calling to see if you received Mr. Schwartz's check for the children."

"Yes, it came yesterday. Please tell him it arrived safely, and say thanks for me."

"I'm afraid there has been a little mix up, and the bank draft was drawn on the wrong account. Would you mind terribly checking to see if it was deposited yet?"

I called down to the house, where Judy was preparing to go out for some errands, which would include a bank deposit.

"We're in luck. She hasn't deposited it yet."

"Please put it in an envelope, and send it back to Mr. Schwartz's office. I'll issue you another on the correct account today. I'm awfully sorry to put you to this trouble. I'm in a bit of a bind. I'm the one who prepares checks for him to sign, and it appears that I wrote your check on the wrong bank account. He signed it without looking, and we sent it off to you."

"No problem" I said, but I was concerned. This was odd, and that was important money. We didn't have very many families who could afford to send three children to camp. It was a lot of money.

Ten days into camp it occurred to me that the replacement check had not arrived. I made several calls to the house. The home phone rang and rang, but was never answered. I tried his office next. This time, when the phone was answered, the upper class British voice of my previous conversation was replaced by a hard boiled Brooklyn accent.

"Mr. Schwartz's pretty busy these days, but I'll see if I can raise him." There was a period of silence. Then she came back on. "What'd you say your name was?"

I told her again. The line became silent. The next sound I heard was a click and then dial tone. She hung up. I dialed again. There was no answer this time.

On Visitors' Day I got the story from other camper parents who lived in the Greater Philadelphia area.

"I see the Schwartz kids are still here. I hope you got your money before he left town. It's been all over the News, on all the channels. The police are after him. He skipped town with deposits from hundreds of customers. The place is closed now."

I felt sick. We could ill afford to lose forty-five hundred dollars. I was angry at myself for sending the check back, but, I reasoned, it probably would have bounced anyway. I had no trouble making a decision about his children. They hadn't cheated me. He did. I wouldn't say a word to them. They were our campers and had to be protected. They'd finish out their summer as campers. When the camp season was over, that would be time enough for them to face some major changes in their lives, not the least of which was the humiliating reality that their father was a pariah and apparently even a fugitive.

37
Special Events

Most campers enjoy most camp activities, and are happy to do them day in and day out. Many can and will enjoy the similar programming day after day, week after week, and even year after year. But all campers are not created equal. There is a significant minority who never achieve success or satisfaction in many traditional camp activities. To create a program, whose goal is to satisfy the needs of all, requires imagination and a willingness to experiment.

At the end of our very difficult 1969 camp season I knew we had to make a lot of changes. I credit Brenda Lichtman, our waterfront director, whose remarks late in the 1969 camp season made an impression on me and inspired me to rethink our program.

"Arthur," she said "you run a good camp, but if I was a camper, I wouldn't keep coming back year after year. I'd be bored. The program looks a little different from week to week, but basically it is always the same. And from what the kids have told me, after they've been here a few summers, the only surprise they have to look forward to is how you'll break Color War. You've got to do new things and change the pace." It was her challenge that got me going.

I resolved that from that time on there would be something new every summer; some event or activity that nobody had ever seen, at least not in our camp. Year after year I came to love the creative process, but I didn't realize when I started just how challenging the task of annually producing new programs and activities would get to be a few decades down the line. I invented, improvised and appropriated (ie. borrowed? stole?) games and ideas from every available source.

I introduced our first new events and activities in 1970 and didn't find the well of ideas running dry until the mid1990s. I continued to work at creating new programs in those later years, but I couldn't fool myself. I realized I was no longer creating, just reworking old ones. That was one of the clues that told me it was time to think about selling, and turning the camp over to somebody with a new perspective and a younger mind. But I had lots of fun in the meantime.

Our special events became the things our campers wrote home about; the things they bragged about when boasting about camp to their friends at home. Creating them became my thing. Within just a few years our camp became well known within the camping industry for our unusual all-camp activities. I love special events. As they evolved they served our camp wonderfully well in many important ways.

First and most importantly, they provided a series of needed breaks in camp program. By definition, they took our camp and campers out of the normal routine of daily activities, and immersed them in a different atmosphere and a somewhat different camp world. Second, it was my intention to create activities that would provide the less gifted athletes among our campers not only with a less pressured situation, but with an actual chance to shine. Many of these creations emphasized using the brain as least as much as the body.

It was a delight to observe the psychological boost they provided for some of our less likely stars. It gave me a thrill to see an undersized twelve year old boy, who would probably never succeed in hitting a baseball, have half of the camp stand up and cheer him because he won the spelling bee for his team. How great it must have felt for that socially awkward fifteen year girl to be surrounded by her team-mates and pounded on the back because her insightful rebuttal won the debate for her team.

Special Events are great for other reasons too. Though our boys and girls do many of the same activities, they do them on a single sex basis. I personally have never believed in coed sports. I don't think they are good for either boys or girls. However, our Special Events are almost all coed. They provide a way for boys and girls to get to know one another in a far less pressured situation than at formal "socials" or dances. What a lovely thing it was to give them these opportunities to interact with one another without pressure to become part of a couple.

Special Events also provided a break for our counselors, giving them a chance to play different roles in camp than they did on a daily basis. Our most experienced counselors took on the role of Judges or referees, while the leadership roles went to our most promising younger counselors. They were given the opportunity to take responsibility for a whole team. They really enjoyed frantic preparation for costumed skits where they would play starring roles as characters in our "break-outs." Kids loved and looked forward to the "break outs."

It also gave them a chance to get to know campers from all parts of camp rather than just the campers they worked with on a daily basis.

When I started "inventing" and "creating" I actually did create some activities from somewhere deep inside a convoluted portion of my mind ... a concept would come to me while lying in bed at night, and I would spend the next day trying to transform that concept into an activity or a program. I remember one completely sleepless night in the middle of the Winter when the idea came to me to create an obstacle course where campers would be challenged by the need to demonstrate skills rather than obstacles. How to create this to give all of the campers a chance to succeed was what drove me crazy. Ultimately it resulted in an activity that I called "Decathalon" with twenty-two events. I made a fairly simple rotation schedule which allowed every camper to go through the entire course, participating in as many or as few of the events as they felt comfortable trying. Frequently, my creations came about by borrowing disparate elements from books, from activities I heard about at other camps, or from our own past activities and combing them into a brand new event. The "New Games" movement was a bonanza for me. I borrowed and reworked ideas from the New Games books shamelessly.

Over the years I created a whole raft of "Special Events", some for a weekend, some for a day, several for a few hours, and lots for Evenings Activities. Among these were names like Super Sleuth Day, Clue, Monopoly, Oddlympics, Anything Goes, Revolutionary War, and Battle of the Wits. Descriptions of these can be found on this book's web page.

38
Work Week

Every camp season started with "Work Week", a full seven days of labor that preceded Counselor Orientation Period. Our work week laborers were counselors, who had accepted my invitation to come to camp a week early, earn extra money, and help get the camp in shape. It was one of the most crucial weeks in the entire camp calendar.

Our full time maintenance staff was responsible for construction projects and repairs on buildings, as well as major landscaping. We also had professionals to do the heavy duty cleaning of cabins, dining room, infirmary and recreation hall. I gave myself and my crew of amateur laborers the less skilled jobs. We installed docks at both waterfronts, resurfaced tennis courts, mowed ball fields, hauled athletic equipment out of storage and into position, moved the right numbers of beds from cabin to cabin, and received incoming deliveries. There was "no tomorrow" on any of these jobs. Whether I had a crew of strong workers or cream puffs, whether it was sunny and beautiful or rainy and dismal, somehow these jobs had to be completed that week.

Work week was all mine, and I loved it. Judy was home in Lexington with our kids during the years they were still in school. Even after our children no longer lived at home, she was never quite ready to make the move to camp the first day of work week. Nor were our Head Counselors. They had teaching jobs, and weren't free that early. The first few days of the week it was just me and my hearty group. Work week signaled the start of the real camp season, the fun season. I considered the things I did the rest of the year as actual work, things like enrolling campers and hiring staff. By contrast, the summer was the payoff. It was challenging. It was exciting. It was often frustrating, but it was never routine. Work week was the start of that excitement. The spirit and sense of community that united our counselor workers was a wonderful part of the week.

During work week I worked side by side with our counselors and discovered them as human beings. We worked together, sweated it out together, and collapsed together by late afternoon. I enjoyed the banter at mealtimes. I even enjoyed comparing my own aches and pains with those of my amateur laborers, most of whom were upper middle class kids, whose previous experience with physical effort had been confined to sports. On the other hand, they were both younger and in better shape than I was when the week started.

It never ceased to amaze me that the same counselors who were ready to drop with exhaustion by four o'clock in the afternoon were completely revived and filled with energy after supper. They would leave the dining room and run to the ball field to hit fly balls or play a pick up softball game. Some would dash over to our gym and play basketball. After that, they would shower and head out of camp for whatever outside entertainment they could find in our little deserted corner of the universe. For me, the therapeutic highlight of each day was my late afternoon shower, after which my ever aging body demanded a complete cessation of physical activity.

Every morning at breakfast I would read off the job assignments I had carefully worked out the night before, and then we negotiated. We all sat around the big kitchen serving table, eating and talking.

Conversation at lunch was always livelier than at breakfast. The mail and newspapers were on the table when we got to the kitchen. The boys grabbed the sports pages. The big sports news was the phenomenal free agent contract signing of Catfish Hunter by the New York Yankees. He was being given an incredible million and a half dollars for each of three years.

Fred Offenberg piped up. "You know, Arthur, I haven't signed my contract for the summer yet. I'll settle right now for a modest raise to two hundred thousand. (His salary for the summer was $400.) You think you can swing that?"

"Why don't you try Camp Winaukee. They're richer than we are. I'll give you a good reference." We went back and forth on that and other equally important conversations through the rest of the meal.

There were lots of funny moments during the many years of work week. Some I remember fondly.

A choice work week job was always putting the docks together. There were many aspects to this job, but the crucial skill job when the various sections were in position was bolting the docks together. This was done in an excruciatingly awkward manner, with two of us lying on opposite docks, one with a hammer and wrench, and the other with two bolts, four giant washers, two lock washers, two nuts and a socket wrench. It was an exceedingly difficult operation every time we did it, and on windy days even more so. One summer in the 1980s, I was in the midst of this operation, and Scott Brody was my partner on the other end of the bolts. Needless to say, the wind was strong that day, making it tough just to hold the docks together, never mind actually bolting them together. Scott was good with tools, but an hour earlier had dropped and lost one adjustable wrench. We replaced that wrench with the last one we had. As we got to the crucial point in the operation I said to Scott … "Okay, Scott, it's all up to you. Drop it and you die." That was a prescription for failure. Within seconds the wrench slipped out of his hands, and descended rapidly into the muck twelve feet below. We looked at each other and burst out laughing. Several years later, when Scott bought the camp from me, we were still laughing about "drop it and you die."

****

Then there was the night we moved the piano…. We needed a new old piano for Hemlock Lodge. A large family of mice had made its home among the felt pads that strike the piano wires. Unfortunately, that family had eaten much of its winter bed on its road to starvation. The result was the need for a new old piano. We never bought a new piano for the girls' lodges. Between the mice, the dampness and the winter freeze fine pianos didn't stand a chance.

I saw the ad in the Concord Monitor. "Upright piano in perfect condition" Bristol, NH (768-3333).

"What do you say, Boys. Who will come with me to pick up the piano tonight after supper? The piano is in Bristol. After we load it on the truck we'll go get some ice cream. I'll need at least three of you plus myself. "

I had a great crew that year, and they all decided to come. There were eleven of them plus me. We all piled into Ansel's pickup truck, nine of them sitting in the bed of the truck and two up front with me. When we got to the house I thought it best if I knocked and stood at the door alone. I didn't want to frighten the poor woman to death.

A nice Yankee lady came to the door, tall and spindly with tight white hair and sparkle in her dark eyes. "Let me show you where it is. We've had this piano forever, but I remember they had a hard time getting it in."

The front hall was about eight feet square. She led the way through a narrow door on the right into a kind of sitting room. That room was like a Currier & Ives painting with the title "Fine country living." In the back corner of this picturesque room was a narrow staircase.

"You might have a little trouble on the stairs. I hope you brought some help with you." I laughed. If there was one thing I had plenty of it was help. I stopped laughing when I saw that the staircase took a sharp right angle turn with a very narrow landing on its way to the second floor. I followed her up to another sitting room, and there it was, a regular beauty. It was just as she said on the phone, perfect, without a scratch. I couldn't imagine how they ever got that piano up there, but somehow they had, so we could surely get it down.

After preparing her for the size of my crew, I brought them all in. They all filed in, quietly and on their best behavior. The twelve of us could barely fit into the siting room at the top of the stairs. We divided into three groups of four; four of us to get it started down the stairs, four on the staircase just as the stairs took their right angle turn, and four below that. In theory we could all work that way, passing the piano along and nobody would be in anybody's way. That was the theory. One hour later we made it to the bottom. We were very careful and didn't leave a single mark on her walls. However, collectively we had several jammed fingers, a few sore toes,and one very swollen jaw.

With twelve of us, the lift on to the tailgate was a relative breeze. We tied the piano in place with our camp Tug of War rope. They picked numbers to see who would get to ride inside the cab with me. The rest were in the rear, helping to hold the piano in place, and hoping it would not fall on them. As soon as I started rolling, the music started. There we were driving through downtown Bristol, New Hampshire, with the piano playing in the back. Two of them were playing "chopsticks." I went very slowly for fear I would lose either the piano or one of the boys. Unfortunately, the nearby Millstream Restaurant, where I had assumed we would get ice cream, had closed early that night…. So I drove on to Franklin. It was ten o'clock by the time we reached the big city, but luckily I found one restaurant that had ice cream still open.

The road from Franklin back to camp has some terrible sharp turns and several steep hills. If I was a little concerned about losing someone from the back of the truck as I drove through Bristol, I was even more so as we wended our way home. At 11:15 we pulled in to camp. We left the piano in the truck. Tomorrow would be another day.

One night during a work week in the early 1980s the boys invited me to join them on the senior ball field after supper for a little batting practice. Baseball was my sport. Foolishly, I said

"Yes, I'll get up there after I make a few phone calls."

Most work week nights I sat in the living room of our rustic cabin with a clipboard on my lap, making up our work lists for the following day. I relished this time alone. It was a pleasure to check off the things that were accomplished that day and to realize that camp was getting closer to the state of readiness necessary for opening day. Every year I worried that we might not be ready in time, but I knew that somehow we always were. The night in question, I was bone weary, and regretted my earlier agreement to play ball. But, I had a great group of boys working with me, and I didn't want to disappoint them.

I grabbed my glove, and made my way from our cabin across the Junior Ball Field. I slowly climbed the steep hill that led from the junior to the senior ball field. Just as I reached the crest of the hill, I heard the crack of bat meeting ball, looked up and saw the ball high in the air headed my way, ready to sail over my head and down to the field below. I couldn't let that happen. Without thinking, I charged up the couple of remaining feet to the top of the hill, leapt in the air, and snared the ball in the web of my glove. As I grabbed the ball, I stumbled, fell forward, did a partial somersault, and came up ready to throw the ball into the infield. I didn't notice the pain until I transferred the ball from my glove to my throwing hand. Somehow I threw the ball, but my body betrayed me with a scream of pain. I looked at my hand, and saw my little finger was now headed away from my right hand, backward, at an impossible angle.

I stood there looking at my hand. I was at least partially in shock. The boys saw me standing there, and realized something was wrong. First they yelled to me. "Are you all right?" I didn't answer immediately. They ran out to see to see for themselves. I had partially recovered by the time Mike Gordon and Steve Marrow reached me. I felt foolish, but even more than foolish, I was angry with myself for doing something so stupid.

"I'm okay, boys. I just fell wrong, and hurt my finger.

Steve took one look and said

"That looks bad. It's probably broken. You should go to the hospital. I'll run down and get my car. Stay right here. I'll be back in a minute." He turned as though to run to the parking lot.

"No, no, Steve, just wait a minute. I'll be able to drive myself. Just give me a couple of minutes to recover. This really does hurt a lot, but it's not as bad as it was."

Driving myself to the hospital was my second dumb decision of the night. Because I was older and presumably wiser, and probably because I was boss, they listened to me, and watched as I started slowly down the hill. I felt very wobbly, but I wasn't going to show them that. At the bottom of the hill, feeling a little steadier, I crossed the junior ball field, and went back toward our cabin where I retrieved my wallet and car keys. I used my gloved left hand as a fairly effective sling for my throbbing right hand. I felt a little faint as I made my way to the car, but stubbornly continued on alone.

I was lucky. I made it to the New London Hospital emergency room without a second more serious accident. They put me in a wheel chair and one of the nurses parked my car. I was in the hospital only an hour. The doctor saw me right away. He took an X-ray. He called me over to look at the X-ray with him on a screen. We looked at it together. Normally when I look at an X-ray, I nod my head knowingly as the Doctors show me light areas and dark areas, which mean nothing to me. This time it was clear enough even to my untutored eye. My little finger went off at an angle, far from its proper position.

"Just as I thought," he said. "It's dislocated and I've got to reset it. This may hurt a bit, but it's the only way."

He sat me down in a chair.

"Brace yourself." As he said it, he grabbed my finger and gave it a yank. I screamed. He slowly released the finger, easing it into its proper socket. He secured it with a splint, gave me a sling, and then lectured me on everything I had done wrong. He made me sit for quite a while. Finally, he gave me back my car keys.

The next morning, as the boys trooped into the kitchen, each of them asked how I felt. I had already formulated a standard reply.

"I'm really Okay. It looked a lot worse than it turned out to be. The finger was dislocated, but the doctor put it back where it belongs. Believe me. I'm going to be fine. Let's eat. Who is waiter this morning?" After breakfast the boys and I went back to work. I never did play ball again during work week.

Part Five
The 1980s and 1990s

39
Organized At Last

The 1980s and early 1990s were good years for camp. Our camper enrollment reached my desired goal of about two hundred campers. I liked our size. It was large enough for all groups to be able to plays games and yet small enough so that I could know all of our campers and counselors. Our counselor staff was becoming solid in both camps. Though the wonderful counselors from the 1970s eventually left camp, their numbers were replaced by mostly home grown counselors in both Kenwood and Evergreen. Our boys and girls aspired to come back as counselors, and so they made up the heart of the staff in both camps. We supplemented our staff needs with imports from the British Isles, Australia and New Zealand. They added a new ingredient and flavor to the camp. We also found some colorful new staff members.

Things were good, but even in the best of times camps face challenges. During those years we faced our first Deaths in camp. Three times we lost wonderful young counselors. In the 1980s more of our campers came from broken families and more of our children came from emotionally needy backgrounds. During the eighties we dealt with our lake mysteriously turning orange; with staff members disappearing under unusual circumstances; and with neighbors who became more important factors in our camp lives.

Finally, as we got into the nineties we faced the reality that at some point we were going to have to turn over our baby, our camp, to other hands.

40
Death At Camp

Death is never a welcome visitor, least of all in a childrens' summer camp. My very first glimpse of Death in Camp occurred in 1960. It was my first summer as a Camp Director. The camp season started with a shock. The shock was delivered to me innocently enough as part of the day's mail. It was a picture postcard. The picture was of a cemetery. The card was addressed to

Camp Director
Camp Kenwood
Potter Place, New Hampshire

The hand writing was shaky and the message was short.

It is very quiet here. I can't wait for you to join me soon.

It was signed *Sheldon.*

It literally gave me chills when I read it. Shelly was the boy who had been killed in a fatal auto accident on a camp trip two summers before. The accident had happened before we bought the camp. I had just graduated from law school, taken my bar exam, and Judy and I were on a cross-country trip when it occurred, but we had heard about it when we came to visit camp at the end of that summer.

After I got over the initial shock I brought the card to Ken, who had been the owner and camp director when the accident occurred. He nodded knowingly. He sighed. His voice was heavy.

"I meant to warn you. It's from Shelly's Mother. She sent the same card to me last year. She had a nervous breakdown after Shelly died. She's been in a mental institution since. I don't know how she gets out to a store to buy the cards, or who sends them for her."

I had heard the details. It had happened early in the morning one day in the middle of July. Our boys had been on their way to a big camp softball tournament which was held on the grounds of Dartmouth College. They were in a camp station wagon, driven by a twenty-one year old counselor. They were traveling North on Route Four. To this day that section of road is a winding narrow two lane road. According to the testimony of the boys in the camp wagon, they had been passing a milk truck on one of the short straight sections when the truck unexpectedly swerved. The camp driver swerved to avoid collision. He hit a soft shoulder on the side of the road, and the station wagon turned over. The Counselor who was driving was killed as well as thirteen year old Sheldon. Four other boys in the van were injured.

I knew that the accident was one of the reasons that Ken had agreed to sell the camp. He never got over the emotional toll those deaths had taken on the families, on the campers and counselors and on him. I knew about that accident, but I was not emotionally involved.

When I recovered from the shock I had a little time to think and to absorb the pain that would have motivated such a card. Prior to receiving the card, I understood there had been an accident, and that it was sad, but I thought more in business terms. How would such an accident impact the camp? Now I was faced with the reality of the impact on the effected family. Then and now, thinking about it sends chills up and down my spin. It made me realize the enormity of the responsibility I had taken on for so many lives. I received that same chilling card at the start of each of the next three camp seasons, and then, thankfully, they stopped coming.

In the subsequent years we experienced our share of heartaches and scares, of camper accidents and serious illness. Accidents could and did happen anywhere. They occurred most frequently on the ball fields, but almost as often at campfires, on hikes, on canoe trips, in arts & crafts or even during rest period when campers are in their bunks. Fortunately we never experienced the death of a camper. I use the word "Fortunately" because I came to understand that no matter how careful we were, it could happen. Luck plays its role. I know because we were not so lucky with our counselors.

It wasn't until the 1981 that I experienced first hand the reality of Death in Camp. Twenty-one years had passed. It was ten O'clock that mid July night when the phone rang. The call came from the emergency room of the hospital in Manchester, New Hampshire. It was Allie, one of our Evergreen counselors. She was crying, almost hysterical. She was trying to tell me something, but I could barely understand what she was talking about.

"Allie, calm down. Catch your breath. Slowly now, tell me what happened."

"We were driving back to camp. Stan's car went off the road. We're at the hospital now. They won't let us see Stan. Something terrible ..."

She couldn't continue. She was crying and gasping for breath. She put down the phone, but I could still hear her crying in the background. There was a pause and then a calm controlled voice came on the phone. The new voice identified herself as an emergency room nurse.

"I have several of your campers here (referring to our counselors). Three of them are hurt pretty badly. One of them is in critical condition. His name is

Stan. They're operating on him now. I don't know whether they can save him. I think the others will be all right."

"Does that mean you don't think Stan will make it?"

"No. He was apparently thrown from the car."

"Can the others come back to camp?"

"Altogether we have eight of your kids here. They were apparently in two cars. The ones in the car that was not involved in the accident will be able to return to camp with us, but they're really shaken up. It's too early to say whether any of the ones in the car that crashed can go back with you. You'd better get some people down here as soon as you can. And we need to contact the parents of the children we're treating. We need that information as soon as you can get it to us."

"I'm putting my wife on the phone. Give her the names, and she will call you back within a few minutes with the phone numbers. I'm coming down there right now. Tell the counselors that I'm on my way. I'm leaving camp this minute."

I've always been good at organizing things and swinging into action. My mind was swirling with uncertainty and fear, but I got myself going. Other than Stan, I didn't even know who was in the car that was in the crash. I didn't know what condition they were in. I didn't know how many would be able to return to camp that night. I left my wife Judy with the job of getting the phone numbers for the all of the counselors who were on a day off that day. It was clear that the cars had been returning to camp from somewhere South of New Hampshire, probably Boston.

We took two cars down to the hospital in Manchester. Phyllis, our girls' head counselor, drove down to Manchester with me. The other car was driver by Ben Siegel, our camp doctor. By the time we started down to Manchester we already had a list of the counselors who had been off that day. We assumed that the car Stan drove was beyond repair. But, other than Stan, we had no idea who had been in the car that crashed and who in the undamaged car. On the way down, Phyllis and I talked about the kids we assumed were in the accident. We knew them all so well.

Stan had been with us since he was eight years old. He was a boy from my home town, Lexington, Massachusetts. He was part of a group of friends from Lexington who had started camp together when they were eight and nine years old. He had been an outstanding camper and was now a wonderful and well loved counselor. A lot of his friends, who were also counselors, would be devastated.

Most of the others who were together on that day off were also former campers, who had grown up in camp. Some had been with us in camp for ten summers. They were all college students and counselors in the summer. These were kids we knew and cared about. We knew their families. We knew some of them would not be returning to camp that night.

We went into the Trauma Center, and right up to the Nurse's station, introduced ourselves, and explained who we were. She gave us a quick run down.

Stan is still in surgery. It does not look good for him. He was thrown from the car, and hit his head hard on the embankment. The injury to his head is life threatening. He also has injuries to his neck, shoulder, his arm and both legs. The other three will eventually be alright. Ruth has pretty severe injuries to her back and neck. Catherine is pretty banged up all around. They're stitching her up now. Alan has several abrasions and cuts, and they'll be sewing some of those cuts for him too. He'll probably be able to return to camp with you tonight. I don't think the others will."

"Can we get to see any of them?"

"I'm sure you can go in to see Catherine and Alan. They're in rooms three and four."

"I hoped I could see them before I called their parents."

The nurse replied, "We've already reached their parents, and they were both able to talk. We reached Ruth's parents too. They're driving here right now from Worcester. We weren't able to reach Stan's parents. I hope you can reach them. He is in critical condition. It would be best if you could reach them while he still has a chance. If there are any life and death decisions to be made we would all like to have his parents permission to do whatever has to be done."

"Yes, of course, I'll call them now. Can I use your phone?"

"You can use the one behind the desk. Your other campers, the ones who weren't hurt, are in the waiting room down the hall. We told them you were coming."

I placed a call to Stan's parents. This is the call I had been dreading, the kind of phone call I hoped never to have to make as a Camp Director. I couldn't even imagine being a parent receiving the news I was going to have to deliver. Judy and I had lost our oldest daughter just six months before the start of that very camp season. Losing a child is the most terrible loss a parent can imagine. But we had time to adjust. Our daughter Amy had battled Cancer for two and a half years before she died. How much worse must it be to send a healthy child off to camp and then get a devastating phone call like the one they were about to receive. In a few short words I would be delivering the news that they would never see their son again; they would never again see the child into whom they had poured so much love, and for whom they had so many plans for the future, a future he would never see.

The telephone rang and rang. There was no answer. They lived in Lexington. So we knew some of their friends. One of their closest friends agreed to track them down for us. I gave them the hospital number. Stan was still alive then. By the time we left the hospital he had died.

A group of four counselors was huddled together in the waiting room. We saw them through the glass partition before they saw us. Allie was still sobbing in the corner. David and Rick were trying to console her. Nathan sat staring at the TV set on the far wall. He was just staring, but not seeing.

When they saw us come in they all crowded around, asking questions.

"What's happening with Stan? How's Alan? What do they say about Catherine? Is Ruth going to be OK? She looked paralyzed when they brought her in."

We gave them whatever information we had, and then they all started to talk at once. They all wanted to tell the story. Finally Nathan became the spokesman. He was having trouble getting through it. I could see he was again picturing what he told us. He began to visibly shake as he relived the accident.

"You know where the highway turns, after you pass Manchester and approach Concord ... We saw it happen. We were right behind them. Stan's car just didn't turn with the road. He went straight, off the road and hit the embankment. He never hit the brakes. He must have been asleep at the wheel. We pulled off the road as close as we could get. Other cars did too. Then the police came. It was terrible. I got to Stan first. I held his head on my lap. I thought he stopped breathing. The ambulance guys put him on a stretcher. They said he wasn't dead. After they put him in the ambulance I looked around. They had the others all stretched out on the grass. They were all bleeding from different parts of their bodies. They were bleeding and hurt and crying. But at least I could see they were alive. Two more ambulances came. They told us to follow them. Now since we got here, nobody will tell us anything. I don't know why they won't tell us about Stan. A while ago the police came in to get statements from us. I told them just what I told you."

Phyllis and Ben and I were there for a couple of hours. When we learned that Stan died, I knew it was time to return to camp. Ruth was going to have to stay in the hospital. Her injuries were serious. But Catherine and Alan were able to return to camp along with us and the four who had been in the other car. I never spoke to Stan's parents that night. Their friends tracked them down in New Jersey where they had gone to attend a special family event. By the time they called the hospital it was over. They got the final terrible news from the Emergency room doctor.

Back at camp we had arranged for the returning counselors to spend the night in the infirmary. We had Jr. Counselors and Specialty Counselors sleeping in the vacant beds of the eight counselors who would be missing when their campers woke up the next morning.

We held a planning session in the living room of our cabin the remaining hours of the night. Judy and I and Phyllis and Norm sat around drinking coffee, and trying to figure out how to take care of our campers and our camp. Dr. Ben was there too along with Judy's brother and our sister-in-law, both of whom are doctors. They had come up from Boston to lend moral support and to help out in our infirmary if needed. We had no time for grieving. The three doctors had made sure Alan and Catherine were settled for the night before they joined us in our living room.

We started making phone calls at one o'clock in the morning to former counselors who had not been able to return to camp that summer. It was most important to get a really experienced counselor into Stan's bunk to work with the kids and help them deal with the awful upset and loss they would experience. Jay Swartz, who had been a wonderful counselor with us for several camp seasons, was now a school teacher. We reached him at two o'clock in the morning. It took no coaxing at all. He said he would be there before reveille. He could only stay for a few days, but that would give us time to think and to find a permanent replacement from among other former counselors we would try to reach.

We called the camp together the next morning right after Reveille. I wanted to tell the campers and staff before rumors took over. We knew the campers would speculate immediately when they woke up and found their counselors missing and Jr. Counselors sleeping in their beds. The truth was terrible enough. I wanted to make sure it wasn't compounded by bad guesses. The campers gathered quickly and very quietly on the girls' ball field. Usually when we have that many campers in one place it is a job just getting them quiet. But they knew before I said a word that something was very wrong. I don't remember my words that day. But they sat quietly and listened. I told them about the accident and about Stan and about the other three who were badly injured. I told them about the counselors asleep in the infirmary, and that they would be back with them later that day.

The meeting ended. We all walked quietly up to the dining room. The boys in Stan's bunk were crying. Jay Swartz had taken over with them, and was holding his own meeting, giving them a chance to express their sorrow. It was a terrible day and a difficult aftermath. My wife, Judy, and some of Stan's closest friends on the counselor staff went back home to the funeral service the following day. We held a memorial service at camp for all the rest of us who could not go to the funeral.

Then we went back to being a camp. For those of us running the camp there was still no time for grieving. We had a responsibility to our campers to make the rest of their summer as good and as positive as possible. We did all of our activities. We sang our songs. We shouted our cheers. Eventually we had our laughter as well. But nobody forgot! Stan's death had a profound and lasting effect on camp.

As devastating a loss as it was for Stan's parents, they never found it necessary to find a scapegoat. They never blamed or second guessed the camp or the hospital. They received a huge number of cards from Stan's camp friends and their families. Many people wanted to make donations in his memory. Stan's parents set up a Camp Scholarship fund in his name to provide a camp experience for poor children, an experience like the one their son had enjoyed for so many years. They were pretty special people.

That was not our final encounter with death at camp. Twice more over the next ten years we had counselors die during the camp season. One young man, Chris Gordon, a Junior counselor who had been with us for years as a camper, just collapsed on the camp waterfront for no apparent reason. I had a frightening ride to the hospital with Chris in the back of our station wagon. Our camp doctor, who happened to be an emergency room doctor the rest of the year, and the camp nurse, were in the back with him, giving him artificial respiration all the way from the beach to the hospital. I was afraid we wouldn't make it in time. We made it in time, but we didn't save his life.

He had suffered a stroke at age eighteen. His parents were able to get to the hospital while he was still alive, and make whatever decisions had to be made. He never regained consciousness. It was shattering to them, his sister and his two brothers, all of whom were at camp that summer, two as counselors and one as a camper.

The Gordon family all went home for the funeral, and some of Chris' closest friends from camp went as well. His brothers and sister returned to camp after a few days, and stayed for the rest of the season. I thought surely none of them would be back the following year. Though I knew they didn't blame us for his loss, I thought Chris' parents and siblings would not be able to face a return to the site of such a family tragedy. When I think back, even now, so many years after the fact, I am still amazed at their courage. Mike, Carol and Evan continued at camp as many years as they could, and their children are all campers at Kenwood and Evergreen, as I write.

Just a few years later there was another auto accident with counselors on their time off. It was 9:30 at night. I was sitting at my desk beginning my evening paper work, when there was a knock on my door. David Lawrence came in. He looked pale and upset. David was a counselor for our youngest boys and a very sensitive young man.

"Arthur, there's been a terrible accident." He paused. "It was a car full of our counselors. It's out on Route 11. I'm not sure how bad it is. I'm not even sure who was in that car, but it looks bad. The car is in a ditch and there are some of our younger counselors outside the car. There were seven or eight of them. A couple of them were on their feet, some were sitting in the grass. One is lying in the grass. There's already an ambulance and police car there."

Phyllis and I got in a car. The accident site was only five minutes from camp. When we got there, two ambulances were on site. Counselors, bleeding and bandaged were being helped into them. Two EMTs were hovering over the girl lying on the ground. I was relieved. That meant she was still alive. But a moment later, as they transferred her to a gurney, they pulled up the blanket that had been covering her body so that it also covered her face. I realized then she had died.

A car filled with counselors had just left camp, and were going to New London for pizza. Only a mile or two from camp a deer darted across the road in front of their car. The driver swerved. His right front tire hit a soft shoulder and the car went off the road. It turned over. One young girl, a seventeen-year-old Jr. Counselor, was thrown from the car. I was told later that she had been killed on impact with the ground.

Several of the other young counselors who had been in that car had life threatening injuries. We all went to the hospital in New London. The most serious cases were to be transferred to Concord. Once again I had to make that awful series of phone calls from the hospital. I will never forget the piercing scream of that young woman's Mother when she realized what I was saying, that she would never see her wonderful girl again.

It was after this accident that I realized what my predecessor Ken had gone through, and why he was willing to sell the camp he had built. I had also come to realize that we could protect our campers, but there was little we could do to insure that counselors would be safe on their time off away from camp. Neither of the auto accidents involved liquor. Nor did they involve drugs of any sort. But both involved counselors on time off in cars. Counselors were always going to need time off. They were always going to go in cars. I knew it could happen again. As much as I loved camp, I wasn't sure that I wanted to be there if there was a next time.

41
Unforgettable Specialty Counselors

Those of us who have been fortunate enough to run a camp know the joys and challenges that come with creating our own private world, putting the pieces together and making it work the whole summer long. We certainly cannot make it happen alone. We must have key senior staff members who share the responsibility and help set the tone for all that happens. But most of all we must have an annual infusion of new counselors whose sense of fun and excitement spreads like a contagion to the campers. Some of them are with us only a year or two. Others become perennials. They come in all sizes and shapes, no two ever alike. All are important, but some are more memorable than others. We were so fortunate during the 1980s not only to have wonderful cabin counselors, but also to come across some spectacular specialists.

Stan Graham

In my mind, I have a picture of Stan. He's half submerged in the shallow water on the Kenwood waterfront. He sits astride a fifteen foot long inflated dragon, wearing a bathing suit and a huge smile. He is chasing, attacking, and being attacked by a swarm of little boys, who laugh and scream with the absurdity of the battle. Each of his adversaries is less than four feet tall and none weigh as much as seventy-five pounds. Stan, the dragon, stands six feet on dry land and weighs at least two hundred twenty pounds. Somehow, despite the disparity, the little boys defeat the dragon. He swims and crawls to shore, collapses on the beach exhausted, while his inflated alter ego floats harmlessly nearby. After a minute or two, he suddenly leaps to his feet, gives a gigantic roar, and plunges back into the water. The battle resumes!

When I first met Stan Graham I was captivated by his charm, his wonderful wide-angle smile and his enthusiasm about absolutely everything. His smile and effusive personality persuaded me to overlook his somewhat limited language skills and to ignore my own bias against men who look as though they could play tackle in the line of a pro football team. He was a big effusive young man, and one of the very few black men, not former campers, who ever applied for a counselor job at our camp. Stan wanted to be our arts & crafts counselor. He showed me newspaper clippings from the Boston Globe and references from the Museum School in Boston. It seemed he'd already made something of a name for himself in Boston art circles. He was a sculptor who created massive works, the kind that grace courtyards and lawns of public buildings. But, in our interview, the thing that he held in reserve, the thing about which he was most proud, was his distinction of being the first black player ever to play in the National Hockey League. That was a very impressive fact, particularly when viewed in light of his artistic talent. Years later I tried to verify this fact, and drew a blank.

Stan was with us for six summers in the late 1980s and early 1990s. His first season at camp, he was not very successful as our arts & crafts counselor. Though a talented sculptor, his communications skills were not up to holding the interest of his classes. But we loved Stan's spirit and he loved camp, so the next summer he made the move from Specialty Counselor to General Counselor in Senior Camp. For the next five camp seasons he was a cabin counselor, leading and socializing with our thirteen to fifteen year old boys, helping with a great variety of sports. Stan was a bundle of energy and enthusiasm, and activities he ran were infused with his sense of fun.

He had a number of interesting memory issues, the most endearing of these was his seeming inability to remember people's names. The first day he met Scott Brody he couldn't remember his name so he called him "Big Guy." For a while Scott thought he was the only "Big Guy", but it seemed that "Big Guy" was Stan's default name for any counselor whose actual name he could not conjure up. Instead of "Big Guy" he sometimes gave out a military rank. To Stan, our staff was filled with people named Captain, General, Sergeant and Admiral. He always greeted people with a big smile and a warm welcome. He was always happy to see everyone. He would never insult anyone by remembering them as Privates or Corporals, always as upper echelon officers. Interestingly, though he couldn't remember their real names, he never forgot the rank he had assigned them in lieu of a name. If he called someone Captain once, he always remembered him as Captain, and called him that. Occasionally he just garbled a name completely, but then always remembered the garbled version. One of our young men, a senior camp counselor, who had been in camp since he was seven years old, was universally known in camp as "Chubber". Stan transformed Chubber into Trevor, and always called him Trevor through six camp seasons. When Stan spoke to me I could see he was struggling to tap his memory bank trying to come up with my name. Usually he remembered and, with a big smile, he called me Artha. I was flattered.

But Stan had an untamed side as well, a side that had to be over-looked if we were to invite him to return year after year. Once, or perhaps twice a summer, he would don his complete hockey uniform, including his goalie mask, the same kind worn by Jason in the horror movie *Friday the 13th*. He would go around Senior Camp, from bunk to bunk, waking and terrifying sleeping campers. He was always apologetic afterward, and could never explain why he did it.

Nobody else would ever have gotten away with such outrageous behavior, but the boys always forgave him because they loved him. Each time I heard of it, I would think to myself. "That's it. We just can't tolerate his nonsense any longer," Then I would catch him doing something wonderful and funny with a group of adoring kids, and I was ready to forgive once again.

Rebecca Buck

I watched a well worn station wagon wend its way slowly down our interior camp road toward my cabin. The girl who emerged from that wagon was about five feet tall and tiny all around. I remember thinking she had a waif-like appearance. I don't remember what she wore that day, but I have an indelible image of Rebecca in her years at camp, her clay stained apron covering shorts and a tee shirt. She is covered, hair to flip flops, with rust colored clay dust. I'm sure she did not appear for our first meeting in her working clothes. Rebecca always put her best foot forward. I'm sure she was sparkling clean that day.

As soon as she spoke, the waif image disappeared. She always spoke with a crisp British accent, though her sentences were punctuated with basic American slang. Her eyes sparkled as she spoke, and she never for a moment doubted that she was right, no matter the subject. She stepped toward me with a very proper business attitude, her right hand extended for a formal handshake. "Hello, Mr. Sharenow. I'm Rebecca. I've come to see about teaching sculpture at your camp."

I swung open the door to the ceramics shop, and she danced in. "It's wonderful!! I can't wait to get to work. What a great place. I hope all of those screens open up so I can work in the fresh air. I see you have a kick wheel in addition to electric wheels. That's so superior. I'll be able to do my own work on the kick wheel. I can control the speed better for fine work. Oh, and look at this," she said, as she went over to the corner to inspect one of our ancient kilns. She lifted the lid and made a face as she looked down into its depth. "I'm afraid you'll have to get me a new kiln. Half your elements are burned out and the insulation is crumbling. Come, look for yourself." My eyes followed her finger as she pointed down into its interior. "See, there and there and there. I love your studio, but I cannot work with that kiln. It simply is not safe." I did think she was getting a bit ahead of herself. I liked her enthusiasm, but I hadn't offered her a job yet and she was already telling me to buy new equipment.

After she completed her inspection of the ceramics shop, we went into my cabin for a traditional interview. It didn't take long for her to convince me that she was just the person we needed to run our ceramics program. She showed me slides of her work and I admired her stunning abstracts, exotic bowls, and life like figures. Though she was only in her early twenties, I could see she was already a very talented sculptor. Someone who combined that kind of talent and her enthusiasm could not miss being a wonderful instructor.

"There's just one favor I have to ask" she said. For the first time there was hesitation in her voice. "I need a place to live between now and the start of the job. I just arrived back in the United States a few days ago, and I have been bunking in with some old friends in Boston. Yesterday they hinted rather broadly that I should find someplace else. I think they're probably about ready to throw me out. I'm not very big, but neither is their apartment."

I thought about it for a moment. I knew it wouldn't really be a problem. Her timing was good. "Yes, we can work that out. You can move in tomorrow. We have a group of counselors coming up tomorrow to help get camp in shape before our formal staff orientation period. It's a week we call work week. As it happens, we have two female counselors in the group this year. You can live with them in one of our girls' lodges. And you can join our crew for Work Week."

"I'll look for you tomorrow. Plan to get here around noon. I'll be back before lunch and we'll get you settled in. The others will be coming in through the afternoon. I think you'll enjoy working with them."

"Oh, do I have to join your work crew? I'd sooner get my studio in shape so that it will be ready for the campers when they arrive."

"OK, you can come up, and work in your shop, but you'll live with the other two girls. One thing I want you to understand, all of the other counselors who come in tomorrow will be doing physical labor, and they may resent you if they see you're not working."

"You can be sure I'll work more hours every day than any of your crew. Is it settled then?"

"Yes, it's a deal. I'll see you tomorrow."

By dinner the next night my Work Week boys were falling all over one another trying to get close to Rebecca. I think seven of them fell in love with her that night. Her dynamic personality captured them, but her looks didn't hurt either. It was a general consensus among the boys that she reminded them of Audrey Hepburn, a popular movie star in the 1950s, 60s and 70s. The following night she had four of them sweeping her shop and washing down her work tables. But it wasn't just the boys. She had also enchanted the two female counselors. Her third night in camp she ran a ceramics clinic for our staff, male and female. I'm not sure whether they were actually working or just sitting around socializing, but I am sure there was more laughing and many more happy noises coming from that shop than I had ever heard before. A new camp social center had been established.

By the end of the week Rebecca and Stan, also new to camp that summer, appeared to be a couple. Probably they were never more than friends, but they spent a great deal of time together, and came to be regarded as such. All I could think of was the show "The Odd Couple." She was slender, small, white, high strung and amazingly articulate. He was hefty, tall, black, relaxed and anything but articulate. Of course, it was not so unusual for artists to be drawn together by mutual interests. Once camp started they would have similar positions in the camp program, she as Ceramics and he as Arts and Crafts Instructors. The one personal characteristic they shared was a ready appreciation for the humor in every situation. They even saw the humor in themselves as a couple. But as colorful as they were as a couple, it did not last. The "couple" phase of their relationship ended by mid-season, but they remained good friends through their six shared summers at camp.

Rebecca came back to us year after year, and always from a different direction. One summer it might be from Long Island, where she was visiting her American father, another from a visit in London with her English Mum. Other years she returned in the spring from Indonesia, North Carolina and New Mexico. Each spring she arrived a little earlier and each fall she packed up and left a little later. She had long since overcome my resistance to her living alone in camp. One fall she never really left. She stayed in camp as long as possible, and then found an apartment in the home of an eccentric woman just a few miles from camp. Rebecca became one of our regulars, whose only settled place in life seemed to be camp, a safe haven where she was universally respected and adored.

Rebecca's life as a wandering free spirit didn't change a few years later just because she had a baby. It was only when her son Daniel approached school age that she felt she must settle down. There were many tearful hugs and goodbyes when Rebecca left us after her final season at camp. She was going "home" to England, where she would build a life for herself and Daniel. Her plan was to open her own Ceramics studio, where she could work, exhibit and teach. I have followed her career with interest, as her sculptures appear frequently in prominent exhibits throughout the British Isles.

Jill and Philippe

Mid-way in the summer of 1986 our camp kitchen was in a ghastly state of disarray, the kind of disarray that occurs when the Head Chef had to be fired, having appeared in the kitchen drunk and incoherent; the kind that occurs when the second cook, a nice young man named Paul, was promoted to chef and turned out to be both an inadequate cook and a hopelessly inept manager. To add to the chaos, Angel, Paul's replacement as second cook, was anything but an angel. He was a man with wild mood swings, a bad temper and a switch blade knife. Angel's stay in the camp kitchen was short lived. One day he reacted angrily to one of Paul's orders, pulled his knife and swung it toward his boss. The wound to Paul's neck was just a slight nick, but it was obvious that our knife wielding second cook had to go at once. The only real issue was whether or not to call the police. Paul, the victim of the attack, begged me not to call. He had his own reasons for not wanting anything to do with them. Our third cook, Simon, was a local kid from nearby Danbury, NH, whose native language may have been English, but whose words were indecipherable to everyone in camp. With this limited cast of characters, we needed a new cook in a hurry. There was no time for ads or interviews. We needed a living and breathing cook instantly.

I called the American Camping Association office in Boston. On occasion, I had hired counselors through their placement service, but never a cook. I didn't have too much hope. It was, after all, mid-season, and anybody who was any good should have been placed in a job long before. At this point in the summer anyone available on the placement office list would almost certainly have been fired from another job.

Terry Phinney, the head of the New England Region, answered the phone with her usual greeting. "American Camping Association, Terry speaking, How may I help you?"

"Terry, I need a cook. Do you have anyone in your files?"

"No, we placed our last cook weeks ago. It's been very quiet here the past couple of weeks. My only activity has been answering phone calls from camp directors. You're all looking for replacements. As it happens, I have a young man filling out an application in the office right now. He's from France. He's spent the summer touring the country taking pictures. He just arrived in Boston. Apparently he's run out of money, and he's looking for a job at a camp. He seems like a nice young man. He said he wants to be a photography counselor. He's unlikely to also be a cook, but I'll ask if you like. "

"Yes, yes, please." I was sure nothing would come of it, but there was no harm in having her ask. She put the phone down, and I was left hanging a few minutes. Then she came back on.

"Boy, are you lucky. He wants to be a photographer, but he has actually made a living for the past couple of years as a cook. Of course, the restaurants he mentioned are in France and I never heard of them. But he seems like such a nice young man, I tend to believe him. I can question him more on the kind of experience he has."

"He doesn't have to be a master chef. The job we have open is for a second cook. We really just need a short order man, someone with experience working with fryalators and grills. Oh, and of course there will be some prep work, chopping vegetables and salad. Could you interview him for me, and call me back with an opinion?"

"I'll be glad to give you an opinion, but I refuse to take responsibility for actual hiring."

"I know. I understand. If you give him a positive rating, I'll still want to talk to him on the phone. The decision has to be mine, but I have faith in your judgment. Incidentally, how's his English?"

"His English is beautiful. In fact, he's pretty beautiful too. The girls will go crazy over him."

Philippe came into New London on the 4:15 bus. Judy met the bus and brought him back to camp. When I came into the kitchen before dinner that night, it was clear that this small corner of the universe was at least slightly improved. Paul was slicing roast beef and Philippe, the new man, was working the fryalators. A small mountain of French fries was growing in the roast pan by his side.

I went over to introduce myself. He smiled, said hello, and excused himself to get back to work. I watched as he simultaneously lowered a basket of frozen fries into one fryalator with his left hand, while his right pulled a cooked basket out of the other.

I barely got to know Philippe that summer. He worked hard, and helped bring the kitchen back to a semblance of order. In his time off, he didn't go back to his cabin to fall asleep, as most cooks do when they get out of the kitchen. Instead, I would see him here and there around camp, watching the camp activities and taking pictures. He seemed happy to be by himself, and spoke little as he made his way around camp. But Terry Phinney was right when she said he would attract attention. He did, particularly the attention of the Evergreen counselors and our senior girls, who constantly popped up in front of his camera, asking him to take their picture.

At the end of the camp season, when Philippe came in for his final check, and "goodbye conference" he asked if I had a few minutes. I looked at the young man sitting across from me.

"Yes, of course, what can I do for you? I know Paul's been very happy to have you and so have I. If you want to come back next summer, the job is yours and you'll get a good raise too."

"Thank you, but I don't think I want to return as a cook. I like your camp, and, other than a few people who work in the kitchen, I like everybody I met here. But your camp is missing an important activity. I see there was once a dark room under the Recreation Hall, but you don't have a photography program. I could run that program for you"

"It's been a long time since we've had a photography program here. I remember we did have one when I was a counselor, but my predecessor closed it down a couple of years before I bought the camp. I just haven't thought to start it up again."

"If you would consider it, I'm your man."

"Philippe, I can't really think about this now. I have a lot of people to say goodbye to, and I'm still focused on the events of this summer. My mind is not ready to think seriously about next summer just yet. But I will be happy to consider your suggestion when the time is right. Why don't you take a good look at that darkroom before you leave camp. Figure out what modifications we would need to make it usable again. Then you could make a list of equipment and supplies we would need to start a decent program. Oh, and prices too, I'll need prices. I want to know if we can afford a good program. I don't want to do it at all unless we can do it right. Give me a call at home a month from now, and we can give it some serious consideration."

Philippe arrived very early the next summer, even before work week, to make sure that Forrest understood and had made the renovations he'd had outlined for our new darkroom. He said he was satisfied with what had been done, but he wound up doing a lot of carpentry himself, the small details he hadn't thought of at our meeting in the winter. When the supplies and equipment he had ordered arrived, he was there to check them in, and he immediately started setting up his shop. Once work week began, he joined my crew during the day, worked in the darkroom by night, and even helped in the kitchen, volunteering to run the dish machine every night after supper. I'm sure he would have washed the floors and cleaned the toilets too if anybody had asked him.

Camp started, and Photography was an instant hit. The small maximum capacity of our darkroom dictated a class size of only twelve campers, half of whom could fit into the darkroom at one time. The other half, supervised by a cabin counselor from each assigned group, would be out and around camp, snapping pictures everywhere. The next time that group had photography the campers would switch off so that all of them ultimately got to develop and print the pictures they had taken at a previous session. Some days Philippe would discuss composition with the entire group and then send them off in pairs, each with their own photo assignments. They loved their "work" as photo journalists. Many of Philippe's photo assistants also became photo enthusiasts, and asked to be assigned there as frequently as possible.

Philippe was busy all of the time, with three classes of boys every morning and three capacity classes of girls every afternoon, Monday through Friday. In between times, I could always find him in the darkroom, developing and printing campers' photos they hadn't had time to complete during class. On the weekends, when our Special Events program supplanted regular activities, Philippe would be out and around camp, snapping pictures for use in the camp brochure and for a slide show for the campers at the end of the season.

There was no question, Philippe earned his salary. That had been my primary consideration when determining whether or not to start such a program. If it was a success, the cost of an additional specialty counselor would be added to the payroll year after year, and would far exceed the cost of equipment and supplies. He had sold me on the value of the program, and, I was sure, that once started, we would want to continue it into the indefinite future. But until he actually started I couldn't estimate whether it would have wide appeal. It didn't need to have wide appeal to be a success. From my standpoint all it needed to do was help satisfy the needs of campers who did not do well in sports, and for whom photography would be a non-competitive opportunity for success. Happily, it was a popular hit, and Philippe somehow found extra time to spend with those kids who needed it most.

Then along came Jill.

Waterfront Director for NH Boys Camp.
Young man must be 21+have WSI, SLS and Camp WF Exp.
Girls' Camp associated. Call 617-862-7537

"What do you mean I can't say "Young man? How can that be discriminating? Half the people I hire are young women for jobs working with girls. The other half are young men to work with boys. This happens to be a job for a young man."

"I'm sorry, we just cannot accept the ad the way you have submitted it. Nobody else will either. It's against the law." (A year or two later, I was no longer permitted to use "young" or "21+", both phrases being considered age discrimination.)

"This is ridiculous. What if it was an ad for a cabin counselor, to live in the same room with the kids? Would the law want me to have a young man as a cabin counselor living with teen age girls or vice versa? I think such a result would certainly be absurd. If we didn't discriminate in reasonable ways we would have some mighty upset parents."

"I'm very sorry, I see your point, but the law is the law, and I can no longer accept an employment ad specifically for a man or a woman."

"Okay, I'll re-word it. I'll call you back." For an hour I toyed with wording that would get my message across, without actually using the forbidden words. I couldn't come up with the right combination. At any rate, I decided it was unlikely that I would be overwhelmed with female applicants for this job. If I did get one I would have to deal with her very carefully. My politically correct ad read

Waterfront Director for NH Boys' Camp.
Must be 21+ have WSI, SLS and Camp WF Exp.
Girls' Camp associated. Call 617-862-7537

When Jill Sweezey responded to my ad I tried to figure out how to put her off, but it was obvious she was very well qualified for the job. She was twenty-one years old, was about to graduate from college, had taught swimming for the past four summers, and was a Red Cross Water Safety Instructor and Senior Life Saver. I couldn't figure out how to avoid interviewing her.

So she came to my house for an interview. After just a few minutes I was able to add a few more positives to her list of qualifications. She was bright, enthusiastic, full of ideas, and preferred teaching boys.

"I enjoy working with young girls, but I find it very difficult getting the teen-age girls to pay attention. They're always more interested in what they have to say to one another than listening to anything I might have to say. Boys all listen. I enjoy working with them."

"I do understand. I've been coaching baseball and softball to kids since I graduated from college, and I prefer working with the girls for the same reason you like working with the boys. The girls treat me like a baseball oracle, and hang on my every word."

While we were talking I tried to figure out where we would house her. Even more important, I pondered the reaction of some of our Kenwood staff if I hired a woman for the Kenwood waterfront. I was particularly concerned about Norm's reaction. He had been waterfront director for nine years before he was promoted to Head Counselor. The waterfront was still his emotional home base at camp. No matter who the waterfront director was, Norm spent a lot of time down there. He would have to buy into this and be ready to support her if she needed help. I called Norm that night. Happily, his reaction was much better than I thought it would be.

"You know I was waterfront director at Camp Matoka before I came to Kenwood. I had no trouble running a girls' waterfront and I don't see why a girl can't run the boys' waterfront. She certainly can't do any worse than the clown we had there last year."

Jill's first summer was a revelation. The boys loved her and the Kenwood counselors immediately became her enthusiastic lifeguards, swim instructors and beach assistants. Though they recognized her as a normally attractive female, both the campers and the counselors working at the Kenwood waterfront treated her as one of the boys. She was just so pleasant as well as being sensible and solid in her job. They responded positively to anything she wanted. A strong plus for her was the unpopularity of her immediate predecessor in the job.

She didn't ask kids to do stupid things. For example, on really cold days, she automatically turned swim instruction into a boating period. On days that were cool, she would do all of her explanations and demonstrations on dry land before anybody got in the water. Once a camper was in the water he stayed in until he achieved a level of competence. That accomplished, he was allowed to go onto land and cover up. On cool days she never asked them to go in and out of the water, leaving them shivering on the dock in between lessons. This may seem like simple logic, but a surprising number of waterfront people simply didn't get it. There has always been resistance to swim instruction, particularly among boys. Understandably, resistance is higher on cooler days. During Jill's eight year tenure on the Kenwood waterfront, there was still resistance, but much less cajoling was required to get the boys to the waterfront.

During Jill's first summer at camp I visited the waterfront frequently. Her General Swim periods were great. The counselors assigned to lifeguard positions on the dock all seemed to have their eyes where they should be, on the swimming area. When Jill blew her whistle and yelled "Buddy Up" the kids got together with their buddies, and counted off with very little wasted time or energy, and when she called "All Out" they all got out.

Swim instruction periods in the afternoon were really a showcase for her organizational ability. When I walked down to the waterfront, typically I would see Jill working with one group of campers, her waterfront assistants working with another group, and each of the regular cabin counselors working with one or two campers who needed special help mastering a single swim stroke. Counselors who had no particular swimming expertise became excellent instructors, one stroke at a time, for the one or two boys with whom they worked.

Other than her ability to make friends with everyone in camp, the thing that impressed me most in Jill's first summer was her ability to create an exciting all camp waterfront afternoon program. We had a "waterfront afternoon" on the camp schedule one Sunday afternoon each summer, year after year forever, even going back to when I was a camper.

As a kid, I hated them. Mostly we sat on benches, either sweltering or freezing depending upon the day, and waited our turn to race against our friends in one or two races during the long afternoon. I had absolutely no interest in the outcome of any of the races that did not directly involve me. There would be an occasional novelty event, like canoe jousting, involving senior boys, or a pajama race, designed to entertain those on the beach. But basically it was a two to three hour bore. That exact pattern continued through my years as counselor, head counselor and director until finally someone came along with enough imagination to create something different. That someone was, of course, Jill. Her annual waterfront afternoons were a three or four ring circus, involving three quarters of the boys in camp at every given moment. She set up stations, with three or four different activities running simultaneously, with boys rotating from one activity to the next. One might be a kayak race across the lake and back, another hand paddling canoes over a slalom course, the third a relay race, involving every boy in an age group as part of a giant relay team. One at a time each had his turn as the team's "swimmer." As such, he held onto a rope, and their teammates reeled him in from one dock to the other until each member of the team had his turn being towed. A fourth group, working in the shallow water section, would be having a multi-team duel, using styrofoam noodles. After her first waterfront afternoon campers looked forward to the next.

Jill and Philippe seemed to be working all of the time. I'm not sure when they found time to get to know one another, but somehow they did. By the end of Jill's first summer at camp they were a couple. After their second summer they got married. They skipped one summer at camp, and we had to make do. Both programs suffered in their absence. When they returned for the 1990 season they came with their newborn son, Nikola, and a very large dog, whose name I don't remember. Jill and Philippe were with us through the 1996 camp season. Neither of them was quirky, an oddball or sensational in any way. They were just wonderful people to have in camp, people who enriched the camp program and the lives of those with whom they came in contact.

42
Dramatic Beat Goes On

Through the years, evening rehearsals for our big Senior musicals were tough on all of our drama counselors. During the regular activity day they could arrange time for their few lead characters to rehearse specific scenes. In the evenings, when all of the ball games were over and there were no Seniors out of camp on trips, we would typically have rehearsals for the large chorus numbers. While the campers were on stage they were usually attentive and cooperative. The problem arose when most of them were off stage between the big chorus numbers, while the leads rehearsed. The fifty or sixty boys and girls who sat in the darkened audience would be quiet, and perhaps even attentive, for a while. Then their interest would lag.

During a typical evening rehearsal there would be several lineups of girls who sat straddling Rec Hall benches. They sat one behind the other. On one bench the girls would be braiding one another's hair. On another they might be giving each other back rubs. Every once in a while a loud laugh would come from one of those benches. Meanwhile, in the darker corners of the Rec Hall, our more socially advanced boys and girls verbally played the teen age courting game, ever more noisily as the rehearsal went on. Then there were the boys who had been "drafted" for chorus roles. These boys tended to be noisy from the start, and their jokes and silliness progressed as the evening went on.

It was no wonder the drama counselors hated the unavoidable all cast rehearsals at night. We gave them as much help as we could. There were always Kenwood and Evergreen counselors in the Rec hall, enthusiastically shushing and hushing the rowdy campers. But, like the campers, their attention flagged as the evening wore on. Phyllis would drop by and watch for a few minutes. I would stop by to see how things were going. Norm would stop by at least once a rehearsal. And for those few minutes, while one of us was there, things got quiet, and you could even hear the actors on stage.

Jim Michaels was drama counselor in the early 1980s. Jim did a good job. Two incidents stand out in my mind from his tenure. One involved Emily R. She was a sweet little eight or nine year old at the time. Emily's group was putting on a one act play where the children sat at small imaginary desks, apparently in school. Each of the girls had a few lines to advance the story. When it came to Emily's turn, she froze. Her mind went blank. You could see the panic on her face. From backstage I could hear Jim stage whispering her lines. I was in the fourth row, and I heard. Emily sat three feet away from him on stage, but either didn't hear or couldn't react. Jim came from backstage, and sat on the floor next to Emily. Using a little girl voice he delivered her lines. He continued to sit next to her on the floor holding her hand and whispering to her. By her next set of lines Emily had recovered, and was able to go on with her part. Once he knew she was alright, Jim crawled off stage, and the play went on.

The Senior Show in 1982 was "West Side Story." David Lawrence was to play the male lead. David was a tall good looking fifteen year old with a good voice and the self confidence to sing in public. He was doing a great job at the early rehearsals. Then disaster struck. He broke his leg in a ball game. It was a serious break, and his parents wanted him to see a specialist in New York. He stayed home to recuperate. It was undoubtedly a good decision for David, but a major problem for "West Side Story" and the Jets.

There was one week to go before Opening Night. Jim cast David's bunk-mate, Nicko Lowry in David's role. Nicko was just as tall and just as good looking as David, but there the resemblance stopped. He had a tentative singing voice and almost no confidence in his ability to sing. He only agreed to play the part because he knew his friends were in a bind without a lead for their show. Jim worked with Nicko to boost his confidence and his voice. Nicko tried, but he just couldn't sing those songs. Opening night Nicko sang like he never sang before, and never would again. He had learned all of his lines and did well with all the acting, but he just mouthed the songs, while Jim sang them back stage.

It wasn't exactly smooth, but it worked, and saved the show.

Jamie Demarest was with us for six summers starting in 1985. Jamie was as close as we ever came to my vision of the ideal drama counselor. I liked Jamie a lot. He was an elementary school teacher, who understood kids and liked them. He was serious about music and his ambition was not only to produce good shows, but to teach kids something about both music and drama. He also understood his role in casting shows. He knew that if he had two girls trying out for a lead role in the Senior Show, and they were reasonably close in talent, the determining factor was which of them would benefit most by getting the lead. The girl who was the best tennis player in camp or the best pitcher on the softball team was unlikely to get the lead unless she was significantly more talented than her competition. He understood this. Many drama counselors did not.

Jamie was perhaps too much of a perfectionist for a camp drama counselor. On the other hand, his Senior shows were among the best ever produced at camp. One of his first was "Joseph & His Amazing Technicolor Dream coat". It was a wonderful camp production. It was light, and fun, and it provided a large number of parts with solos. The show was a smash hit with everybody: the cast, the audience, the parents of the cast and the camp directors. I knew we had found a winner. In the next few camp seasons "Bye Bye Birdie", "Sound of Music", Guys and Dolls" were all wonderful productions. But things got testy toward the end of Jamie's run.

An occasional Senior boy, who normally liked dramatics, refused to be in his shows because he demanded too much time, too much effort and too much excellence. The most obvious example of this came in 1991. We did many Senior shows through the years, and though there were times when the male leads were important, most of the time the girls carried the show. Jamie wanted to do "Fiddler on the Roof". That show requires quite a remarkable male lead. For three years Jamie was grooming an unsuspecting Jason Sebell* to be his Tevya. (*A few years later Jason became Kenwood's head counselor and is now the camp's Associate Director.) Jason was musically talented, imaginative and really interested in drama. This was going to be his last summer as a camper. What made him an even better candidate was that he was not a strong athlete, and he would not have to divide his time and energy between the show and softball or soccer practice. He would be the perfect "Tevya".

Jason arrived at camp that year and announced that he was not going to be in the play. He had been in several Jamie Demarest productions in previous years, and just didn't want to spend his last summer as a camper working that hard. I tried, without success, to talk him into the role. Jamie was very disappointed, and the role was thrown open for try outs. The show went on and was a reasonable success, but there was a message in that casting for Jamie and for all of us who were interested in kids and drama. We were running a camp, not a professional theater company.

Peter Jones was a terrific guy. He joined us in 1990. By then our camp had grown some and our drama department now boasted two full time drama counselors. Jamie Demarest was Head of Drama and Peter was hired as his assistant. Jamie was to continue doing the Senior Show and a big musical with the Juniors. Peter would take care of all the smaller one act plays for our younger boys and girls. He was well organized and his rehearsals were fun for the kids. It was not surprising that he was a very popular addition to our camp staff with campers and counselors alike.

In 1991 Peter returned. Somehow he seemed different. He was still pleasant and well organized, but he seemed distracted and uneasy. His most relaxed times came when he was in the prop room under the Rec Hall, painting scenery and singing along with Jean Valjean, as "Les Miserables" blasted away on his tape player. He had a good voice too. I often looked in on him there, and stayed a while because I too loved the music from "Les Mis"

His shows were usually on Tuesday nights and his day off was Wednesday. In the fifth week of camp, he took his scheduled day off, but failed to return to camp. His clothes were still in his bunk. He had only one more show to direct. He had cast the show with our Intermediate boys, and was scheduled to have his first rehearsal with the boys that Thursday. When he didn't appear, Jamie took over the rehearsal, and we awaited further word from Peter. It never came. About a week after his mysterious disappearance we received a phone call from his brother, who was trying to locate him.

"I'm sorry. We don't know where he is. He was due back here a few days ago. I tried his apartment number, but there was no answer there."

"That's what I was afraid of. He's done this before. It's usually a bad sign. He had a breakdown last year. He was treated for depression. That seemed to help for a while, and then he disappeared for a month. Please let me know when you hear from him."

"Yes, I certainly will. We're almost at the end of our camp season now. We have just a little more than a week to go. If he doesn't return, what should I do with his things? He has a locker full of clothes. I know his precious tape player is somewhere in the Rec Hall. I don't know what else is his, but I'm sure he has other belongings back in his cabin."

"Just hold on to them. He'll turn up. I know he will. He'll get back there some time. If he doesn't, I'll collect his things."

Peter returned on the last day of camp. The campers had all just left for home when he drove right up to the dining hall. His brother was with him. Peter looked like a beaten man. He looked down. He wouldn't meet my eyes. He was all apologies, and was clearly terribly upset that he had broken his contract. I had a check and W-2 form ready for him.

"I don't want it. I don't deserve it. I let you down."

"Peter, it's yours. You've got to take it. If you don't, I'll just mail it to you. We were worried about you, but we were OK from the camp standpoint. Jamie took over the Inters' play, and everything was fine. You just take care of yourself, and don't worry about us. You earned your salary."

"Does this mean I can come back next summer?"

"I don't want to talk about next summer yet. I'm just finishing up this one. Meanwhile, you just take care of yourself." I truly never expected to hear from him again. He was a nice guy and I wished him well.

It was January when Peter called. He wanted to come back. I felt really foolish even entertaining the idea. But I invited him to the house to talk. I've always had a soft spot and lots of sympathy for people with mental and emotional problems. When he walked in the next day, I was thrilled. It was the old Peter. He was filled with good cheer and bursting with new ideas. He told me about his breakdown and his rehab, and assured me he was fine.

"Can I please have another chance? I'll never disappoint you again."

I probably should have had my head examined, but I said "Yes". As soon as I did I was angry with myself. He was going to have to play a far more important role that next summer because Jamie was not returning. Peter would be the one in charge of the Senior Show, and would be running the whole program. He would have an assistant, but what was I thinking?

It happened again. Peter started off like dynamite, full of pep and enthusiasm. He got the Senior show going early. He held tryouts the 2nd day of camp. He had the show cast by the end of the first week of camp. Meanwhile he was casting and rehearsing three other shows with younger campers. He was an absolute dynamo. Then he disappeared again, just like the first time. I had only myself to blame.

Phyllis and I took over directing the Senior show. It wasn't the first time we had wound up as battle field replacements for failed drama counselors. Peter's assistant carried on with the rest of the camp drama program, and did an excellent job.

Jay and Linda Lambert took over the drama program in the early 1990s. They were two of my favorite people. They did a great job. They understood our program. Jay had been in our plays. He had helped with drama in the past. Linda had helped with little girls shows. They had both seen the best and worst of camp drama counselors, and they knew what had to be done to avoid the pitfalls of so many of their predecessors..

I can't begin to guess the numbers of hours the two of them spent planning their rehearsal schedule in order to minimize the need for many of those huge night rehearsals. But they did it. We didn't have to get those huge rehearsals until two days before show time. And by then most of the cast, even those with very small chorus parts, were invested in the plays enough to try to be quiet when they were asked.

But even the two of them, as organized and calm as they were, struggled with our challenging schedule. The last summer they were with us as drama counselors, Jay became so frustrated; he was furious with me. He had every right to be frustrated and upset because I had scheduled so many trips and other competing activities that he found it very difficult (He said impossible) to find rehearsal time for some of his cast. He had carefully orchestrated his rehearsal schedule. It was maddening to them both, but, despite the difficulties, somehow, they pulled it off. The Senior Show was always a success. From my standpoint, the measure of success was always the same. A show was a success if the boys and girls in the play felt successful. They always felt that success in Jay and Linda's shows.

Our camp is an athletic camp, and though a number of our graduates made high school teams and a few were even on college teams, none has ever made a professional sports team. On the other hand, Hollywood and television studios are filled with our graduates, several of whom have become important writers, directors and producers. One of our former staff members was for a time the head of a Disney Studios. We've even have had several successful performers. On a personal note, we had one group of four boys who were bunk-mates through camp, all of whom wound up in television. Nicko Lowry is a "Poster Expert" on *Antique Road Show*. That is not his real job, but he is on the air frequently. Jaime Greenberg had his own night time cable show in New York, but is now in Hollywood. My son Robert started as a writer on the History channel and is currently Program Director at *Lifetime* channel. Sam Mettler is the creator and producer of "Intervention." Sam and Robert, working together, both won Emmys as Producer and Executive Producer of "Intervention".

43
In Forrest We Trust

In the early 1980s Ansel's son Forrest took over as head of maintenance. Ansel's health had been deteriorating for several years. Though he tried valiantly, and wanted desperately to continue, he knew he could no longer work full time. His son Forrest applied for the job. He was in his mid-thirties, a responsible contractor with a wife and three children to support. Additionally, I had seen his work. I knew he had the knowledge and skills for the job.

I first met Forrest when he was a teen-ager. He worked at camp in the summer, as his Dad's helper. His primary camp job was rolling tennis courts. We had clay courts, and it was Forrest's job to be there at dawn to brush and roll the eleven courts so that they would all be ready for play by 9:30. It was many years prior to power rollers. He pulled a heavy water filled hand roller behind him until the courts were solid. This was grueling work on mornings after heavy rain, and his day was not over when he finished work on the courts. He spent the remainder of the day working with his father on a variety of maintenance jobs.

Ansel and his wife Edna had somehow scraped together enough money to send their two older children, Forrest and Bertha, on to higher education. Forrest attended Wentworth Institute in Boston. It was his goal, and his Father's goal for him, to become a contractor. He did it. Coming back to his roots in Danbury, New Hampshire, Forrest built a business as an independent contractor. He started with renovations and wound up building houses. He had done this successfully for more than ten years. Then the home building business slowed and finally came to a virtual standstill during one of our country's periodic economic recessions. The country's misfortune happened to coincide with our need. Forrest came to me and asked whether he could take on the head maintenance job at camp. A steady income from camp seemed a better bet to him than waiting for the economy to turn around.

Forrest was as different from his father as he could be. Where Ansel was quiet and self effacing, Forrest was bombastic. Where Ansel was timid, Forrest was filled with self confidence. Where Ansel would run away from conflict, Forrest would invite it. During Ansel's long tenure, I always worried that people would hurt his feelings. In Forrest's twenty plus years at the helm, I had to put out many flames he had ignited with his short temper and loud bellowing voice. His temper presented serious issues, at a rate of about one or two a camp season. His targets were counselors, delivery men, and, most frequently, kitchen workers. But I never doubted that his many positives made it well worth dealing with the problems. Like his Dad, Forrest was a completely conscientious worker who was willing to take on anything at all that needed to be done. With his experience and education, he knew how to get things done, even complicated projects his Father could never have attempted.

With Forrest as our in-house maintenance man, we accelerated a building program that, within a few years, had replaced all but two of Kenwood's original cabins and added Cedar and Laurel Lodges to Evergreen. Where Ansel had worked in the living room of the Red House during the winter on small portable projects, Forrest made our camp gymnasium into a winter factory. That was his work site on all but the most bitter winter days. He seemed oblivious to the cold breezes that permeated and whistled through the siding of the unheated building. There he built the walls of new cabins, painted dock sections, and repaired camp equipment.

Forrest was a builder. As soon as camp was over, and he completed our closing procedures, he started the foundation and deck work on the next summer's new cabins. He was quite remarkable as a builder. He would have several projects going simultaneously, and drove me slightly crazy worrying that none would be complete by the start of the camp season. More than once, the final nails were hammered into a new cabin or a renovation as the busses filled with campers arrived at camp the first day of the season.

"Don't worry, Arthur. It will be ready."

There was a price to be paid for Forrest using the gym as his winter factory. Not only did the gym get used as a storage depot for tools, lumber and building materials, but it was used as housing for our camp boats, docks sections awaiting refurbishing, ping pong tables, gymnastics equipment, dining room tables and anything else that needed an indoor winter home. As each winter progressed the gym also became the repository for Forrest's personal things he didn't have room for at home. It was not unusual for me to find the Gym not only chock full with our camp goods, but also with perhaps a pile of truck tires, a motor boat of unknown origin, a rusty old freezer, a portable counter from some ancient general store or perhaps a rotting Wurlitzer juke box he had picked up at a sale somewhere.

When Spring came, Forrest started extracting the lumber and building materials, moving them to actual work sites. It became my job, along with the counselors who came to help out at "Work Week", to get all of the other camp equipment out of the gym and into position for camp use. That left Forrest's personal belongings strewn about the gym.

"Forrest, you know I have to have that gym cleared by the first day of Orientation. When are you going to get all of your junk out of there?"

"You tell me what day you need it, and I'll have all my things out."

He knew my deadline was the first day of staff orientation. But, until I asked and he answered, those things sat. The day before the start of staff orientation he began hauling. When necessary, he worked through the day and night, but the gym was always clear and usable by the time we needed it.

Through the years, Forrest made a lot of friends among permanent staff and counselors. He also intimidated and alienated lots of people. He had complete respect for any of our counselors who were good at physical labor, but barely concealed contempt for those who were physical bunglers. Many of our counselor volunteers who came to help at Work Week tried hard, but fell into his bungler category.

"What's the matter with that one? Doesn't he even know how to put a paint brush away?" ..... "I can't have these kids banging nails everywhere. Come and just see what he did.".... "That guy you have on the Gravely (our tractor mower) is gonna kill someone. Have you seen the Junior Ball field since he finished?".... "Steven (Forrest's son) can't do it all. You've got to give him somebody who knows how to use a wrench if you want to get those dock sections together.".... "That girl you have using the flame thrower on the Senior Tennis courts is gonna burn the whole camp down. You better get up there right away, and show her how to do it." (He was almost right on that one. Joanna Silver, one of the first few female counselors to break the tradition of an all male work week, was in a panic by the time I reached her. The flames had reached the grass beyond the tennis fence on the edge of the ball field, and her efforts with the hose were not very effective.)

I could usually hear a problem with Forrest before I could see it. One day mid- summer I was watching boys playing on the Junior Tennis courts, when I heard Forrest's voice bellowing at somebody. It was coming from Evergreen. I ran in that direction until I approached the near end of Spruce Lodge. Forrest was there, with a helper. They were both standing, shovels in hand, over an open septic tank. I could smell the source of the dispute before I got close.

"Don't you people have any sense at all? You can't flush underpants and hair brushes down toilets and expect them to work. Is that what you all learn in college? If you think its fun trying to clear these pipes, you come here and try it."

He had been shouting for a couple of minutes before I got there, and was quite prepared to continue as long as our young counselor stood terrified outside her lodge door, not knowing what to answer or being able to answer at all. I could see she was near tears by the time I arrived.

Phyllis and I arrived on the scene almost simultaneously. She came from another direction, put her arm around the girl's shoulder, and led her into the lodge. I signaled Forrest to follow me. We stopped on the girls' ball field, just far enough from the girls' lodges so that our conversation would not be overheard.

Before we even got to the field, Forrest realized that his anger had taken him too far. He calmed down and listened. He nodded his head in agreement, but I knew he would never apologize to the girl. He would never admit to being sufficiently wrong to have to apologize. I had to do it for him on his behalf. On the other hand, that was the last time I heard him shouting at anyone that summer.

Another day in another camp season I heard Forrest's angry shouts coming from our "counselor lounge", a barely habitable former arts & crafts building which we had moved to a position near the camp entrance. When I arrived at the scene, Forrest was literally pulling two scruffy looking teen age boys out of the building. They reeked of beer. Forrest knew them and I recognized them. They were local kids who either had no summer jobs or had already been fired from the jobs they had. With time on their hands, and full knowledge of the layout of our camp, they had made themselves at home in our counselor lodge, watching television, hoping to socialize with one of our female counselors or kitchen girls on a break.

"If I ever catch either one of you back here again, I'll call the police! Now get out, and don't even think about coming back!"

They nearly stumbled as he pushed them away. Then they turned and ran. That day, in his rough way, Forrest took care of a problem that would have been much more challenging for me to handle had I happened on the scene first. This was Forrest, the good and the bad, a long term dependable, and a diplomatic challenge for a camp director.

When I turned the camp operation over to my successor, Scott Brody, there were still many jobs to be done, but the physical plant was in much better condition than the camp I bought thirty-seven years earlier. Between them, from 1959 through 1996, Ansel and Forrest had rebuilt the camp for me, and for future generations.

44
Nightmare in Orange

Saturday, June 30th
Camp Season Started that Afternoon

Orange has never been my favorite color. When I woke up that morning and looked out our bedroom window, I couldn't believe my eyes. Our beautiful blue-black lake was orange. It had turned orange overnight. I leaped out of bed and ran to the living room. Maybe the lake would look blue from that window. No such luck.

"Judy, wake up." There was no reaction from my sleeping wife.

"Judy, please get up. I need you to look out the window and tell me what you see." She turned to her side lifting her head enough to get a clear view of our bedside clock.

"Why do you want me to get up now? What's wrong?" She got out of bed and pulled the curtains open. She gasped. Now we were both wide awake with a nightmare. This was the first day of camp. Our campers were due to arrive that very afternoon.

That Afternoon

After the busses rolled in and we welcomed all of the campers, I made my way to the waterfront to see their reactions.

I heard two old campers, ten year old boys, with their first reaction.

"What happened to the lake? Jesus! It's red!"

"It's not red at all. It's orange. Well, whatever, it's certainly not blue. It looks pretty awful."

One thirteen year old boy told his friend "I'm not swimming in that. They can't make me."

Jenny, an outspoken fourteen year old, had a group around her.

"There's no way I'm going into that water. If they try to make us go in I'll call my Mother to come and get me. Can you imagine what that will do to your hair...or your bathing suit?" She had unanimous support from her friends. They made a pact.

"Nobody goes in the water! Agreed?"

"Agreed!"

From a new camper, an eight year old girl ... "I don't think I'm going to like this camp. It won't be any fun without swimming..... I want to go home."

There was no doubt in my mind, clearly we were facing enormous difficulties. This could wind up putting us right out of business. I truly loved running a camp, but had always worried about the inherent dangers. I had always understood that there are enormous risks involved when you take responsibility for the lives of other people's children. I knew I was in a business where one irresponsible act or failure by an eighteen or nineteen year old counselor could put a camper's life in jeopardy and possibly cost the life of the camp as well. But my camp nightmare scenarios never included the vision of an orange lake, or worse still, the possibility of a toxic lake.

Monday, July 2nd

We had one important piece of good luck. Our next door neighbor at home in Lexington was a talented Marine Biologist, a man whose business was repairing damaged lakes, ponds and waterways. Jay was also a friend. He was away from home for the weekend, but I reached him at his office Monday morning.

"Jay, I need your help. Our camp lake has turned orange. I woke up Saturday morning, and the lake was orange."

"Don't panic, Arthur. If the lake is orange it's probably just iron oxide. It's not harmful in any way. So don't worry about that."

"Thank God. Are you sure?"

"I'm sure there's iron oxide just from what you've described. But I can't be sure until we test the water that there aren't any toxic elements as well. Send somebody down with water samples today, and I'll have them analyzed by tomorrow morning. I'll be able to tell you then if there is anything harmful in addition to the iron. I'm pretty sure it will just turn out to be iron." Jay went on to give detailed instructions on how many samples would be needed and how to take them.

"I hope you're right, but even so, it looks awful, and our camp season just started. None of the kids want to go in the water, and I don't even want them to go in unless I'm sure it's safe. How could this have happened overnight?"

I really knew better than this. I knew it wasn't overnight. For the last three years I had been writing and calling the New Hampshire Water Supply and Pollution Control as well as the Bureau of Solid Waste to complain that the landfill, a few miles upstream of our pond, was leaching ugly looking stuff. Our normal black-blue water lake had been getting murkier each year. The landfill was now closed, but I knew that it was the source of our troubles. But I had no idea why the lake was suddenly orange.

Jay gave me my first lesson in marine biology.

"It didn't happen overnight. That iron oxide has been seeping into your lake from somewhere, and lying on the bottom where it looks black. If you have dark water you might not have even noticed it. What happens is the lake turns over about once a month. The bottom water rises to the surface and the top water goes down. When the water with the iron oxide comes in contact with the air it turns orange."

"If I'm correct, and that is your only problem, we can treat it right away, and your lake will look better than it ever has. I'll send a team up as soon as you get a permit from Concord. It shouldn't be a problem. We're licensed to do business in New Hampshire. We cleaned up a few lakes in New Hampshire over the past five years. You know Kezar Lake near you? We cleaned that for the state a couple of years ago. The Water Supply Commission people know us. They trust us."

Three Weeks Later: July 23rd

The whistle sounded. Paula, our waterfront director, shouted "All out! "All out now!!!"

Little orange girls started emerging from the water. Most of them had kept their faces and hair out of the water, but their bodies shone orange in the sunlight. Their bathing suits, no matter what color they started, were all covered by an orange film. Lori and Karen were handling the hoses. By this time in the summer there was a well established routine. Dutifully each of the girls did a pirouette as the hoses splayed them with cold cleansing water. The orange dripped off them and disappeared into the sand, soon to be returned to the pond from which it came. The girls ran for their towels. The girls were no longer orange, but their bathing suits were and all of their towels now had a permanent orange cast as well.

I stood above the girls' waterfront with Phyllis, our Head Counselor. Together we looked out at the Orange lake and the strangely colored girls who emerged. We looked at one another and started to giggle. The giggle turned into loud laughter. What else could we do? The situation was beginning to look hopeless.

The night before, as all of the senior staff sat around in our living room discussing our problem and trying to put a positive face on it, our serious session deteriorated into gallows humor. The prize winning suggestion was that we build a fence around the lake, put signs up all over the state telling people to come and visit the Orange Sea. We'd charge admission and make a fortune.

It had been almost three weeks since Mickey Dank had delivered samples of our water to Jay's labs in Waltham. Jay called us the next day to assure us that there was no danger from the water; the issue was purely aesthetic. Despite his assurance those three weeks were unbelievable. The kids and counselors were all reluctant to go in the water. Upset Parents called in a panic that their children were swimming in a polluted lake. But worst of all, we dealt with a state bureaucracy that was straight out of a Kafka novel.

The agency in charge of lakes, water testing and coincidently children's summer camps was and still is New Hampshire Water Supply and Pollution Control Commission.

It was Judy's job to deal with the state bureaucracy. I never left camp while it was in session unless I was out with a group of kids. I felt that if there were ever critical decisions to be made I wanted to be physically present to make them. So Judy got stuck with all of the dirty work that required leaving camp. This was certainly dirty work. Judy is very thorough and organized. She made notes on all of the important conversations. I have paraphrased her notes below.

"Yes, we are the agency that issues permits to treat lakes, but I'm sorry we can't issue a permit to treat Your Lake with chemicals. Yes, we know the company you have employed. Yes, we know they are reliable. But you know as well as I do that your problem started with the Sanitary Landfill upstream from you in Danbury. The iron from the landfill leached into the ground water and then into Walker Brook, and finally to Eagle Pond. We're convinced the problem came from there. Since it is a landfill issue, you have to take it up with the Bureau of Solid Waste. I understand that they've been on the case with that Landfill for two or three years. The Fish and Game department has to be in on the decision too. They're worried that your chemicals may kill the fish. I don't see how we can issue a permit without a public hearing involving all three agencies. For now our hands are tied."

Judy was furious when she heard that the Fish and Game Department was a part of the delay. She scolded them. "Do you think we would put any chemicals in our lake that would harm our campers, never mind your fish. What's the matter with you people?"

We knew all about the landfill. For the last three years I had been writing and calling both the Water Supply and Pollution Control office and the Bureau of Solid Waste to complain that the landfill was leaching ugly looking stuff into the stream and that it was only a matter of time before it would reach our lake. Now it had happened, and it was time for one of these procrastinating agencies to take responsibility. Judy left Water Supply frustrated and angry. She next went through the maze of the state office complex to the Bureau of Solid Waste.

"Sorry we can't do a thing for you. We have already ordered the landfill closed. But we have nothing to do with issuing permits for chemical lake treatment. Water Supply and Pollution Control makes those decisions."

Judy was beside herself with upset at those people. "They either didn't understand or they didn't care what was at stake here."

"Can you imagine, now they are worried about fish! It doesn't seem to matter to them that our concerns are children and the camp. I can't deal with these people any more."

Finally we went to the State's Attorney General's office. By happy chance, one of our former campers was now an Assistant Attorney General in charge of Environmental affairs. Jeremy came up to camp to look for himself. He was shocked. He had swum in that lake as a little boy and as a young man. He found himself looking at a very different lake than the one he remembered. Until he saw it for himself I'm sure he thought I was exaggerating.

"Wow, it really is orange!" He thought for a minute. "Since there is nothing dangerous in the water we don't have authority to order an environmental clean up, but I will personally call the people at Water Supply. I'll let them know that I think you have a reasonable case for damages against them as well as the landfill company if they don't get that permit out right away."

Jeremy did place a call. Suddenly there was action. They held an emergency hearing the next day. Judy and a man from Jay's office testified for us. Later that day they issued the permit. I called Jay. He came through immediately.

"I'll have my men there tomorrow morning. You will have to find another place for your kids to swim tomorrow while we treat your lake. It will be perfectly safe the next day." We hurriedly arranged a trip day for our whole camp, and waited eagerly for morning.

Jay's men arrived before nine. He sent Al, his Operation Manager who had twenty-five years experience and Carlton, his Chief Aquatic Biologist with 15 years experience, to supervise the operation. He had prescribed and they prepared a large cocktail for our lake. The ingredients were 5,200 gallons of Aluminum Sulphate and 400 pounds of Potassium Permanganate. Jay's men and three of our Junior Counselors, working from "Spray Boats" distributed the chemicals at key points in the lake. Frank Morse, who ran our water ski program, was enlisted to use his ski boat as a mix-master, to stir the contents and spread them throughout the lake. I think Frank had a lot of fun that day using his trusty old boat in a new and different way. It was fascinating to watch the whole operation. The idea was that these chemicals would precipitate the iron oxide out of the water. I had absolutely no idea what that meant. I only hoped that it would work.

It took several hours, but they were finished well before our various groups of campers returned from their trip day destinations. At assembly that morning we had told the whole camp that we were having the lake treated that day. When the busses pulled back into camp late that afternoon, there was a mass movement down to the lake. Their disappointment mirrored my own. The lake looked the same as it had when they left in the morning. By the time the sun went down the lake still looked orange. I went to bed with a heavy heart. I kept repeating Jay's reassurance on the phone that evening like a mantra.

"Wait till you see that Lake in the morning. You won't believe it. Your lake will be beautiful." That is what Jay had promised. I couldn't wait.

July 25th

"Wonder of wonders ... Miracle of miracles ..."

"Oh, what a beautiful morning! Oh, what a beautiful day. I've got a wonderful feeling, everything's going my way."

These songs came into my head unbidden. I always did love musicals and now I felt like singing out loud. I felt like shouting my joy to the world. I was so relieved. I practically danced out to the end of the dock. I couldn't believe what I saw. I saw everything. I saw the bottom of the lake from the end of the dock. Nobody had ever seen the bottom of that lake from the end of the dock. It just wasn't ever that kind of lake. But there it was. I could see half buried sticks and stones.

I laughed out loud when I got to the deep water point where the dock sections meet at right angles. I looked down and saw years' worth of dropped wrenches where they had lain dormant and undiscovered since they slipped out of the hands of our enthusiastic but inexperienced counselors who put the docks together each year. I remembered all of those dropped wrenches well. I had seen all of them slip out of hands and out of sight. I had dropped some of them myself. I would have shouted out loud, but it was only 5:30 AM, and I hoped that our camp was still asleep.

That was not the end of the saga, just of the drama. There were court battles and injunctions and suits for damages. The landfill was closed. The landfill was "capped". Finally they had to dig out their rubbish and move it all to another safer location far away from ground water. We won, but we still had to deal with leachate from the landfill for years. The next year it was not nearly as bad, but bad enough so we needed another treatment. Each succeeding year it was less and less of a problem. The lake took seven or eight years to clear completely, but finally it did. If you visited our lake now you would never suspect that it had once been a nightmare in orange.

45
Parents Who Present Challenges

Psychiatrist?

In the nineteen seventies and even more in the eighties we noticed a disturbing trend, an ever increasing numbers of campers who were receiving psychiatric help. We received long detailed letters attached to the camper confidential reports. Most of the letters were entirely reasonable, and expressed the parents love and concern for their children entering a brand new environment. In addition to the letters, there was an accompanying increase in medications that arrived at camp to be administered to children on a daily basis. Sometimes we wondered if these children needed all of the emotional and mind altering medications they received, we speculated what their personalities might be if they just were allowed to grow up and work through their problems. On occasion we found out.

Sheryl was an experienced counselor, so when she came to the Evergreen office, visibly upset, I knew she had a real problem.
"She's impossible. I can't deal with her anymore."
"Sheryl, this is only the fourth day of camp. It's a little too soon to give up on a camper."
"I know, I know it's early, but she's not going to change."
"I don't know her at all. Tell me something about her. What does she do that is so terrible?"
"All right, take this morning. It's clean up time, everyone else is working, while Liz is sitting on her bed reading "True Romance." I go over and tell her she has to do her part or the other girls will be upset with her. She agrees. Then she goes into the bathroom. I figure she'll come back and start to make her bed, but no, she disappears. She's not in the bunk. She's not in the bathroom. She's not in the living room. I go outside and eventually find her playing with the Freshman girls down at Hemlock Lodge. When she looks up and sees me, she's not embarrassed or upset. She just looks puzzled, like what am I doing there."
"I said to her, Liz, what are you doing here? You know what her answer was?" I shook my head no. "She said "playing". I said what about cleanup. She said 'I forgot.' She came right along back to the bunk with me, no argument. Of course, by then the other girls had all finished their jobs, and it was time for activities. I had to go to soccer with the rest of the girls. I left Liz making her

bed. Carrie agreed to watch her, and bring her along when she was ready. We were about half way through the soccer period when Carrie came into the Hollow. She looked frantic. She had lost Liz again on the short walk from Pine Lodge down to the Hollow.

"Jacki (our athletic director) was running the activity anyway. She said she could handle it alone if I needed to find Liz. So Carrie and I went searching. We found her at Ceramics. Again, when she looked up and saw me, she had that puzzled look on her face. When I questioned her she said 'of course I'm here. I like ceramics.' That was just one example. It's been like that every day since camp started."

I suggested we look over Liz' Confidential Report, and see if there were any clues there. My wife Judy, Phyllis, Sheryl & I passed the Parent Confidential Report around trying to find a hint from Liz' parents of the kind of behavior Sheryl had just reported. There was nothing there. The closest was a note that "she sometimes needs reminding."

"Well, that clears things up, doesn't it? Who wants to make the call to her Mother? Phyllis? Judy?" I looked back and fourth, hoping one of them would volunteer. But that was not to be. Judy said "You're the only one who has ever met the woman. This is your call."

"You're right. I'll call. Sheryl, I'd like you to stand by while I try to reach Mrs. Goldstein. I may want to put you on the phone to give her a first hand report." It seemed unlikely that I would reach her mid-morning at her home number, but was pleasantly surprised when she picked up on the second ring. After I introduced myself, and assured her that her daughter was healthy and had not been in any kind of accident, I got right to the point.

"Mrs. Goldstein, we need your help trying to figure out what's going on with Liz"

"I can't imagine that you would be having a problem with Elizabeth. Are you sure the problem isn't with your counselor?" She didn't wait for an answer. "Liz has been wonderful at home lately."

"That's good to hear, but it's not what we're seeing here. Have there been any changes at home recently that might have upset her?" She thought for a few seconds, and then replied.

"Now, we did make one change before she left for camp. We decided she could use a break from her daily meds. We thought camp would be such a nice relaxing change for her after the pressure at school that she wouldn't need them. We stopped it a few days before she left. I'm sure that's not the issue. But let me give you her psychiatrist's number. You can discuss it with her. Whatever you two decide will be fine with me."

I was amazed. All I could do was take the psychiatrist's phone number, and end the conversation. There was no point in telling her what I thought. It would only put her on the defensive. I found it hard to believe that they enrolled her in camp, filled out confidential reports as well as medical forms and never once mentioned either medication or that their daughter was receiving psychiatric care. That was totally unreasonable. Perhaps worse, from a practical standpoint, was their decision to change her medication regime just before camp.

Liz's psychiatrist agreed that she should be put back on her medication right away. Within two days after she resumed her meds, Liz acted like a different girl. Though hardly a perfect camper, she was well within the norm. She was able to function in her cabin and in activities. She had a good summer, and returned to camp for three more camp seasons.

Mrs. Goldstein was neither the first nor the last parent to suspend her child's behavior modifying medication before her child left home for the very first time. On almost every occasion when this was done, it resulted in the child starting camp unable to cope with her new situation.

Camp Battleground

In nineteen sixty we had two children in camp whose parents were divorced. We recognized that those children might have special problems and issues. We understood that the breakup of a family was likely to create victims, and that the children were apt to bear scars. Through the sixties the numbers increased little by little. By the mid seventies perhaps twenty or thirty of our campers had parents who were separated or divorced. By the mid nineteen eighties perhaps as many as a quarter of our campers came from split families. In many of these situations camp played a stabilizing role in the children's lives. They looked upon camp as a safe place, a place that could serve comfortably as home for seven weeks. But there were many side issues that came along with divorce. More than once I was caught in a battle between parents who had favored different camps for their children. Once I was even asked to come to family court so that a judge could decide which of two competing camps the child should attend. The story that follows was unusual, but hardly unique.

The Green family lived on the South side of Newton, Massachusetts in a neighborhood I knew well. They lived just a couple of blocks from my Father's house, where I had spent weekends in my high school years. Though my Dad had long since moved to Florida, I felt comfortable coming back to the streets where I had learned to drive, streets I knew so intimately as a teen-ager. This was home territory.

Very early in my visit with the Greens, it became obvious that there was serious tension between husband and wife. It was evidenced by negative glances and barely audible asides. Their daughter Joanne seemed oblivious to the tension. She appeared to be a really nice girl, who would surely be a happy camper. Mr. Green was anything but subtle in letting me know he did not want his daughter coming to Evergreen. Mrs. Green just as obviously did. This battle of the camps was not so unusual with divorced couples, but, with an apparently intact family, it was strange that it hadn't been resolved before I was asked to come. Dad was decidedly antagonistic toward me and my camp. I had an uncomfortable hour and a half, but all things come to an end, and I was happy to make my exit, leaving an application for them to debate in my absence.

Two weeks later the application and deposit reached me, and I was pleased to learn Joanne would be with us. The application was signed by Harriett Green, and the deposit check, though written on a joint account, was also signed by her. Shortly before the start of the camp season, Joanne's "Parents Confidential Report Form" arrived at camp. Parents were asked to respond to all sorts of questions about their children. Under the "Special Considerations" portion of the report came this gem.

"Phillip and I are in the process of a divorce. It has been a terrible strain on Joanne, and I am glad she will be away from all of the anger and upset for the summer. It is very important that Mr. Green not be allowed to upset her by visiting her at camp. The court has issued a restraining order against him. If he comes to camp, and tries to visit Joanne I want you to call the police and have him arrested right away."

Camp started, and Joanne fit right in. She was a quiet girl, but seemed to have established herself with a circle of friends. Her counselors reported that she liked camp activities, and happily participated in everything. Our mid-summer Parents' Visiting Day went well. Mrs. Green visited Joanne, and appeared to be happy with her daughter's camp experience.

The following Saturday morning I received a phone call from Mr. Green.

"Mr. Sharenow, Phil Green calling, remember me? We met at my house when you came to show slides to my daughter Joanne."

"Certainly I remember you, Mr. Green. What can I do for you?"

"I'm coming up to visit my girl this morning. I'm planning to take her out to lunch."

"I'm afraid that won't be possible. We had parents' visiting day last Sunday."

"I knew about that, but I didn't want to come when Harriett was there. It would put too much pressure on Joanne. It's not good for her to see us fighting, and apparently that's all the two of us can do when we get together these days."

"I certainly understand, and I'm sure it was best that you did not visit at the same time. But, Mr. Green, your ex-wife told us that there's a restraining order against you, and that you're not allowed to visit with Joanne at all."

"What! That bitch! There's no restraining order! Take my word for it. We're still negotiating about custody. I have every right to see my daughter, and, I'm going to. Please don't give me a hard time. I called as a courtesy to you. I want to abide by your rules, and I don't want to cause any disruption, but she is my daughter too, and I can certainly visit her. I'm leaving Boston now, and I'll be there before noon. I'm warning you, you had better not make it difficult for me. If you do, you'll be sorry. I'm the one who pays the camp bill." With that, he hung up.

This presented me with an interesting dilemma, one I would have to resolve quickly. Mrs. Green had instructed us to call the police. Mr. Green asserted there was no restraining order. I hadn't seen the order. I couldn't ask the police to come and arrest him without any documentation or evidence of a crime. Yet it was Mrs. Green who had taken responsibility for her daughter at camp, and I at least wanted to alert her. I picked up the phone.

"Mrs. Green, I just got a call from your husband. He's on his way up here to visit Joanne and he's planning to take her out to lunch."

"Call the police at once."

"I can't do that. I never saw your restraining order. Can you fax me a copy of the judge's order?"

"I'll never find that piece of paper in time. Just call the Police and hold him. I'll bring the order with me. I'm getting dressed now. I'll be there by noon."

"I can ask him to wait in the office with me, but I have no authority to call the police."

"All right, just don't let him get to Joanne. We'll call the police when I get there." She hung up.

It was almost twelve thirty. Mr. Green was with me in my office. My tiny office was on the driveway side of the dining room. In five minutes, the bugle would blow, and the entire camp would converge on that same dining room. I was stalling Mr. Green, explaining that this would be a difficult time for us to reach Joanne. She'd be heading up to the Mess Hall with all of the other girls in a few minutes. He needed to be patient.

Mess call blasted out over the PA system. In the background another sound pierced through the familiar bugle call. The sound of the siren was piercing and grew louder the closer it came. The police car came up the hill and rolled into the small lot next to the dining room. A state trooper stepped out. New Hampshire state troopers all looked as though they were stamped from a mold. This one was typical, all spit and polish, pants creased, shoes shined, and his trooper hat perched on his head at a rakish angle. As he strode purposefully toward my office door, a few of our senior boys, making their way to lunch from Senior camp, crossed through the parking area and next to the police cruiser. Their eyes popped. They were excited to see a state trooper in camp, and enjoyed speculating about what had brought him.

I met him on the small porch outside the office. I wanted to talk to him before he came in. I was afraid he might do something rash, like handcuffing or arresting Mr. Green on the basis of a call from his wife.

"Hello, officer, what can I do for you?"

"Your name, Sir?"

"I'm Arthur Sharenow. I'm the director. This is my camp."

"I'm here about the kidnapping. A woman named Harriett Green called, and reported her daughter was kidnapped from this camp within the last hour. You must know all about this. First, I need to know just what time it was when he grabbed the little girl. Next, I need a description of Green and his car. "

"Hold for a minute, officer. Nobody's been kidnapped. Mrs. Green must have been a little hysterical when she called you. This is a custody dispute. I'm not happy being in the middle, but believe me, nobody has been kidnapped. I don't know the legal situation, but I have the husband here with me in the office, and I know his wife is on the way. I talked to her this morning on the phone, and promised her I wouldn't let him go anywhere with their daughter before Mrs. Green gets to camp. She says there is a restraining order against him. He says that's a lie."

"Meanwhile, their daughter, Joanne, is safe in camp. She's with her friends on the way up to the dining room to have lunch. She knows nothing about what's going on. She doesn't know her Father is here. I'm hoping we can resolve this mess without an emotional scene for the little girl. You can talk to Mr. Green and get your own sense. I don't think he's a dangerous character, just an unhappy anxious father."

The trooper stepped into the office. Mr. Green, displaying restraint for which I would not have given him credit, stood up, offered his hand, and introduced himself. Just then I heard the crunch of another set of tires rolling into our gravel parking area. I looked out the window, as Mrs. Green pulled in next to the police car. Her face was red with fury as she stormed up the side stairs to the office porch. I met her at the door. She screamed at me.

"Where is he? How long ago did he take her? Why aren't the police chasing him? You can't just sit around and talk when my child has been kidnapped."

"Calm down, Mrs. Green. Joanne's fine. She's with her group. Your husband didn't take her anywhere. He's in the office talking to the state trooper now." I watched as the blood drained from her face. She didn't say a word, but she was swaying. She grabbed onto the porch railing. I held onto her, as she crumpled slowly onto the landing.

The camp nurse held a cold compress to her forehead. The color started returning to her face. Along with it came an awareness of her situation. In another minute she looked up and thanked the nurse, while removing her hand and the compress. She pulled herself up using the porch railing as a support.

"I'm sorry to create a scene like that. I've never fainted before. I was just so relieved I don't know what came over me."

Mrs. Green came face to face with her husband as soon as I opened the office door. He stood aside and she squeezed past. My office was now filled wall to wall. There was little room to separate the feuding parties. The room was small by any standard, but it was made smaller by its furnishings: my battered double desk took up one wall, two desk chairs, two folding chairs, and a file cabinet. The remaining wall space was cluttered by several milk crates filled with softballs, an old style umpire's inflated chest protector, and a stack of boxes filled with our campers' favorite candy bars. The four of us stood together briefly, in the center of the room, making a close knit tableau. It could only have been a few seconds, but it seemed longer until it occurred to me to pull out one of the desk chairs for Mrs. Green. She sat down heavily. Her husband took that as an invitation, and sat in the other. He pushed it back as far as his chair would take him.

The trooper was the first to speak.

"Mrs. Green, I'm here because you called state police headquarters, and reported a kidnapping? It doesn't look like there was any kidnapping. Are you aware that falsely reporting a kidnapping is a crime?"

"It wasn't a false report. If you didn't get here that man would have been out of here with my daughter."

"Maam, there was no kidnapping. When I arrived your husband was here in the office with Mr." turning to me, "tell me your name again."

"Sharenow, Arthur Sharenow." I spelled it out for him as he wrote in his pocket notepad.

"Your husband was talking to Mr. Sharenow, and I understood they were waiting here for your daughter and the rest of the campers to come to the dining room. He didn't take her anywhere."

"He has no right to even be here."

"I understand you have a restraining order. Please let me I see it."

"Well it's not exactly a restraining order. It's an agreement that was drawn up by our lawyers. We both signed it. He agreed not to visit her or take her anywhere without my OK, pending a final settlement in court."

The trooper turned toward Mr. Green.

"Is that true?"

"Yes it's true, but she kept saying no. I didn't get to visit Joanne for weeks. Then she sent her off to camp, and I couldn't even say goodbye or give her a hug before she left. I have a right to see my own little girl. And anyway, that's no court order, and she had no right to call the police."

"You're right about that." He turned back toward Mrs. Green.

"Don't ever call the police and report a kidnapping when there wasn't one. I'm going to let you get away with it this time, but I'll make a record of this. If you ever call in a phony report again in this state, you will be charged."

"I'm sorry, officer. It won't happen again."

I felt superfluous, like a spectator. It was time for me to propose a solution. The trooper had little or no experience with this kind of issue, but I did.

"Officer, before you leave, I'd like to suggest a temporary solution for today. After today the two of them can fight it out with their lawyers." I turned toward Mrs. Green and then toward her husband. Of course, both of them have to agree. Officer, in case they can't agree would you mind staying for another few minutes." He nodded yes.

"I'm going to propose a solution we have used in other similar situations. Mr. Green, we'll bring your daughter to you and you can have three hours to visit with her in camp. You have to agree not to leave the camp grounds. I'll assign a counselor to keep the two of you in sight during your visit. The counselor will stay far enough away so that you can have private conversations with your daughter. This way, Mr. Green, you can visit with Joanne, meet her counselor and bunk-mates, watch her at activities and have a full visit. We've used this procedure several times, and it has worked successfully. Mrs. Green, there will be no possibility of Mr. Green leaving camp with Joanne. What do you say? Could you live with that?"

She thought for a minute, and then turned toward her husband.

"Phil, I'll go along with that if you agree to the restrictions."

"Yes, I agree. I don't like it, but it's better than nothing. Just don't you ever call the police on me again. Call me if there's a problem. Don't call the police."

"That's fine, Phil. Just don't try to sneak behind my back again. Just one other thing, I'm here now and I'd like to stay for a brief visit with Joanne after you leave."

It was agreed. We shook hands all around, and the trooper left the scene. As soon as he drove down the hill and out of camp I felt relieved. Camp was back to normal.

Joanne was delighted to see her Father. He visited with her for a few hours. Mrs. Green spent that time reading magazines in the infirmary living room. After her husband said goodbye, she left too, having second thoughts about the wisdom of staying and possibly confusing Joanne with her visit. After all, she had seen her just a week earlier.

46
A Jewish Bride from the East

John Frank made a wonderful first impression. He was tall, slim and well groomed. His straight brown hair was cut neatly. He wore a collared shirt under his white v-necked tennis sweater. His brown slacks were neatly pressed and even his shoes were polished. He presented a quiet contained demeanor, and his responses were intelligent and thoughtful. He was very articulate. Considering that it was still the 1970s, John appeared to be a throw back from a pre-Vietnam War era.

He had an impeccable background. He had served as a tennis coach at a Boston area university, where he worked with the women's tennis team. He appeared to be a "straight arrow" in every important way. We discussed the drug problem in colleges, and he spoke out strongly against experimentation of any kind. He was appalled by the binge drinking he was witness to in college dormitories. He believed in firm rules, clear directions and good competition. It was true he had never stepped foot in a camp, but he had been working with teen-agers, teaching them tennis from the time he was one of them.

I hired John as a cabin counselor and tennis assistant. I did so with great confidence that he would be a pillar of strength in an already strong Kenwood staff for the 1979 camp season. I was sure that, once he had a little camp experience under his belt, John would be the kind of young man we would want with us in future years as either a unit leader or a head of tennis.

I was right. John was with us from his start in 1979 into the 1986 camp season. His first year at camp he was a counselor in our "Junior Unit ", working with boys eleven and twelve years old, including my son Robert and some of Rob's closest camp friends. During the years our children were campers, I always got a post-camp review of the camp season from their perspective. Rob was less than enthusiastic about John, but he was not negative either. I supposed that John probably asked for tighter discipline from his boys than Rob and his friends were accustomed to.

Despite rather tepid endorsements from Robert and several staff members, I promoted John to Senior Camp, where he became Unit Leader of our largest group of boys. This group was always our most challenging since it spanned three difficult ages, thirteen to fifteen. His quick promotion was made necessary because we had reached the end of a cycle, and many of the young men who had joined us in the early 1970s were finally graduating from their various graduate school programs and going out into the real world of year round employment. Of those who remained, none appeared qualified to be Senior Unit Leader. Only John seemed to have the age and maturity that we needed in that spot. He got the job.

John did a decent, if unspectacular, job over the next few summers. He was hard working, well organized and reliable. The Senior boys seemed to be well directed. There was pretty good evidence that he did his job well in the very high percentage of the Senior Camp boys who returned year after year. Nonetheless, there were rumblings of discontent, murmurs that things were not always as they appeared. The rumblings grew more persistent from year to year. Jacki McCarthy, Evergreen's Senior Unit Leader, had to work with John frequently on coed evening programs. She was outspoken in her criticism. She had heard stories that he was malicious and sometimes even vicious. When I questioned campers after each season, I didn't hear anything to back up Jacki's assertions. Of course, I didn't want to hear bad things. I needed John. He had Senior Camp running well, and we had no experienced replacement in the wings.

By the mid-1980's, we had built a new counselor staff, though slightly younger than our all-star staff of the mid 1970s, they were almost as solid. In fact, many of the counselors on the Kenwood staff had been campers John's first year as a counselor, including my son and two others who had been in his cabin that year.

John had moved from Boston in the early 1980's, and was now an English Instructor at a college in the mid West. His academic career was moving along. It was late in the Spring of 1986 that I received an astonishing letter from him. He did plan to come back to camp, but

"... I have a surprise for you. I'm a married now, and my wife's Jewish. She's a beautiful Jewish girl from the East. She wants to come to camp with me this summer. I'm sure she will make a great counselor for Evergreen, but she doesn't have to be a counselor as long as we can live together. If that's not possible, I can't return."

John was Catholic, but the fact that his bride was Jewish was not a big surprise. He'd been working at our largely Jewish camp for years and had never made a point of going to church Sundays. I was sure that religion was not a major factor in his life. On the other hand, I was astonished that he was married at all. I had always thought of him as being asexual. He had never shown any interest in our Evergreen counselors, and had never spoken about a girlfriend. I assumed his wife "from the east" must have been a rare New York or Philadelphia girl who somehow wound up as a student at his mid-western college.

Once I got over the shock, I reached John by phone that very night. After I expressed my surprise and happiness for him, we got down to business. His wife's name was Joy; she was twenty-one years old, and she had no camp experience. It would be all right if we had no job for her. She would just come and vacation there, as long as they didn't have to live in a bunk with campers.

"Don't you think she'll be bored without a job and you working so many hours? She may not realize that Senior Unit Leader is busy with the kids every night until at least nine thirty or ten o'clock.

"It will work out. She's very independent. She'll find things to do."

"What about you? Do you think being newly married might be a distraction? "I can handle it."

"John, I have to warn you. It can put a strain on your marriage. I can tell you from personal experience. Judy and I came to camp right from our honeymoon. She was Evergreen Head Counselor, and I was Kenwood Senior Unit Leader. Of course, our housing situation was not helpful. We lived upstairs in the Red House (the opposite end of camp). I had to keep a change of clothes in Senior Camp. There was never time enough to run back to the Red house. By the time I got back at night it was usually after ten, and she was prestty upset. Mostly she was lonely. Since she was Head Counselor and married, it put her out of the social swing. Her job was usually over by eight thirty or quarter of nine at the latest, and she couldn't understand why I was so late every night. At that point in time Evergreen was still a very new camp, and the oldest campers were twelve and thirteen, not fifteen like Kenwood's Senior boys."

"Of course, your situation will be better since you'll be right there in that cabin next to Senior Camp, but it won't be easy."

"I can handle it and so can she. She understands that my job will be the priority for the summer. You said it was hard for you and Judy, but it all seemed to work out all right in the end."

"John, you and Joy will have that beautiful staff cabin that faces the lake. I think that cabin is great but it's pretty rustic for a young woman who has never been to camp. It's not a finished cabin, and mice and chipmunks have been a constant problem through the years. We almost lost a Head Counselor one year because his wife found a nest of baby mice in their cabin the first day they moved in. She was hysterical. We had to move them. In fact, we moved them to the Red House."

"Don't worry about Joy. She's a pretty solid girl."

I decided it could work out. By now, we had built a strong staff again in both camps, and we could afford the luxury of a Senior Unit Leader who was not also a cabin counselor.

We were all very curious about this mysterious young woman, who had captivated John. He apparently met her in the Winter and married her in the Spring. That was an amazingly fast decision. There was some speculation among the camp brass that she might be pregnant, which would account for the record courtship. We could hardly wait for her arrival..

Joy and Jack exploded into camp the first day of Orientation. It is hard to make a big entrance when you arrive in a battered eight year old mustard colored Mercury station wagon. It is also challenging to make a big entrance when you are driving on a narrow dust choked dirt road. But, if anyone could do it, it was Joy Frank. Within fifteen minutes, everyone in camp was talking about John's incredible bride. People, who didn't actually see or hear their arrival felt cheated, and positioned themselves so they wouldn't miss the next glimpse.

Joy was driving when their car came into sight, zipped around the bend in the road, and nearly ran down our welcoming committee, stationed on the side of the road by the Camp Evergreen entrance Gate. Andy Tarsy, Gary Saks and Josh Macht jumped nimbly out of the way. According to one version of the episode, John was slumped down in the passenger seat and waved to them from the side window as the car whipped by without stopping. Their car cornered quickly around the gym, and finally slowed some going up the hill toward the dining room and office.

I was in the office when they pulled to a stop in the dirt parking area. John jumped out of the car and ran in the front door of the dining room, and around the corner into the office. I was getting up to shake his hand and welcome him, but he got in the first words.

"Is my cabin unlocked? We have to get up there right away. Joy needs to cool off and change out of her city clothes. The air conditioner isn't working in my car. She's really hot and tired."

He looked and sounded frantic.

"Yes, John, the cabin is open. You go and get settled. I'll meet Joy later."

I watched from my office as he ran back out to the car. I caught a glimpse of her as the car backed and turned to go down the hill away from the dining room. All I saw were tanned arms, very red lips, sunglasses, and a wide-brimmed hat.

Before dinner, we always had assembly and flag lowering in front of the dining room. All of the counselors and the whole administration, even those who were usually late, were gathered around the flagpole when John and his bride came into the assembly area. It is fair to say that heads turned. In fact, they continued to turn right through my welcome speech and a variety of announcements. There was an excited buzz rippling through the ranks. Joy was the focus for all eyes.

She was Asian, probably Korean, and certainly not the New York or Philadelphia Jewish girl I had imagined from John's description of "a Jewish girl from the East". My first impression was that Joy had chosen as her model Madame Nhu, the notorious Dragon Lady of Vietnam. Madame Nhu had been a well known figure to the American public during the early stages of the Vietnam War. Of course, we didn't know Joy Frank at all, and it was unfair to jump to conclusions, but, looking at her in her form fitting dress, floppy hat, unlikely high heel shoes, blood red finger nails and "tanned" face it wasn't too much of a stretch to imagine that she might share Madame Nhu's sharp tongue as well as her ruthlessness and arrogance. It was equally tempting to view her as a visiting movie star, moving among the peasantry. Neither of these interpretations was fair, but it was fun to speculate. One thing was obvious; Joy was not going to bow to the fashion expectations of camp. In fact, after one day she substituted designer jeans and blouses for her silk dress and high heels. Her makeup and her finger nails remained.

That night, after the evening program, our permanent staff members came down to our house to share with Judy and me their impressions of all of the new counselors. Phyllis was there with her husband Mickey, Norm and his wife Shirlee, Jacki McCarthy, our girls' camp Senior Unit Leader, and Jamie Demarest, our long term Drama Counselor, made up the party along with Judy and me. Much of the entertaining discussion centered on Joy, and we really enjoyed ripping her apart and pitying poor John. We had so much fun I almost felt guilty. By the end of the evening we all agreed that she was probably a lot more solid citizen than she appeared. John was no dummy. He wouldn't have married an empty shell.

Mid-way through Orientation week John came to me with a request.

"Arthur, would it be all right if I take off tomorrow? I know it's unusual and I won't go if you feel you need me here, but I would love to take Joy out and around and show her New Hampshire. I know it gets more difficult the closer we get to opening, and we won't have a day off for at least the next ten days."

"How are you two doing up there? Is Joy happy?"

"To tell you the truth, she's a little bored. That's why I want to get her out for a day. I know she'd be happier if you could find something for her to do."

"I'll see what I can come up with. In the meantime, take your day tomorrow and relax. We'll be fine here without you."

I had worried about Joy from the first day she arrived. She was unlikely to fit in anywhere in camp. I was also starting to worry about John. Counselors in Senior Camp were talking about the shouting they heard at night. It came from John's cabin. Of course, this came to me second hand, but I believed it.

I had met Joy the first day she stepped into camp, and we had exchanged pleasantries, but I had never really gotten to talk to her until the day before the campers arrived. I was down in the Evergreen office when she approached me. We sat and talked on the office porch.

"I need to have something to do. I'm going a little stir crazy here. I really need to keep busy. I have nothing to do all day. John is working all the time, and I'm stuck back in the cabin. The nights are even worse. You have those counselor meetings every night, and there's no point in me going to them if I'm not a counselor. It's not good for John either. I'm always upset by the time he gets back to the cabin, and I take it out on him."

"Joy, I'm truly sorry you're bored. I've thought about your situation, and the only real job I could come up with would be for you to help out in the office a few hours every day. Would you like to do that?"

"Well, I suppose I could, but I can't really be expected to do typing with these." She held her hands out for my inspection. Her long red finger nails would certainly not be of much use on a typewriter. I laughed.

"I can see your point. Don't worry about that. We don't have much typing to do anyway. The biggest job is just sitting here to answer the phone, make announcements and take care of whatever comes up. This is not the most exciting job. I can't promise you won't be bored. If people are unhappy with the office job that's the usual complaint. But if you come in, we can shorten the rotation and it won't be such a long day for you or the other girls. The office opens at eight o'clock in the morning and stays open until nine thirty at night. On the positive side, people are always in and out of the office. You'll know everybody in Evergreen within a week."

She thought about it and agreed.

Joy was not a happy office worker. Her litany of complaints grew daily, and she was driving everyone a little bit crazy. She looked for every possible opportunity to leave the office. More and more, she gravitated toward Juniper Lodge, where our fifteen year old girls lived. Missy Laakso was Juniper counselor that summer, and it didn't take long before Missy came to me with her Joy problem.

"You've got to keep her out of our lodge. She comes in, plops herself down on somebody's bed, and starts doing her fingernails. She's giving my girls makeup lessons. Can you imagine Liz Mettler and Nina Lieberson getting makeup lessons? It would be laughable, but they sit there, studying themselves in hand mirrors and listening. I really don't want her in my lodge any more."

Fortunately, Joy solved our Juniper problem by quitting the office job.

"It's just too boring....the children are rude...your office chairs are unbelievably uncomfortable...the counselors are nasty to me....I don't think I can do this any more."

One day, while Joy was still at Evergreen, I dropped into the office, and, since she was the only one there, I stopped for a chat. We talked about how she and John met, their lives together at school, and finally about their respective families. When we got to John's family, Joy sounded very angry.

"I've tried my hardest to get them to like me, but they're cold to me and not very nice. I think they're upset that I'm Jewish."

I could think of lots of reasons that John's parents would not warm up to her, but her religion didn't strike me as being high on the list.

Difficult situations kept coming up, one after the other. Joy was a pain in the neck, for sure, in many ways. Greg, our Kenwood waterfront director, came to me with a Joy dilemma.

"Arthur, would you mind talking to John Frank for me."

"What's the trouble?"

Joy comes down to our waterfront every morning, as soon as it warms up. She's there the rest of the morning and then comes back just in time for swim instruction in the afternoon."

"That doesn't sound too terrible. Does she want to help with instruction? Is she swimming? What's she doing?"

"Mostly she's sunbathing on the dock. She comes down in this tiny bikini, and she's really a distraction. Some of the counselors are busy watching her instead of keeping their eyes on the water during general swim. And when the Senior boys are there, forget it. She parades around just making a play for attention, and she gets it. Of course, John is there when the Senior boys are there. I don't know how he can stand it. I don't know what to say to him. I would appreciate it if you would talk to him for me. It's really difficult with her down there."

My talk with John was uncomfortable for me, and, I could see, very upsetting to him. Very tactfully, I suggested that Joy could spend her time at the girls' waterfront, where at least she wouldn't pose a safety hazard.

"I'll try, but I know she won't want to walk all the way to the girls' waterfront when we live in Kenwood and the beach is just down the path from our cabin. If she doesn't want to do that, how about if I ask her to just leave the waterfront during Senior swim times, explaining that the boys are distracted by her body. That would work. She might even be flattered."

"Let's try the girls' waterfront approach first. That is the better solution."

That night there was a terrific row in their cabin. I heard about it the next morning from Henry Smith. Henry was a veteran counselor, and this was his third summer working under John as Senior Unit Leader.

"It was awful. She was screaming at John. It went on for a long time. All the boys heard it. I'm starting to worry about John. Have you noticed? He hasn't been himself lately?" I nodded, puzzling to myself about how to solve this problem. Henry went on. "John has been very irritable this summer, and he's not paying attention to details like he usually does. The schedule has been screwed up a few times already. Dennis and I have been able to cover for him, but the other counselors certainly have noticed. I don't know what the kids think."

A few days later Dennis Shattner reported to me that Joy had taken to dropping in on their hut just as he was trying to get the boys to change and settle down for the night. Dennis had the oldest boys, fifteen year olds.

"She doesn't knock or anything. She just drops in like she's one of the boys. Sometimes, I come back from the shower house, and she's already in our hut, sitting on one of their beds. She does leave when I ask her to, but this is getting very awkward. And you can be sure the boys are not ready to go to sleep right after Joy leaves the Hut. She is one swift pain in the ass."

By now, I knew we had a huge problem. Not only was Joy difficult everywhere in camp, but she was clearly undermining John's confidence and his ability to do his job. His job was one of our most important in camp. I wondered whether we would be able to get through the camp season with John's problem. But for now, it would have to wait. It was just a couple of days before Parents Visiting Day. I couldn't even contemplate making any kind of change just before then. We would have to muddle through until the Parents came and went, and then figure out what to do.

On Visiting Day, I was not besieged by anxious Senior Camp parents as I had feared. A few of them did ask me about Joy, but nobody actually pinned me down on the subject, so I was able to make light of their boys' comments, and change the subject as quickly as possible.

The crisis came two days after Visiting Day. John came to see me. He was shaking and looked as though he had been crying.

"Arthur, Joy is miserable, and she insists she wants to go home. I tried to talk her out of it, but once she has made up her mind, she never changes it. I need to get her to Logan Airport today. American has a four o'clock flight direct to Chicago. She has a friend who will meet her at the airport and drive her to our apartment."

"John, are you going to be all right with her gone?"

"I don't know. I just know it isn't working out very well here. I told her I would go with her, but she said I should stay here. So, I'm asking for two things. I need the day off and I need to borrow one of the camp cars."

"What's the matter with your car?"

"It's at Currier & Phelps. Clyde said it would be ready in a couple of days, but it's been two weeks already. I called them before I came up here and it still isn't ready."

"John, I'll check but I'm pretty sure all of the camp cars are out on trips today, all but the emergency car and I can't let you take that. Can't she wait one more day, and I'll make sure we have a car available for you tomorrow?"

"No, she's raging back in the cabin. I have to get her out of here today. Don't worry. I'll borrow one from one of the counselors."

By the time the two of them got going it was almost one o'clock. The drive from camp to Logan was only two hours, but that didn't leave much margin for error. With misgivings, one of the Senior Camp counselors had agreed to lend John his car. It was hard for him to say no to John's request. He had been one of John's campers John's first summer at camp, but he was reluctant to lend anyone his new car. The sparkling blue Toyota Celica was a college graduation present from his grandmother.

I don't remember who came running to the office to tell me about the accident. It happened just across the road from the entrance to Senior Camp. Joy had been driving. She was obviously going too fast, and when she came to the left turn onto Eagle Pond Road, the tires lost traction on the dirt road, and the car skidded into a ditch on the far side of the road and wound up crushed against the granite hillside. The right front side of the car looked like a crumpled accordion. By the time I reached the accident site, John and Joy had managed to climb out of the car. There was already a crowd of campers and counselors on the scene. There were no visible injuries but Joy was crying, and John had his arms around her shoulders, trying to comfort her. They were both shaking. Several counselors tried to dislodge the car, but it would not budge. The young man who had lent him the car looked bereft as he looked at his damaged car. The car was eventually towed away.

John and Joy spent the night in the Infirmary. Neither of them was hurt beyond bangs and bruises, but both seemed to need pampering rather than independence at that moment. The next morning, Jamie Demarest drove them to Boston in a camp car. He came back to camp with John late that afternoon. Jamie was our Dramatics Counselor, a school teacher and a very reliable guy. I wanted his opinion on John's emotional state.

"He seemed all right. I think he is relieved that Joy is gone. He'll be okay. Just give him a day or so to calm down."

"I can't give him much more than that. Monday he's supposed to take out the Connecticut River canoe trip. That's a three day trip, and I can't send them out with him as leader unless I know he's himself. The problem is I don't know who else to send. Henry is leading the Androscoggin canoe trip, and we're stretched thin for people qualified to be put in charge."

John was fairly reclusive the next few days. He did his scheduling and ran the activities he was supposed to run, but any sense of fun and excitement seemed to be drained from him. His depressed state was not good for him or the camp. I discussed the coming canoe trip with him. He assured me he would be fine and it was his responsibility to lead that trip.

I was not convinced by his assurances. I wanted this trip to be safe and fun. I questioned whether in his condition I could trust his safety instincts, but there was no question in my mind he was not going to be a fun trip leader. I had Jamie Demarest go along as an additional older staff member, who knew all of the kids, and who could be trusted to take over if he felt the need.

"Jamie, if you sense that he is acting irrationally in any way or makes any decisions that seem dangerous to you, I want you to call me right away. You'll take over as trip leader, and we'll come and get John, no matter where you are. I'll send another counselor, of course, but you have to be ready to be the man in charge."

The worst did not happen. The trip went off safely enough, and Jamie did not have to take over. In our post trip evaluation session, Jamie said that he made a real effort to lighten John's mood, but it turned out to be an impossible task. So he decided to work around him. He thought this might be a problem, but John seemed to be happy enough to have Jamie in charge of communicating with the campers and the other counselors. It was Jamie's assessment that the boys had a good trip.

John left camp two days before the end of the summer. He had his car back, and felt he had to get back home and reestablish his relationship with Joy.

After the summer I wrote to John, but he never replied. I never heard from him again. I have often wondered how their lives have gone, whether they have managed to resolve their problems and to stay together as a married couple. If I were a betting man I know which way I would bet.

47
The Swamp

"Girls, this afternoon we are going to do something nobody has ever done before."

Fifteen girls had elected to join me on an adventure walk. They trusted me. I'd taken them on walks before. They were sitting on the steps of Spruce lodge, most of them dressed as I had instructed. They had on bathing suits, shirts and pants over the bathing suits. All but two wore sneakers on their feet. Those two were wearing Tevas, and they would have to change. My instructions had been that they should all wear clothes that would protect them from being scratched. They should try to pick their least favorite clothes because they would probably get very dirty.

I had confidence that this "First time ever" walk would be a great success. I had the cream of the counselor staff coming with me, Kari Rosenkranz, Lynne Meterparel and Pam Dockser. They were all not only good counselors, but they were all well coordinated athletes and good swimmers, and two of them were lifeguards. The campers who had signed up for our excursion were all great kids. There was only one question mark, Jessica Stone. Jessica had lots of problems in camp and was a little slow in a lot of ways. She was not well coordinated and I wasn't even sure what kind of swimmer she was. I was worried about her, but her counselor Kari assured me she would take care of Jessica. She was, of course, one of the two girls without a second pair of sneakers. They had to wear their Tevas with the understanding that they would have to take them off and put them in their pants pockets at a crucial point in the trip.

"Girls, we are going to be the first people from camp ever to attempt to walk around the lake." This brought smiles to their faces and erased some worried frowns. "It is not as simple as it seems. First, right at the beginning we are going through enemy territory." They giggled.

"You know our neighbors, the Grants, have never been friends of camp." Some of them looked blank. Others nodded. "What you don't know is that they don't welcome anybody walking through their property and they have two large unfriendly German Shepherds who always seem to be prowling around." Now the girls looked a little worried.

"We're going to be walking across a small corner of their property that they never use. We'll get through it as fast as possible. So, when I tell you that you have to be absolutely quiet and not talk at all, you really have to do what I say. Does everybody agree?" I looked around as heads bobbed up and down in assent.

"After we leave the Grant's property the fun begins. I mean it. It will be fun. But it will be hard going and you will all get wet and dirty, and I'm not even sure we can make it around the lake. We might have to turn back. Now, is there anybody who wants to drop out? This is your last chance." I looked around at a small sea of smiling eager faces.

"OK, let's go. Kari, you bring up the rear. Nobody gets behind you at any point. Lynn, I'll need your help up front with me. Pam, you stay in the middle. There will be times when we get out of sight of one another. You have to keep us together by checking to make sure that you can always hear those of us in the front and those at the end of the line. We'll stop and wait whenever we spread out too much. I'll count on you to make sure we don't get spread too far."

I led them on the path next to the lake that circled the senior boys' area. We walked to the end of the camp property. I showed them our long since abandoned camp rifle range, which was right next to the Grant's property line. We gave the girls a short "time out" to look for ancient bullet shells. Not one shell came to the surface. After the shell search, I gave them the quietness lecture again and I pointed out the various strands of barbed wire ahead, demonstrating how to get through them without being touched. That barbed wire had been there for a very long time. It had been strung generations earlier by a sheep farmer who wanted to keep his sheep from wandering into the lake.

We crossed as quickly and quietly as possible through the Grant property. I had called Stacey Grant earlier that day to tell her we would be crossing that afternoon so there was no real concern about their dogs. We progressed steadily uphill, through the scraggly woods and finally came to a cautious stop. We were at the very edge of a thirty foot sheer hillside that led down to the stream below. The stream was littered with broken trees that had fallen from that hillside. The hillside itself was composed of unstable gravel and sand. There was evidence of recent small landslides etched in the hillside on either side of my chosen point of descent.

The girls at first thought I was joking when I told them we were going down right there. They realized I was serious when I demonstrated how we would go down. We would start down on our sides with a kind of half walk, half slide while leaning up hill.

"Nobody get near the edge until I am in position to help you."

With that, the demonstration was over and I started down. I half slid down the first ten feet, moving a little faster than I had planned, but I was able to stop at the first place I had counted on stopping, a fortuitously placed tree. Without that tree, there was nothing below to break a slide or fall for at least another eight or ten feet. I braced my feet against the tree, and stretched myself as far up hill as possible. I saw tiny Leslie Segal first in line at the brink of the hill.

"Leslie, don't even try to walk down. Just sit on your rear end, and slide toward me. Use your feet as brakes to slow you down. " Leslie weighed almost nothing and as she slid into my outstretched arms it was an easy catch. I stowed Leslie next to me with her back against the tree, and Jodi Heyman slid my way. Jodi was a little bigger girl and, though well coordinated, not quite as agile as Leslie. I felt the jolt when she slid past my outstretched hands and landed safely against my shoulder. Now that their immediate danger was past, they were full of encouragement for their friends.

"Come on guys. Its great fun....Don't worry, he'll catch you... Its really cool sliding down...Don't be nervous." Randy Dank came next followed by Joanna Silver. I was now better prepared for each new downward hurtling body. There were four girls holding on to the tree behind me now, and we were running out of space.

"Lynne, I want you to come down next and take my place, while I move further down." Lynn a top athlete, was not a skinny adolescent, but a fully grown young woman. I really had to brace myself when she came slipping and sliding down at me. Fortunately she was also much better at applying her own brakes than the girls had been. I briefed Lynn on the best way to catch the next group without getting dislodged herself.

Then I moved down in the same fashion to the next stopping point. It was a little steeper and more slippery as I went down. The next stopping place was a large bush that tenaciously clung to its eroding place on the side of the hill. Next to the bush was a mini plateau about six feet wide. On the other side of the bush was a straight drop into the water. The girls would have to slide down at an angle for me to stop them and to secure them on the small landing. One by one they came. Lynne replaced me and I went to the last catching spot ... Pam replaced Lynne, and so on.

From the last stopping place on the hillside there was a four or five foot drop into the water. As each of the girls hit the icy water there was a dramatic scream. They had all been in colder water before, but it was quite a contrast after the nervous sweaty climb down the side of the hill. Looking up from the stream it looked like we had made it down a sheer cliff.

Finally we were all down in the water shivering, all but three. Pam was still two thirds of the way down the hill while Kari was hugging and coaxing a terrified Jessica Stone just above Pam's safety spot. With a lot of energy and patience the two counselors got Jessica down to the water where her screams of terror were replaced by tears of relief.

Once I was sure they would be able to get her down without my help, Lynn and I led the other girls over a tangle of submerged branches. We felt our way through the water, conscious of the hazard presented by sharp branches. Finally we carefully climbed over a beaver dam. The water on the other side of the dam was only a few inches deep and much warmer. The girls were happy to play in the warm water. We waited there until Pam and Kari were able to get Jessica over the beaver dam and back with the group. Jessica had stopped crying, but was still whimpering. Kari had brought a life jacket for her for the water part of the trip so she knew she was not in any danger, but that didn't keep her from being afraid.

"Now, girls, we get to the difficult part of the trip. I have done this part of the trip before, but I have never gone further. I know we have a small swamp ahead of us, but after we cross through that swamp I have no idea how to get around the lake. I'm not even sure we can do it. If it looks too dangerous to me we'll have to turn back. Is everybody ready?"

The girls rushed to be first, jostling one another for position in the shallow water. After a couple of minutes of disorder, Kari had the winning formula.

"Everyone should be in the same order as when we went down the hill." That seemed to settle it. It was time for important instructions.

"Now girls, if you are wearing sneakers tie them as tight as you can. If you have on Tevas or any other kind of shoe that fits loosely, take them off, and put them in your pants pockets. Just a few feet ahead of us it gets pretty mucky. Your feet may get stuck. You may find yourselves sinking in. Don't panic if that happens. Just call one of us and we'll pull you out."

I started forward, the girls following close behind. At the start, the water was just a few inches deep and quite transparent. Just ahead of us I saw dark murky water. I stepped forward and my left foot went in and in and in. I put my right foot down hard to try to pull the left out, and it sunk in. My left leg was now in muck up to my knee. The right was only slightly less stuck. All around me girls were sinking in, screaming and laughing nervously. Some of them seemed to be stuck almost up to the waist. Others were not in quite so deep. There were a few in the rear who had not yet taken the plunge. From their point on high ground they were having a good laugh at our discomfort.

Kari yelled out to me. "Is there any way around this?"

"I don't think so. Just step right in and join the fun."

"All right, girls. Don't panic. This is not quicksand. It's just mud. Here's what you do. Slowly, point your foot down. Now use your leg muscle to lift that leg."

The legs started coming out of the muck, and you could hear the suction pop as a foot came free. As the muck released legs, it also released a terrible stench. And as soon as one leg came free and stepped forward it got caught all over again. We had to help a few girls free their legs. Two girls were able to pull their feet out only to realize that their sneakers were still below the surface of the mud and would never be found.

"We don't have too far to go this way, and then it will get more solid again." It was true. I knew it was true. I had been through this particular patch before. I loved watching the girls wade through it screaming, yelling and laughing. When we came out of the dense mud and reached a semi solid plot of witch grass, we all collapsed breathless but laughing. They all made it through without any real panic. Happily even Jessica Stone, attached though she was to Kari, seemed to take that portion of the trip in stride.

The girls were caked with mud. None of them had ever been so dirty or smelled so bad in their lives. I wished their Mothers could have seen them. They would have had trouble recognizing the well scrubbed, well dressed daughters they had kissed goodbye just a few short weeks earlier. They had certainly not looked anything like these wonderful laughing and incredibly dirty creatures. I took out my disposable camera, and took our first group picture. Unfortunately the lens was so smeared by the muddy water that this picture never saw the light of day.

"OK girls, now I have to pick a path to get us where we are going. Before we started, I checked the topographical map, and discovered that there is a small lake, totally hidden from people, between where we are now and the camp lake. I'd never seen it, but I've decided to call it "Lost Lake" because I don't know anybody who has ever seen it. We have to get around Lost Lake to get to the camp lake. If we don't we will probably wind up in "Lost Lake". I have no idea what that will be like."

The land we were crossing next could properly be called "wetlands". Virtually all of it was under water at least part of the year and some of it was under water all year. There were small patches of relatively solid ground here and there, and there were lots of rivulets running, seemingly at random, but all headed eventually toward our lake. I felt safe in following the most promising rivulet. It seemed to be heading directly toward the lake.

We started down the narrow stream bed. It had a few inches of water where we started. There were lots of vines and small branches crossing our path, but we moved along pretty well for a while. I used my arms as a kind of dull machete, pushing and pulling branches down and away to keep them from the faces of the girls right behind me. My brave girls were still up front, Leslie, Jodi, Randy, and Joanna. I heard but could no longer see Lynne and the next group of girls. We were only walking for about three minutes when Pam called out. Pam was the next to last counselor in our strung out line.

"Arthur, can you hear me?"

"Yes, Pam, what's up?"

"I've lost the trail. There was kind of a fork, and I took the left fork. Was that right? The stream seems to have petered out."

"Pam, we're all going to stop now. You retrace your steps and take the fork on the right. Tell me when you've caught up to Lynne. Kari can you still hear me?" Kari was the counselor bringing up the rear.

"Yes, we're turning back now. I took the same wrong turn Pam did."

Less than a minute later the group was back together. We started moving again. It wasn't very long before my stream seemed to come to a dead end with a thicket of thorny branches just ahead. Through the thicket I could see our stream continuing, wider and looking deeper. My advance guard of girls waited patiently as I looked for and finally found a reasonable detour that would get us back on track.

We took our short detour and came back to the stream, I stepped into the stream bed, and immediately dropped about four feet deeper than I expected. The water was now up to my arm pits, and would be over Leslie's head. They all saw me go down so they were not surprised as they stepped in, one after another. We were all in a narrow channel now with bare bushes on either side. The shorter girls, who could no longer walk, were able to pull themselves along by the bushes. This was hard going. I could see they were getting tired. But it did move us forward for a while, and then our rivulet widened just enough so that it almost seemed like a real stream.

I wasn't sure where we were in relation to the lake. I tried to pull myself onto the patch of apparently solid land next to me so that I could see the lay of the land. I got my knee up on land and my little island started to sink. The more weight I put on it the lower it went. It wasn't solid after all. I lifted Leslie up onto the patch of land. She was light enough so it didn't sink, but she couldn't see anything.

"Okay, girls, I don't really need to see where we are. I know we are headed for a body of water. We'll know which one soon enough." And we did. Our stream got wider and wider, and finally around a bend I saw a small pond I had never seen before. We had arrived at "Lost Lake". I knew our lake was dead ahead. I could see a stream leading from the other side of "Lost Lake" through bushes and trees directly toward the camp lake. We could hear Frank, our water ski man, giving instructions to one of his skiers. All of the girls heard it and cheered.

"Lost Lake" was not exactly choice water for swimming. Much of it was clogged by water lilies and other serpentine vegetation that seemed to grab our legs just enough to make progress really hard. The girls were following me like baby ducks follow their Mother on the assumption that Mother must know where she is going.

I looked at my watch. We had started at about 2:30 PM and it was now 4:30. I was getting tired and I knew the girls were tired. We had to get back in time to get cleaned up before dinner. It was time to find an easy end to this adventure. We stayed on the right side of Lost Lake until I found some semi solid ground on the right. I got up with difficulty. Then, with the help of all of the counselors, we managed to get all of the girls up on land. Now we were able to walk through real woods to the mouth of "Beaver Dam", the stream we had dropped into at the start of our trip.

We were on a sand bar at the Mouth of Beaver Dam, and could see the boys' waterfront. We yelled and waved. Finally Jill, our waterfront director, figured out who we were, and sent counselors with row boats across the lake to pick us up, and return us to civilization. We trooped into camp disgustingly dirty.

By assembly that night our little trek had become a legend. The girls on the trip all rated it their best activity of the summer. Many of the Senior boys and girls were begging for the chance to join me on the famous "Swamp Walk". I did take a group of our oldest boys later that summer. Over the next several years I led that trip two or three times each summer. Each year conditions were different and I had to find a new path from the muddy quagmire to Lost Lake. But I was smart enough on those subsequent trips to know I had to wind up at the mouth of Beaver Dam Stream and to alert the waterfront director ahead of time so that there would be row boats with life jackets all ready to rescue us when we emerged and started calling.

48
The Case of the Missing Stripper

She looked the picture of Innocence when she walked in my front door. She was about five feet tall, had blond hair, blue eyes and a smile that lit up her whole face. She was dressed as though she had just stepped out of a copy of Seventeen magazine published in 1946. She wore a pleated blue skirt, a light blue sweater with a white collar showing above it. All she was missing were bobby socks and saddle shoes to complete the picture. I didn't often pay much attention to counselor applicants' looks or clothing unless there was something extraordinary about one or the other. I couldn't help paying attention to Pauline Fusco's looks. She was an unusually pretty girl.

It was an interesting interview. Pauline had a little girl's voice that almost persuaded me she would not do well as a counselor. Sometimes, even with eight year olds, you have to be firm and loud. She didn't look as though she had firmness as part of her makeup, and I couldn't imagine her being loud. Pauline applied to be a bunk counselor for our youngest girls. She had no camp experience, and she was clearly not athletic, but she convinced me. She did have other talents to offer. She was perky, and her little girl voice had a breathless excited quality about it.

"I love playing games with little girls. We can make up stories and act them out, and I can teach them songs. They'll have a wonderful time with me."

She told me she had been taking singing lessons and was enrolled in a drama course. She was smart. I posed several counselor hypothetical questions to her, and her responses were usually proactive and always thoughtful. After she left the house, I checked her two references. They were both effusive in their praise. One was an old friend of the family, but the other was her boss in her job two summers before. I hired her. Her salary for the eight weeks was the standard first year counselor salary, $250 plus room, board, and laundry.

The staff arrived for the beginning of Orientation, and Pauline seemed to fit right in. She was invisible to the camp administration for the first day. Prior to the arrival of the staff, we always tentatively placed new counselors in the age groups where we thought they would work best. Pauline's placement was as a co-counselor for our youngest bunk of girls. Before dinner the second night of Orientation, Irene Sternberg, our Freshman unit Leader, came up to me and suggested that we may have placed Pauline wrong.

"She's much too sophisticated for our little girls."

"What do you mean?"

"You might not want to hear the things she talks about."

"What kinds of things? What could be so terrible?"

"I'd rather not repeat some of the things. But if you heard her I think you would be shocked."

"I've been involved with camp for a very long time, and I'm not as easily shocked as you think. But if you don't feel comfortable telling me exactly what she says that's okay. I don't have to know. If you tell me it's bad I believe you. It can't be allowed to continue. Why don't you just talk to her and tell her to watch her language?"

Irene gave a kind of nasty chuckle. This was not like her. I'd never known her to say or do anything nasty.

"I doubt if any talk will change where she's been or the things she talks about. It's her life that's the problem. Well, maybe I'm over-stating it. I like her, but I think you ought to keep an eye on her these next few days. We still have five days before the kids arrive."

Before supper that night I repeated Irene's observations to Phyllis. I was sure she would watch and pick up any bad vibes.

I didn't have to wait long to be introduced to a very different Pauline Fusco. That night after our staff meeting, the entire staff gathered in the Rec Hall for a first discussion of our Counselor show. We always put on an Opening Counselor Show the night the campers arrived. Through the years, this show evolved into a variety show, loosely stitched together by one or two entertaining counselors who served as Masters of Ceremonies. The idea of the first night show was not just to entertain our campers and take their minds off home the first night of camp. The more important benefit came from involving our counselors, as a group, with a fun project, a project in which no counselor would be or feel left out. Orientation period has the potential to be lonely for new counselors during unscheduled social time. Counselor show rehearsals were a way to extend the program in a non-threatening way. This also provided Phyllis with an annual opportunity to exercise her directorial talents.

After Phyllis explained the show for the benefit of the new counselors, all of them were asked to get together into groups to try to create acts. After a few minutes, there were various sized groups scattered around the Rec Hall. Some seemed already to be working on acts. Others were just chatting and getting acquainted. Phyllis and I roamed about the Rec Hall making sure that none of the counselors was alone and uninvolved. First run through was to be the next night after our counselor meeting.

On that first run through the next night most acts were missing all of their props and most of the actors were in jeans, chinos and sweat shirts. Not Pauline! Jaws dropped when she exploded onto the stage with two sidekicks, Keith Garte and Chuck Silverston. She was in a Madonna look-alike outfit that left little to the imagination, and she opened her act with Madonna's "Like a Virgin". She belted out the song, while preening back and forth across the stage. She played with her boys, mussing their hair and brushing against them suggestively. Both boys were turning from light blush to deep red. The audience of counselors howled and applauded wildly. This was clearly not our typical counselor song and dance act. The innocent girl I hired had disappeared.

At our urging, some of the older counselors talked to Pauline, and by the rehearsal the next night she had modified her act just enough to pass the censors (Phyllis and me). It was still easily the most suggestive and explosive act we had ever had in a counselor show. When Opening Night came, her act was the hit of the show. It didn't hurt a bit that Chuck Silverston, one of her supporting cast, was so flustered he tripped and fell face down onto the stage. The campers roared, thinking it was all part of the act.

Off stage it was clear the other counselors liked Pauline. She was quiet and enthusiastic and was obviously trying hard to become a camp counselor. She did everything she was asked to do. The other counselors decided early that she was a fun person. There was a lot of laughing going on whenever I saw her sitting with a group of friends. It was apparent to me that, whatever her background, she was a winner and would be a very good counselor.

The evening before the campers arrived was a night off for the counselors. It was a night we typically did a final review of any unsettled issues. Though Pauline was no longer an issue in my mind, she had been an issue. So she was on the list of people to discuss. Phyllis, Judy and I had already decided that she would do very well with the youngest girls, but we wanted to bring her Unit Leader, Irene, into the decision, particularly since Irene had issued the very early alert about her. Irene was just waiting for our call, and she joined us on the porch of the office.

"I think she'll do fine with the kids. I know she wants to very badly. She's told me a little about her past, and this is really important to her. Camp is a whole new world for her. She said she's never been anywhere before where the people were so nice to one another. She sees camp as the beginning of a new life for her."

"What about her language?"

"She's more careful now. I'm sure she understands that. She's really a great girl, and we've become good friends"

That was the end of the discussion. Camp opened the next day. Camp ran very well the first few days, as it usually does. Those first few days of camp the counselors are charged up from Orientation Period; filled with energy, enthusiasm and good cheer. The younger campers are in awe of their counselors. The older campers are still a little wary, weighing and judging which counselors are worth respecting, which will be pals, and which ones deserve to be flouted. Pauline did very well with her little girls. Though far from a talented athlete, she did her best to teach sports and was a willing assistant everywhere. She proved to be pretty imaginative and a good motivator. Her bunk finished in first place with their Fourth of July skit. Her girls were adorable and the skit was clever. Everybody liked Pauline.

The third week of camp Phyllis agreed to give Pauline two days off instead of the customary one day that ended at midnight. In exchange, Pauline would skip her day off the following week. She got a ride to Boston with a group of other counselors on Tuesday morning. She was due back in camp Wednesday before Taps (the time when the campers go bed). Wednesday night came, but Pauline did not. Phyllis was really angry with her for breaking her word. The Junior counselor who was covering her bunk stayed in her place. Thursday night Pauline was still missing and unaccounted for. Now we started to worry. Phyllis called the "Home number" that was on her counselor application and was told the disquieting news that we must have the wrong number because nobody by that name had ever lived there. Phyllis tried to call Pauline's two references. The first number had been disconnected. At the second, a business, it seemed nobody had ever heard of her. It was puzzling since I had reached a reference at that same phone number before I hired her.

Phyllis called Irene into the office, hoping she could shed some light on Pauline's whereabouts. That conference started in the office, but quickly moved to the living room of my house. All private things had to be discussed there. Our office was a bee hive of activity, and no conversation there was ever really far from listening ears.

"Pauline told me that she needed to stay over in Boston one night so that she could earn some money. She said she owed some people money, and needed to pay them back right away."

I did not like the sound of that.

"Is that all she told you? It sounds like she has gambling debts or something. Can you tell us anything else? I'm worried about her. We've been thinking about calling the police."

There was a long pause while Irene looked at the three of us. She made her decision.

"I guess I just have to tell. I promised her I wouldn't, but I'm worried about her too. She really loves it here, and I was sure you would fire her if you knew." She hesitated for a bit and then went on.

"For the past two years Pauline's been making a living as an Exotic dancer in the Combat Zone in Boston. Right up to the time she came to camp she was working at a club called 'The Naked Eye.'" Irene paused for a few seconds to give us a chance to absorb that and then went on.

"She's been living with a guy she doesn't love or even like very much. But she's stayed with him because he takes care of her and makes her feel safe. But she wants to get out of that life. She wants this job. She ran away from her boyfriend and her job in Boston without telling anybody where she was going. I'm not sure what happened to change her mind, but I know she needed the extra night off to go to Boston to make money dancing. She said she made more money in one night dancing than she would as a counselor for the whole summer."

She paused to give us a chance to react. I laughed. It was incredible. It was unbelievable. It was astounding.

"Oh, my God!" That was out loud. My mind was playing its own internal theater. My first picture was

of Pauline lying dead in an alley. The second picture she was drunk or stoned, flopped over a table in a sleazy dive.

"What will her campers' parents think if they find out that their daughters' counselor is a stripper? You read about strippers in the newspapers. You see them on TV shows. They're usually the dead bodies people stumble on at the beginning of "Law and Order". There's a slim line between strippers and whores in the public mind. Whores have pimps and use drugs. They get arrested. They're certainly not camp counselors. They don't play "Duck, Duck Goose" with eight year olds. There's no way, just no way we can let her stay, but in the meantime something has gone very wrong or she would have called."

"Irene, why didn't you tell us about this earlier? Don't you think we deserved to know? When you were a camper, what do you think your Mother would have said if she found out your counselor was a stripper?"

"I know. I'm sorry. I should have told you, but she is really so nice, and seemed so determined to leave that life behind. I wanted her to have a chance."

A new bad thought occurred to me. "Irene, how many other counselors know about her? Is this common knowledge?"

"No, I think I'm the only one, but I am worried about her." Irene started to sob, softly at first and then with a great gush of tears and wails. Judy and Phyllis tried to comfort her.

"We're all worried about her too, but we have to worry about camp and her campers as well."

We excused Irene after she calmed down a little. Then the three of us talked in circles for the next hour or so, going over every conceivable possibility. I wanted to call the police because I was worried about Pauline. But I was afraid to call the police because, if they took it seriously, they would storm into camp in police cars, sirens blaring, and try to question everybody who ever had contact with her. This would be a disaster for camp and would almost certainly be problematic for her campers. We had already told them that Pauline had to go home to visit her sick grandmother. I was also reasonably sure that if something bad had happened to her it was already too late for the police to help. In the end I decided we should do nothing but wait.

Days passed, and still no word. We moved another counselor into her bunk, and packed her things. Finally, there was a phone call. It wasn't Pauline. It was a man on the other end.

"Mr. Sharenow, I'm calling for Pauline Fusco. She asked me to call to tell you she's sorry she won't be able to come back to camp. She's made other plans."

"Where is she? We've been worried about her. Why are you calling me instead of her? Can I speak to her?"

"She asked me to call because she is embarrassed to talk to you."

"All right, I understand that. But we're over that now. I would like to speak to her."

"I'm sorry that is not possible. She's not here."

"Where is she?"

"I'm afraid I can't tell you that."

"Look, give me a phone number where I can reach her or have her call me herself. If not, you'll be talking to the police not me."

"I'm telling you, Pauline's fine. I'll have her call you."

"Good, you have until six PM tomorrow. If I have not spoken to her by then, I will call the police."

At five o'clock the next day a call came in for me. It was a girl's voice, but it didn't sound like Pauline.

"Arthur, it's me Pauline. I'm fine. Don't worry about me."

She spoke in a monotone. There was no sign of life or vivacity or even energy in her voice. She sounded very tired or drugged. But it must have been her. I asked her to name the girls in her bunk, and she knew them all. She named a lot of counselors as well.

After a couple of minutes of questions and answers, the phone call was over. I told myself it was time to stop worrying about Pauline and to stop feeling guilty for not calling the police.

A week or so later a young man drove into camp, and identified himself as Pauline's friend. He had come to get her things. I suppose I was still suspicious about what had happened to her. His story was that she was in perfect health and had decided to go back to school in the fall. That was why he was coming for her things. She still felt badly leaving as she had. We followed him out to his car with her things, hoping that we might catch sight of Pauline ducking down in the back seat. But the car was empty. That was the last we ever heard of her.

49
New Sheriff in Town

I met Scott Brody the 2nd night of Hanukkah when he was nine years old. His cousins were campers with us, and Scott's mother wanted him to go to camp with his cousins. She and Scott's father were divorced, and she felt there was a need for some strong male influences in his life. Scott's cousins were good kids, well coordinated and enthusiastic about sports. My first impression of Scott, during that night's visit, was that he was a nice and sensitive young boy. A lot of years have passed, and that first impression remains true.

I showed him slides of camp and answered his questions. He proudly took me into his room to show off his Hanukkah presents. He also wanted to have a private minute with me. In his bedroom he let me know he was "a little worried" about camp because he knew his cousins were athletes, and he was not. I reassured him then and his Mother later that, though our program had lots of sports, it had many other areas, and that a boy didn't have to be a great athlete to be a happy camper at Camp Kenwood. Scotts' ears perked up when he learned that we actually had a vegetable garden at camp. It had been planted during the school year by the environmental education classes we ran with school groups. I had to warn him that the garden would probably be overgrown with weeds by the time he arrived in camp because there would have been nobody to tend to it between the end of the environmental programs and the start of the camp season. His enthusiasm was undaunted, and he looked forward to that garden.

Scott, like so many other little boys, only needed to find something which he could do well. That something would make him feel good about himself. The vegetable garden was his, but only for the beginning of that first summer. Drama, music and crafts all became more important. But more significant to him than the vegetable garden, drama, crafts or music were the friends he started to make. For a seemingly quiet boy, he had a magnetic appeal that allowed him to gather an ever increasing circle of close friends. Many of them have become his lifelong friends.

When Scott was fourteen years old, he did not return to camp. His Mom, Sheila, explained to me that Scott was going to have the chance to spend the summer with his Dad. She hoped that this would provide a basis for a solid father-son relationship. As much as I hated to lose him as a camper, I admired his Mother who wanted to give his absent Father back to him.

That marked the beginning of his absence from camp for several years. I didn't forget him, but I did lose track of him, and it came as a pleasant surprise when I received a letter from him his freshman year in college. He wrote asking about a counselor job. "Yes, we have a spot for you." And I knew we did. I hadn't seen him in a several years, but had confidence that this sensitive boy would have grown into a fine young man, perfect to work with for younger campers. It was 1984 when Scott returned to camp as a counselor.

Young boys, whether they are athletic, artistic, bright or slow all need a sensitive counselor. Scott was the man for them. I was sure he would have been good, but he was even better than I anticipated. Intuitively he knew which kids needed more time or more affection or more patience or more prodding. Though he was only a first year counselor, he exhibited stronger leadership than the young man who was their group's Unit Leader that summer. He became the person we looked to when the Freshmen and Sophomores had a special trip or anything out of the ordinary to do. He also exhibited a highly unusual characteristic for somebody his age. It was almost unheard of for a counselor to come, unbidden, to the camp office just to find out how things worked. He was interested. He always arrived with bits of information to share about particular campers or activities, but he managed to leave the office having garnered a good deal more information about how camp worked than the tidbits of information he had brought with him as a kind of admission ticket.

By his second year as a Counselor I promoted Scott to Unit Leader for our little boys. Admittedly Unit Leader in our camp does not connote high administrative responsibility (except for our Senior Units), but there is an enormous difference between the way a unit runs with a wonderful unit leader and one who is just adequate. That summer, and the next, our Freshman/ Sophomore units were a spectacular success. Every new camper was happy and every single boy returned to camp from those units.

Of course, Scott was helped along the way with a wonderful supporting cast of young counselors. There was my son Rob, Who would have made a wonderful camp director, if he hadn't set as his goal being a writer for movies and television. He is a successful novelist and an even more successful television producer. There was Zach Fisher, who should have become a camp director, or at the very least, a teacher instead of the lawyer that he is. I'm sure Zach is a fine lawyer, but he would have been sensational had he spent his life working with kids. Sam Mettler was also in Scott's unit. Sam too would have been a wonderful choice for a camp director if he hadn't had his heart set on becoming a Hollywood producer. Sam created and produces *Intervention,* a heart-breaking reality show about addicts. It is ironic that he produces such an emotional show, since he was one of the funniest young men we have ever had in camp. But, good as they were, it was Scott who guided them into being our best younger boys' staff since the early 1970s. Scott proved his leadership potential.

He came to me after his first year as a unit leader, and asked when I was planning to retire, because he was planning to buy the camp from me. I laughed and told him he would have to be patient. I wasn't nearly ready yet.

The next summer we promoted Scott to Senior Unit Leader. His appointment broke a tradition as old as Senior Camp. Senior Unit Leaders, from the beginning of time, had been strong athletic counselors, people who could not only work well with teen age boys and run a staff of six or seven other counselors, but who could also provide competent coaching for one or more of our team sports. I knew Scott was not capable of coaching Seniors in any of the sports, and it was even questionable if he could run a good activity with them. But I had no doubt he had the most important skill of all, the ability to relate to people and communicate with both campers and staff.

Scott helped to "reform" Senior camp. Senior camp has to be "reformed" periodically. In our camp our senior boys live in an area that is physically separate from the rest of camp. As a consequence, the Head Counselor spends less time in Senior Camp than anywhere else. The Senior Unit Leader becomes essentially a Head Counselor for his unit. There is a macho tradition that seems to rear its head with groups of teen-age boys, and at camp it is difficult to keep it in abeyance for more than a few years at a time. This tradition has sometimes included initiations, hazing, and unacceptable degrees of physical roughness. It is not easily detected by people who do not actually live in Senior Camp. But it could not go on without the tacit approval of the Senior Unit Leader. Scott's immediate predecessor clearly had given that approval.

It was Scott's job to change minds and attitudes. During his first year as Senior unit leader he made great inroads in eliminating these unhappy vestiges that belonged to another era and another kind of camp. By the end of his second year, the job was done, at least for a while. Many years earlier, I had been Senior Unit Leader and had to achieve the same kind of reformation. I appreciated the difficulty and the importance of the job he successfully undertook.

By then Scott was in law school, and still talking to me about buying camp. "Not yet Scott". Eventually he graduated from Law School, and had to spend a part of that summer studying for and taking his Bar Exam. As soon as the Bar exam was over, he returned to camp for the rest of the camp season. He just couldn't stay away. After the summer, he went to work for a law firm in Boston. The following summer he spent his vacation weeks at camp. When his vacation was over, he went back to work, but joined us at camp every weekend.

While he was a part timer for a couple of summers, we used him wherever our needs were greatest. He could do almost any job in camp. He became our boys' White water canoe specialist, our Montreal trip leader, and our Assistant

Head Counselor. During his years at camp, Scott established closer ties with more Kenwood Senior campers and with more staff members than anyone else in camp history. He seemed to "care" about everyone. He was everyone's confidante. He was the guy they came to when they had a problem.

He left his law firm, and moved to the Czech Republic to explore business possibilities. Before he left, he explained to me that he wanted to come up with some business that would earn him enough money to buy the camp as soon as I was ready to sell. While doing business in the Czech Republic, he carved out time during the summer to rejoin us at camp. He now shared the Head Counselor position with Norm Laakso, our long time Kenwood Head Counselor. When he returned from the Czech Republic for the final time, he came back with a product. He called it "Tiger Ties". To me it didn't look much different than bungee chords. But he was enthusiastic about his ability to develop and sell the product. He was at least moderately successful in his fledgling business.

"Is it time yet?" he asked.

"Yes" the time had come to start talking. We did start talking about the transfer of ownership, and within two years the deed was done. In September of 1996, money changed hands and documents were delivered. The Camp, our camp, now belonged to Scott. I hated to give it up. But I had to face reality.

First, it was getting physically more difficult for me every summer. My self defined job as a camp director was to be everywhere and know everything. This meant doing as little paper work as possible during the day. Instead, I would arrive at my office at 5:30 or 6:00 every morning to work undisturbed until the camp day started at 7:30. I spent weekdays walking around, watching some activities and running others. On weekends I usually ran camp wide special events. After the campers went to bed, four or five nights a week I would be back at my desk until midnight or later. I recognized that it was getting more and more difficult to maintain that pace as I approached age sixty and beyond. My body gave me unmistakable messages that my energy level was no longer where it needed to be.

Second, my primary Winter activity was camper recruitment. Recruiting, and its associated travel, were becoming more tedious each passing year. It was a necessary means to an end. Even with seventy-five to eighty-five percent of our campers returning every summer, camp could not survive long without an annual infusion of new campers. Not only was I bored with selling, but I knew I was not getting as good results as I had a few years earlier.

A third factor was Scott himself. He was ready, and he was the perfect buyer. He loved camp. But as much as he loved camp, he was not likely to wait around indefinitely. I felt certain he would do a great job as a camp director; that he would keep our camp alive and well into the foreseeable future. As a bonus, I was confident that if we sold the camp to Scott, Judy and I would still be able to stay active and play important roles in camp.

In fact, we helped Scott long beyond a typical transition, spending an additional eight summers, working at camp, doing things we loved. The transition years are over now. During those years I watched Scott go from an enthusiastic neophyte to a competent and successful camp director. We left camp after the 2004 camp season with confidence that our camp (and to me it will always be our camp) is in good and loving hands.

About Arthur Sharenow

Arthur Sharenow spent virtually all of the summers of his life in camp. He started as a camper at age five, and, barring a couple of years out in his late teens, his summers prior to retirement were spent at camp, as camper, counselor, unit leader, Head Counselor and finally Director. Following a short foray in the practice of law, he has spent all of his working life as a camp director. He and his wife Judy, owned and directed a brother-sister summer camp in New Hampshire for thirty-six years. Even after they sold the camp, they continued on for an additional eight summers as associate directors.

Sharenow joined the American Camping Association in 1963, and has maintained his membership in that camp umbrella organization to this day. The ACA sets the standards for fine camping across the country. For several years, Arthur was on the Executive Board of the New Hampshire Camp Association. He also served as a member of a standards revision committee for the New England Camping Association. Under the auspices of the ACA he directed a "New Camp Directors Workshop." In his later years in camping he took on the role of ACA Visitor, visiting other camps, and evaluating the extent to which they complied with the ACA health and safety standards.

"Camp was my life for forty-four summers, and even now, in retirement, camp, is never far from my thoughts."

About Zorba Press

Zorba Press is an independent publisher of books, multimedia books and audio books (forthcoming), and user-friendly ebooks in many formats. From the gorgeous gorges of Ithaca, New York, we publish the paperback books The Zorba Anthology of Love Stories; The Ithaca Manual of Style; the anthology Zenlightenment!; and a wild comic novel about love and eros (for adults) Thoreau Bound: A Utopian Romance in the Isles of Greece.

Currently, we offer about 30 titles — fiction and non-fiction — and we are eager to build our list with quality authors and books. Our recent publications include The Terrestrial Gospel of Nikos Kazantzakis by Thanasis Maskaleris; 50 Benefits of Ebooks: A Thinking Person's Guide to the Digital Reading Revolution; and Michael Tobias's extraordinary novels, The Adventures of Mr Marigold and Professor Parrot and the Secret of the Blue Cupboard.

At Zorba Press, we practice what we call "Sustainable Publishing": publishing with a greater sense of awareness and responsibility. Sustainable Publishing is the attempt to bring to the work of publishing a healthy balance between four essential elements: Culture, Commerce, Technology (humanized), and the Environment.

Zorba's mission is to promote the innovative ideas and the daring books that nourish children and childhood, point the way to a culture of non-violence, create a sustainable future, and nurture — for every living being — a new world of love, kindness, courage, creativity, sincerity, and peace.

Visit Zorba Press at www.ZorbaPress.com

22086986R00167

Made in the USA
Middletown, DE
19 July 2015